*"A new series that promises to b
research with popular appeal.... co
authoritative,...excellent references.*

—Clarence Pete,
Chicago Tribune

Bantam/Britannica Books

Unique, authoritative guides
to acquiring human knowledge

What motivates people and nations? What
makes things work? What laws and history lie
behind the strivings and conflicts of
contemporary man?

One of mankind's greatest natural endowments is the urge to learn. Bantam/Britannica
books were created to help make that goal a
reality. Distilled and edited from the vast
Britannica files, these compact introductory
volumes offer uniquely accessible summaries
of human knowledge. Technology and science,
politics, natural disasters, world events—just
about everything that the inquisitive person
wants to know about is fully explained and
explored.

BANTAM/BRITANNICA BOOKS

Catastrophe!
When Man Loses Control

Prepared by
the Editors of
Encyclopaedia
Britannica

The Encyclopaedia Britannica staff for
BANTAM/BRITANNICA BOOKS

Editor	Frank Gibney
Executive Editor	Richard Pope

CATASTROPHE! WHEN MAN LOSES CONTROL

Editorial Assistants	Robert Beran
	Marc I. Davis
	Bruce L. Felknor
	Robert Rauch
	John Robinson
	Thelma White
Art Director	Cynthia Peterson
Picture Editor	Holly Harrington
Layout Artist	Richard Batchelor
Editorial Production Manager	J. Thomas Beatty
Production Coordinator	Elizabeth A. Blowers
Index Supervisor	Frances E. Latham
Indexer	Mary Neumann

Encyclopaedia Britannica, Inc.

Chairman of the Board	Robert P. Gwinn
President	Charles E. Swanson

Bantam edition/August 1979

Printed in the United States of America

Foreword:
Knowledge for Today's World

One of mankind's greatest natural endowments is the urge to learn. Whether we call it knowledge-seeking, intellectual curiosity, or plain nosiness, most people feel a need to get behind the newspaper page or the TV newscast and seek out the background events: What motivates people and nations? What makes things work? How is science explained? What laws and history lie behind the strivings and conflicts of contemporary man? Yet the very richness of information that bombards us daily often makes it hard to acquire such knowledge, given with authority, about the forces and factors influencing our lives.

The editors at Britannica have spent a great deal of time, over the years, pondering this problem. Their ultimate answer, the 15th Edition of the *Encyclopaedia Britannica*, has been lauded not merely as a vast, comprehensive collection of information but also as a unique, informed summary of human knowledge in an orderly and innovative form. Besides this work, they have also thought to produce a series of compact introductory volumes providing essential information about a wide variety of peoples and problems, cultures, crafts, and disciplines. Hence the birth of these Bantam/Britannica books.

The Bantam/Britannica books, prepared under the guidance of the Britannica's Board of Editors, have been distilled and edited from the vast repository of information in the Britannica archives. The editors have also used the mine of material in the 14th Edition, a great work in its own right, which is no longer being published because much of its material did not fit the design imposed by the 15th. In addition to these sources, current Britannica files and reports—including those for annual yearbooks and for publications in other languages—were made available for this new series.

All of the Bantam/Britannica books are prepared by Britannica editors in our Chicago headquarters with the assistance of specialized subject editors for some volumes. The Bantam/Britannica books cover the widest possible range of topics. They are current and contemporary as well as cultural and historical. They are designed to provide *knowledge for today*—for students anxious to grasp the essentials of a subject, for concerned citizens who want to know more about how their world works, for the intellectually curious who like good reading in concise form. They are a stepping stone to the thirty-volume *Encyclopaedia Britannica*, not a substitute for it. That is why references to the 15th Edition, also known as *Britannica 3* because of its three distinct parts, are included in the bibliographies. While additional research is always recommended, these books are complete unto themselves. Just about everything that the inquisitive person needs to catch up on a subject is contained within their pages. They make good companions, as well as good teachers. Read them.

The Editors,
Encyclopaedia Britannica

Contents

Introduction:
Death by Chance

Devastation, destruction on an epic scale, vies with creation to dominate the lore of the human race. If all living beings fear death, or at least try instinctively, desperately, to avoid it, humans are also fascinated by death and by those dramatic confrontations with destruction wherein death is the probable outcome.

The spectacle of chaos rehearses for us the ultimate challenge, reminds us that we are not only mortal but vulnerable —vulnerable to our own carelessness, to expert miscalculation, to mechanical failure, to what some have called evil spirits and others bad luck. Such reminders often lead to the invention of safety devices that can prevent tragic recurrences of catastrophic events—until the next "attack" of carelessness or metal fatigue or bad luck or. . . .

Danger, or its representation in the arts or the news media, sets our adrenaline to coursing, rivets our attention as other humans face the ultimate challenge, and when that last choice is made we settle back with a sigh: *there but for the grace of God went I.*

"Life is intrinsically boring and dangerous at the same time," writer-artist Edward Gorey observed. "At any given moment, the floor may open up. Of course, it almost never does; that's what makes it so boring. Every day is new and perilous." Television owes much of its popularity to its "on the spot, live coverage," to its ability to transform the passive viewer into an active eyewitness to the excitement and the drama of the world's daily "floor openings," whether they reveal the hell of a collapsed and gas-filled mine, the awesome spectacle of a raging fire, or the mute wreckage of an aerial disaster.

The enormity of catastrophic events and the recounting of their details lend a mythic quality. Virtually in our own day the burning of Chicago, the sinking of the *Titanic*, and the explosion of the *Hindenburg* have evolved as legends.

At one time or another everyone is exposed to various kinds of accidents. *Accident*, in its root Latin definition, means something that happens to you. Every person who boards an airplane, a bus, a ship, or a train, who gets into a car to take a drive, or who even walks across the street runs

A catastrophe may serve as a catalyst for preventive safety measures that are designed to lessen the frequency of future disasters. In the aftermath of a fatal train derailing (above) at Angola, New York, in 1867, railroad gauges were standardized on all U.S. railroads. Following a tragic grain-elevator explosion on the Galveston wharves (left) during the 1977 Christmas holidays, the U.S. Occupational Safety and Health Administration issued a "hazard alert" to the grain industry and more than doubled the number of grain-elevator inspections during the following months.

the risk of injury or death resulting from miscalculation, carelessness, ignorance, or an unforeseen combination of circumstances. The risk of losing control is inevitable. It is universal, no matter how safe or how orderly a life we think we are creating for ourselves.

Yet experience of catastrophe, immediate or vicarious, stimulates the intelligent foresight and preventive measures that can help diminish the frequency of destructive misadventures. This book offers a number of examples of different kinds of disastrous man-made accidents and reveals how they affected the human beings immediately involved, and indeed how some of those catastrophes have worked to shape the way all of us live today.

1.
Aviation Disasters

To many people the most frightening thing about aviation accidents is that they are most likely to occur thousands of feet in the air. It is ironic that the worst aviation disaster in history—on Tenerife Island in 1977—took place on the ground.

Accidents on major domestic and international flights are actually quite rare, and those with very high death tolls are even more unusual. Between 1960 and 1975, the world's yearly average of deaths from air accidents was only about 1,500, as compared with a yearly average of about 30,000 deaths from auto accidents in the United States alone. Although few in number, however, air accidents are usually dramatic.

The Hindenburg

When the dirigible airship LZ-129—better known as the *Hindenburg*—was built by the German Zeppelin Transport Company in 1936, its designers considered it to be the last word in long-distance air transportation. Others were not quite as sure. Lighter-than-air craft had been in use since the turn of the century, but their safety record was far from encouraging. Usually filled with highly inflammable hydrogen gas, the great balloons were especially vulnerable to fire. On the other hand, for trans-Atlantic flights they afforded a degree of comfort and convenience not yet available in airplanes.

The *Hindenburg* was a rigid airship—one that maintained its shape through a rigid structural framework. It was 800 feet long, with thirty-six longitudinal girders, fifteen wire-braced transverse frames, and an outer cover of linen. Powered by four 1,100-horsepower diesel engines, it had a cruising speed of seventy-eight miles an hour, and accommodations for fifty passengers. Its facilities included individual private cabins like Pullman compartments, a shower bath, a kitchen, a dining room, and a lounge with a grand piano. The ship's cargo space was large enough to accommodate automobiles and small airplanes.

In 1936 regular service was inaugurated between Germany and the United States. Westbound crossings averaged sixty-five hours; eastbound, fifty-two hours. A "millionaires' flight" in October of 1936 was arranged to convince the leaders of

American finance and industry of the merits of airship travel. Winthrop Aldrich of the Chase National Bank; Paul Litchfield, president of Goodyear; Byron Foy, head of De Soto Motors; John Royal, vice-president of the National Broadcasting Company (NBC), and dozens of other influential persons were taken on a ten-hour flight as guests of Dr. Hugo Eckener, head of the Zeppelin company, and they were suitably impressed. The *Hindenburg* received a great deal of favorable publicity, and the future of the dirigible as a commercial carrier began to look much brighter.

Having made ten trips to the United States in the spring, summer, and fall of 1936, the pride of Adolf Hitler's Germany took the southern route to Rio de Janeiro, Brazil, during the winter months. On May 3, 1937, the *Hindenburg* left Frankfurt, Germany, on its first North American flight of the new season. It had ninety-seven persons aboard and was commanded by Capt. Max Pruss. After a smooth crossing, the airship arrived over New York City on the afternoon of the sixth. The craft no longer created the sensation it had produced on its maiden flight, but thousands of New Yorkers watched it pass overhead, the huge Nazi swastikas on its tail fins clearly visible from the ground. Ships that were docked at the piers along the Hudson River blew their whistles in greeting as the *Hindenburg* headed away from New York City toward its destination, the Lakehurst Naval Air Station in New Jersey.

On the airship itself, passengers looked down from the observation deck at the panorama of Manhattan Island receding into the distance. Some left the smoking room to make ready for the landing. As they passed through the door, each of them was searched for matches by a steward. Inflammable materials were not allowed anywhere else on the ship. With seven million cubic feet of hydrogen gas over the passengers' quarters, every precaution had to be taken against fire. All equipment in the vicinity of the gas-filled chambers was covered with rubber, and personnel working in those areas had to wear asbestos clothing. Even the engines that drove the dirigible were specially designed to start without ignition.

The *Hindenburg*'s arrival on its first flight of the year was still a newsworthy event; a full complement of reporters and cameramen had been waiting at Lakehurst since eight in the morning, the originally scheduled landing time. Strong head winds had slowed the great ship's progress, and the newsmen were unhappy about the long delay. The landing field, with its huge dome-shaped hangar, was located about a mile outside of town, and there was nothing much to do there. A sizable group of people who had come from New York City to meet clothing manufacturer Philip Mangone, one of the arriving passengers, had driven twenty miles to Asbury Park, New Jersey, for lunch. Finally, at four o'clock, the *Hindenburg* was sighted approaching from the north.

At about the same time, dark storm clouds began to appear, and Captain Pruss, nervous about the weather, notified the field that he was going to wait another two hours before descending. Comdr. Charles Rosendahl, the officer in charge of the air station, felt that Pruss was being overly cautious, but he knew that the Zeppelin company prided itself on its safety record and did not believe in taking chances. To the dismay of the long-suffering crowd, the ship passed over the field and cruised off to the south. Just then it started to rain, and everyone ran for cover. A few minutes after six, Rosendahl sent an "all clear" signal to Pruss, who by that time was south of Philadelphia, Pennsylvania.

Pruss turned his ship around and headed back. The cabin attendants removed the sheets from each bunk and piled them in the corridors. There was not going to be much time to take care of everything that had to be done before they took off again at midnight. The ship was taking a large party to attend the coronation of King George VI in London. A new and faster method of refueling was going to be used, so the crew hoped to have at least an hour or two of liberty despite the tight schedule. The Swedish journalist Birger Brink had an even greater time problem. He had made the trip for the express purpose of interviewing Governor Earle of Pennsylvania, in connection with a story he was writing to mark the 300th anniversary of Swedish settlement in that state. Brink had planned to go to Harrisburg, Pennsylvania, for the interview during the day and then return to Europe on the *Hindenburg* that night. He was still hoping that he could manage the schedule somehow, but with only five hours to spare it was beginning to look hopeless.

At Lakehurst, a ground crew of nearly 250 naval and civilian personnel took their positions for the landing. Mooring an airship was a complex and delicate procedure, but for them it had become fairly routine. The rain had tapered off to a light drizzle by the time the *Hindenburg* arrived, shortly after seven o'clock, and hovered 500 feet above the field. On

Rosendahl's signal it began a slow descent toward the earth.

Comedian-acrobat Joseph Spah looked down to see if he could spot his wife and children, who had come from their home in Douglaston, Long Island, to meet him. An Alsatian by birth, Spah had regular theatrical engagements in both the United States and Germany and was viewed with suspicion by German authorities. SS agents on board the *Hindenburg* had been ordered to keep an eye on him, since there was some concern about threats of sabotage that had been made against the ship.

At 7:20 the landing ropes were picked up by the ground crew, and the final stage of the landing process began. One of the reporters on the scene was Herbert Morrison, a radio announcer from station WLS in Chicago. He and his engineer, Charlie Nelson, had just arrived, and they hurriedly set up their equipment in the Bachelor Officers' Quarters. The men were there to record the landing for a program called "The Dinner Bell." As he left the building with his microphone, Morrison had no way of knowing that his recording would become one of the most famous descriptions of a news event in the history of broadcasting. The *Hindenburg* seemed to be motionless above him; he could see people waving from the windows. Customs, immigration, and public health officials were walking out onto the field, where Pat Dowling, an American representative of the Zeppelin company, stood with a load of dry ice to be delivered to the ship's kitchen. Morrison had begun to record for his radio audience:

> *Here it comes, ladies and gentlemen, and what a sight it is, a thrilling one, a marvelous sight. . . . The sun is striking the windows of the observation deck on the westward side and . . . Oh, oh, oh. . . . It's burst into flames. . . . Get out of the way, please, oh my, this is terrible, oh my, get out of the way, please! It is burning, bursting into flames and is falling!*

Spah's wife thought at first that the mass of flames coming from the dirigible was a fireworks display to mark the landing. Mrs. William Craig, whose husband was in the press group, thought that the flash was the sun coming out after the rain. An explosion followed almost immediately. The noise was hardly noticed by many of the onlookers, but ten miles away it was clearly heard, and a light was seen flashing in the sky.

Captain Pruss felt only a slight shock and thought one of the landing ropes might have broken; then he heard the explosion and the screams of the people below. His radio officer shouted that the ship was on fire, and suddenly they felt the stern drop sharply. People, furniture, and everything not fastened to the decks went tumbling toward the rear. Morrison, sobbing and nearly incoherent, continued to speak into his microphone:

> *This is terrible! This is one of the worst catastrophes in the world! Oh, the humanity and all the passengers. . . . I'm going to step inside where I can't see it. It's terrible. I—I—folks, I'm going to have to stop for a moment because I've lost my voice. This is the worst thing I've ever witnessed!*

Dowling ran for his life, still carrying the dry ice he had brought for the *Hindenburg*'s kitchen. John Eitel and Babe Klaasen, members of the ground crew, struggled to get away through the wet sand with the feeling that the burning dirigible was pursuing them. Associated Press photographer Mur-

Roaring flames destroy the Hindenburg *on May 6, 1937, after an explosion sent the giant dirigible crashing to the ground.*

ray Becker had his lens trained on the ship when the explosion occurred, and he mechanically took shot after shot of the disaster. They are among the best-known news photographs ever taken.

At 7:25, less than one minute after the fire had broken out, the stern hit the ground. To those who watched the flames tearing through the entire length of the *Hindenburg*, it seemed impossible that anyone could survive in such an inferno. But many did. Philip Mangone was thrown down onto the deck at first, but he got to his feet and tried to open one of the windows. It was jammed, but he broke it open with a chair. Mangone climbed out, burning himself on the hot metal, and jumped thirty-five feet to the ground. The flaming wreckage was falling all around him, cutting off his escape. In desperation, Mangone dug a tunnel in the sand and crawled out from underneath the charred framework of the airship.

Engineer Eugene Schäuble's post was in one of the gondolas under the *Hindenburg*'s tail. He was knocked unconscious and woke up on the ground a few minutes later, completely unhurt but without any idea of how he had gotten there.

Mathilde Doehner, one of the passengers, looked around for her husband when she realized something had gone wrong, but she could not find him in the confusion. Deciding that the only way to save her three children was to get them through one of the windows, she tried to lift her ten-year-old daughter out first, but the girl was too heavy for her to manage. The mother grabbed her two smaller boys instead and just threw them out, hoping for the best. The boys survived, and Mrs. Doehner eventually escaped too, helped by two crew members. Her husband and daughter were killed.

The acrobat Spah got outside, but his end of the ship was more than 100 feet above the ground. Knowing that it would have to fall soon, he held on to the ledge as long as he could. Finally he had to let go. The next thing he remembered was crawling away from the blazing wreck on his hands and knees. After jumping to safety, Captain Pruss returned several times to help rescue passengers and crewmen. Badly burned, he was at last forced into an ambulance and taken to a hospital.

Alerted by telephone within minutes of the initial explosion, medical personnel from the hospitals in the vicinity rushed to the air station. A dispensary was set up to care for the injured; for the dead, the airship hangar became a makeshift morgue. There were thirty-six fatalities, a comparatively low figure considering the nature of the disaster.

News of the *Hindenburg*'s destruction created a sensation throughout the world. The complete film record of the tragedy and the numerous eyewitness accounts gave it an impact greater than that of any previous airship accident. Herb Morrison's recording was broadcast by NBC the following afternoon, and the graphic newsreels horrified theater audiences during the next few days. In Germany, Eckener, Zeppelin's director, was awakened in the middle of the night by a phone call from the Berlin correspondent of *The New York Times*, who told him what had happened. At first Eckener could hardly believe it. "Is there a possibility of sabotage, do you think?" asked the voice at the other end of the line. Eckener remembered the bomb threats. "If it was in the air," he replied, "then it might perhaps have been sabotage."

On the day after the crash, a search was made of the ship's twisted wreckage. Not much was left—a few briefcases and handbags, some pieces of mail that had escaped the fire, and a movie camera that the search party was surprised to find was still in perfect working order. A Luger pistol from which one shell had been fired caused considerable speculation, but nothing definite could be determined from it.

The U.S. Department of Commerce appointed a board of inquiry to look into the causes of the catastrophe. For several weeks the investigators questioned witnesses and weighed the evidence, eventually deciding that ball lightning or St. Elmo's Fire generated by the storm were among the most probable causes. Sabotage was apparently not seriously considered, perhaps because it would have been embarrassing to the German government. Nevertheless, many people continued to believe that a bomb may have been planted aboard the *Hindenburg* by an opponent of the Nazi regime among the passengers or crew. Although the cause of the tragedy remains uncertain, there can be no doubt about its result: it marked the end of the dirigible as a means of public transport. The widespread publicity it received completely destroyed public confidence in lighter-than-air craft and ensured the future dominance of the airplane.

Ten Weeks in the Andes

The Old Christians rugby team—so called because most of its members were graduates of the Christian Brothers' Stella Maris School in Montevideo—won the Uruguayan national championship in 1968 and 1970. They had played against teams in Argentina, and in 1971 they played two matches in Chile. The Chilean trip was a great success, and the Old Christians decided to return the following year. They chartered a Fairchild F-227 twin-engine turboprop from the Uruguayan Air Force and filled the extra seats with twenty-five of their relatives and friends for the flight to Santiago.

The plane left Carrasco Airport in Montevideo early in the morning of October 12, 1972, carrying forty passengers and nine crewmen. For a craft like the Fairchild, flying across the Andes Mountains could be quite dangerous. Because it could not reach the altitude of the highest peaks, the plane would have to go by way of one of several passes that were made hazardous by tricky air currents. Only a few weeks before, a four-engine cargo plane had been lost in the mountains.

Weather conditions turned out to be bad on the twelfth, and the pilot, Col. Julio César Ferradas, landed at Mendoza on the Argentine side of the Andes to wait until they could safely make the crossing. On the next day, Friday the thirteenth, there was still a considerable amount of turbulence. But Ferradas and his copilot, Lt. Dante Lagurara, who had been teased for their lack of daring by the young rugby players, decided to chance the flight. The plane took off from Mendoza at 2:18 that afternoon and headed south through the Planchon Pass. The view of the ground was obscured by a cloud layer. At 3:24 Lagurara radioed the Santiago airport that they were over Curicó, a Chilean town west of the Cordillera range of the Andes. They turned north toward Santiago and descended into the clouds for their landing.

When the plane emerged from the clouds a few moments later, the passengers were alarmed to see that they were still in the high Andes and seemed perilously close to the side of a mountain. Ferradas struggled to gain altitude, but before he could the right wing was torn off by projecting rocks. Then the tail and the other wing were lost, and the plane went down in a snow-covered valley, more than eleven thousand feet above sea level, and still on the Argentinian side of the border. The plane's fuselage was relatively intact.

Thirty-two people survived the crash, but several of them were badly injured. Those who were able to move around did what they could to help the others; then, with night coming on, they took steps to protect themselves against the freezing cold. The radio transmitter was dead, but they felt certain that they would be found and rescued soon. The next day came and went, and four of the survivors died. Among them was the copilot Lagurara, who kept repeating in his last delirium, "We passed Curicó. We passed Curicó." Colonel Ferradas had been killed in the crash.

On the third day, the stranded group was organized under the leadership of Marcelo Pérez, the captain of the Old Christians' "first fifteen." The meager supply of food was strictly rationed, and each person was assigned to one of the tasks that had to be performed.

When the Fairchild failed to show up at Santiago, the authorities sent planes to search for it in the area north of Curicó, its last reported position. When the search proved fruitless, they retraced the plane's route from Mendoza and concluded that, flying into a strong headwind, Ferradas and Lagurara could not have reached Curicó in the hour and ten minutes reported. It was realized that they must have turned north in the middle of the Cordillera range. Pilots of the Chilean Aerial Rescue Service flew over the area where the crash had actually occurred, but they saw nothing. The remains of the Fairchild, painted white and half-buried in snow, were invisible from the altitudes at which they were operating. The marooned survivors' attempts to signal aircraft flying over their valley were equally useless. Chilean police and volunteer rescuers tried to get through on foot too, but heavy snows forced them back. The search was finally abandoned on October 21.

Meanwhile, the survivors were growing weaker and weaker on a diet of chocolate, wine, jam, and melted snow. Even the little food they had was rapidly disappearing. There did not seem to be any plant or animal life in the vicinity. When their supplies were gone, there would be only one source of nourishment left—the bodies of their dead companions. At first only a few of the survivors could accept this as a possibility. Most continued to hope and believe that help was on its way. But they had been picking up Chilean broadcasts on a transistor radio, and on October 22 they heard a report that the search for their plane had been called off. This convinced most of the holdouts that if they were going to escape from the valley they would have to do it on their own, and since there was no alternative, they would have to live on human flesh. One by one they overcame their revulsion and did what would have been unthinkable to them only a few days before. The last one to give in was Liliana Methol, the only woman in the group, who refused to eat until she had nearly died.

Sixteen survivors of the Friday the thirteenth plane crash in the Andes Mountains lived for seventy days amongst the wreckage of the turboprop.

In the Southern Hemisphere October is springtime and brings the avalanche season to the mountains. On the night of October 29, while the survivors were asleep in the plane, an avalanche came down the mountain. Snow poured through the wreckage, burying everyone inside. Nineteen dug themselves out or were saved by others. The rest, including Liliana Methol and Marcelo Pérez, were dead by the time anyone could reach them. Fighting against despair in the wake of this new disaster, those who remained decided that the strongest and most determined among them would have to try to cross the mountains into Chile as soon as the snow season ended.

Three were chosen: Nando Parrado, Roberto Canessa, and Antonio Vizintín. They left the crash site on November 17 and headed northeast, expecting the valley to curve toward the west and lead them toward their destination. After two days they realized that they were going the wrong way, and they started back again. But their efforts were not entirely wasted; they found the missing tail of the plane, where the luggage and extra batteries had been stored. They brought back some much-needed heavy clothing, a few more scraps of food, and some cigarettes. Despite this, their return was a great disappointment to those at the site. Two more had died since the avalanche, and the expedition's failure to get out of the valley made things look worse than ever. The group had begun to divide into factions, and there was continual bickering about the allotment of tasks and supplies.

Canessa, Parrado, Vizintín, and Roy Harley took the radio transmitter from the plane to the tail section to see if they could use the batteries to make it work again. They were unsuccessful, but they did hear a report from Montevideo that their relatives had persuaded the Uruguayan Air Force to make one last attempt to find them. Buoyed up by this welcome news, they used suitcases from the luggage compartment to form a large cross in the snow, which they thought should be visible even from several thousand feet.

Renewed hope of rescue caused the "expeditionaries" to put off making another start on their trek to civilization, but when yet another of their companions died on December 11, they decided they could wait no longer. On the morning of the twelfth, the three began climbing the heights on the western side of the valley. They reached the summit on the third day. To their dismay, they saw on the other side, not green valleys and farms, but more snow-covered mountains. Realizing that their journey was going to be a much longer one than they had thought, and that there would not be enough food and water for three, Parrado and Canessa sent Vizintín back to the plane and went on alone.

They chose as their goal a mountain they could see in the distance, which had no snow on it, and started the precipitous descent into the next valley. Canessa, remembering how Tevye had talked with God in *Fiddler on the Roof*, prayed in the same bargaining manner: "You can make it tough, God," he said, "but don't make it impossible." They had brought seat cushions from the Fairchild with them, which they first used as toboggans to slide down the slopes; later, in places where the snow was soft and slushy, they tied the cushions to their feet and used them as snowshoes.

In the valley they were overjoyed to find a stream and some grass, the first vegetation they had seen since the plane crash. As they went on, they began to see birds and animals too, and the snow gradually disappeared. After eight days, they noticed signs of the presence of humans—an empty soup can, cattle dung, and ax marks in trees, but still no people. Finally, on the ninth day, when they had eaten almost all of their food and had just about given up hope, they came to a river and saw horsemen on the other side—Chilean cattle herders. Parrado and Canessa shouted and gesticulated but could not make themselves understood over the noise of the rushing water. The horsemen went away but returned the next day. Parrado tied a written message to a rock and threw it across to them. That night, on December 21, the two men ate a decent meal and slept in beds for the first time in ten weeks.

The next day their hosts notified the local police, who sent for a helicopter to take them back to the scene of the crash. News of their discovery spread quickly, and while they were waiting for the helicopter, a crowd of reporters arrived from Santiago to interview them. Once back in a conventional setting, the boys began to feel uneasy about what they had had to do to survive in the mountains. They did not mention the subject of cannibalism. Two Chilean helicopters left the Chilean village of Los Maitenes on the afternoon of the twenty-second. Parrado went along to help them locate the Fairchild.

The group at the crash site heard the news over the radio that their comrades had gotten through, and they tried to make themselves presentable to greet their rescuers. They were filthy and as thin as scarecrows, but they made an attempt to clean themselves up; some even put on neckties. They knew that the half-eaten corpses scattered around in the snow made a ghastly sight, but they were too weak to try to cover them up.

The helicopters were not built to fly above the 13,000-foot peaks around the valley, and they had a difficult time reaching their destination. When they did get there, they were able to take back only eight of the survivors. The others had to wait until the next day to be picked up, but by the evening of December 23 all had reached safety. What became known as the "Christmas Miracle" was completed.

During the first few days after the rescue, there was no mention of what was to be the most sensational aspect of the story—the fact that they had survived by eating human flesh. But the newspapers soon heard of it, and some of them printed lurid photographs of the bodies found on the mountain. The publicity caused considerable bitterness among the young Uruguayans. What they had come to see as an almost religious act of creating a bond between the living and the dead—some of them had compared it with the sacrament of Holy Communion—was presented as a descent into savagery

Roberto Canessa and Nando Parrado, two of the survivors of the Andean plane crash, managed to climb down the mountains and alert mounted Chilean policemen.

by many of the journalists who wrote about it. Piers Paul Read's best-selling book, *Alive*, which was published in 1974, gave a detailed account of the episode and caused it to take its place beside the loss of the *Hindenburg* as one of the most famous disasters in aviation history.

Paris, France

In 1972 an American Airlines DC-10 jumbo jet, manufactured by McDonnell Douglas, crash-landed at Windsor, Ontario, when a cargo door blew open in flight. Although it was suggested that the cause of the accident lay in the construction of the door's fastening mechanism, no action to correct such a fault was undertaken. DC-10s continued to operate without modification. Within the following two years two additional DC-10s were sold by McDonnell Douglas, one of these to Turkish Airlines.

In March 1974 an engineers' strike was curtailing the number of flights between France and Great Britain. When Turkish Airlines Flight 981 left Paris for London at about 12:30 P.M. on March 3, it was, therefore, filled to capacity; the passengers and crew totaled 346. The passenger list included more than

200 British travelers, 49 Japanese, and individual families, single travelers, and small groups from several other countries.

The door of the lower cargo hold on the DC-10 had not been fastened securely, even though it appeared to be fastened from the outside. Less than ten minutes out of Paris's Orly Airport the door blew open. The hold began to lose its cargo, and the sudden decompression caused the cabin floor of the airliner to collapse. Six passengers, strapped to their seats, were drawn through the buckling floor and pulled to their deaths. The plane began a steep dive; radio transmissions indicated that the pilot tried to, but could not, control the plane. The collapse of the cabin floor had severed the cables to the tail section. There was no action that the pilot could take to prevent the crash of the plane.

Flight 981 smashed into a picnic area of Ermenonville Forest, a few miles from Mortefontaine, reducing many of the trees to stumps. A control tower official at nearby Le Bourget Airport was walking in the forest and witnessed the crash: "It went down very rapidly. . . . I lost it as it went behind some trees. Then there was this big ball of fire. We didn't hear anything. And we didn't see any smoke." A farmer saw something falling toward him: "It was a woman, although I could not be sure that it was a woman because she was completely smashed, completely broken." Horrified picnickers ran from the forest. One witness said, "Through the smoke, I saw blood, blood everywhere." As the plane crashed, it exploded, cracking windows in houses several miles away. The plane disintegrated, scattering pieces of metal and bodies over a wide area. All 346 aboard were killed. Only four bodies were found intact, three miles from the crash site. Every other body was in fragments, as was the craft itself. Pieces of bodies and of clothing were caught in the trees; personal belongings were scattered everywhere. The momentous task of identifying the dead took weeks.

The subsequent investigation of the crash did have some beneficial effects. The U.S. Federal Aviation Administration (FAA), more than a year later, required a technical overhaul of DC-10s, Boeing 747s, and other similar craft. Cargo doors were equipped with safety mechanisms to insure that they were locked.

Two years after the Paris crash, more than $62 million had been paid in damages to more than 1,100 relatives of the victims. The settlements ranged from $10,000 to $900,000—

the latter for the death of a man survived by his wife and four children. Thirty-three cases were settled for more than $500,-000. Although there were suggestions of criminal negligence on the part of both the manufacturers and aviation authorities, all but two plaintiffs waived the right to punitive damages.

The Canary Islands Collision

On March 27, 1977, a group opposed to Spanish rule in the Canary Islands set off a bomb in the terminal building of the island's main airport at Las Palmas. The airport was closed temporarily, and incoming traffic was diverted to Los Rodeos, a smaller field on the neighboring island of Tenerife. One of the airliners that landed at Los Rodeos was a Pan American 747 carrying American passengers on their way to a Mediterranean cruise. Parked next to it was a KLM 747 transporting Dutch vacationers to Las Palmas. The entire area was covered by a dense fog.

When word arrived that the Las Palmas airport was open again, the KLM flight was scheduled to leave first. Its captain, Jacob Veldhuyzen van Zanten, was instructed by the control tower to proceed to the end of Los Rodeos's single runway,

On March 27, 1977, two jumbo jets collided on a fog-shrouded runway on the island of Tenerife in the Canary Islands, killing most of the passengers aboard. The final death toll was the highest in civil aviation history.

turn around, and wait for permission to come back on the runway for takeoff. Veldhuyzen taxied to his position, made a 180-degree turn, and waited. The Pan Am pilot, Victor Grubbs, was told to taxi up the runway too, but to turn off at "the third exit on the left" so that the KLM could take off.

The exits were marked C-1, C-2, C-3, and C-4, but because C-1 was blocked off, Grubbs understood "the third exit" to mean C-4. Just as he was passing C-3, he saw the lights of a plane approaching through the fog. It was the other 747 coming down the runway straight at him at a speed of 160 miles an hour. Both pilots tried to avoid a collision, Grubbs by turning off the runway onto the grass and Veldhuyzen by lifting his plane off the ground. But their actions were too late. As it rose into the air, the KLM plane tore through the Pan Am craft and then crashed onto the field about 300 yards away, where it exploded in a ball of fire. Everyone on the KLM plane and all but sixty-eight on the Pan Am craft were killed. The complete death toll—582—was the highest for any disaster in the history of civil aviation. The taped record of communications with the control tower indicated that Veldhuyzen had not been cleared for takeoff, and why an experienced and responsible pilot would have taken his plane down a fog-shrouded runway without having been told to do so remains a mystery.

San Diego, California

There have been several air disasters in the United States that have killed more than 100 persons. The two worst accidents involving single craft were those of an Alaska Airlines plane, which crashed into a mountain in the Tongass National Forest on Sept. 4, 1971, killing 111 persons, and of an Eastern Airlines plane near New York City on June 24, 1975, which killed 113 persons. Trans World Airlines and United Airlines planes collided over the Grand Canyon in Arizona on June 30, 1956, killing 128 persons. On Dec. 16, 1960, in a collision of Trans World and United planes over Staten Island, New York, 134 persons were killed. Until 1978 the Staten Island collision had been the worst U.S. air disaster in terms of lives lost. But on Sept. 25, 1978, two planes collided over San Diego, California, in what not only became the worst accident in U.S. air history but also one of the most puzzling.

The San Diego collision involved a Pacific Southwest Airlines (PSA) Boeing 727 and a small single-engine Cessna 172. PSA, the largest intrastate carrier in the United States, had never had a fatal accident in its nearly thirty-year history. PSA Flight 182 had originated in Sacramento, California, early in the morning. It was a popular commuter flight to southern California for businessmen and state officials.

On the morning of September 25, Flight 182 was in command of Capt. James McFeron, a veteran pilot. The flight was uneventful from Sacramento to Los Angeles, its first stop. There, about 100 passengers disembarked, but the flight took on new passengers for the half-hour flight to San Diego. Among those on board were 31 PSA employees returning to their San Diego homes or flying there to PSA headquarters. The flight took off from Los Angeles at 8:30 and flew along the Pacific coast. When it reached the area of Lindbergh Field in San Diego, the plane flew eastward in order to turn and approach the airport on the west runway.

While the PSA flight was on the ground in Los Angeles, the Cessna 172 took off from Montgomery Field, eleven miles northeast of Lindbergh. The Cessna was being flown by Marine Sgt. David Lee Boswell, who had a commercial pilot's license but who was working to gain experience in instrument flying so that he could upgrade his license, and flight instructor Martin Kazy, Jr. Because Lindbergh Field is the only airport in the area with the sophisticated equipment necessary for instrument landings, the Cessna headed there.

Sergeant Boswell was wearing a specially designed helmet that obscures a pilot's view of the sky but that allows him to see the instrument panel. The Cessna received permission to make a landing approach to the east runway at Lindbergh Field and then to continue east. At about 8:55 the maneuver was carried out successfully, and permission was granted for a second approach. The Cessna continued east and began to pull up. At the same time PSA Flight 182 was headed east over the airport in preparation for its turnaround and landing.

A series of radio communications, which are perhaps the best evidence of the events, seem to indicate that the pilots did not see one another until it was too late. The PSA flight was tuned to the frequencies of both Lindbergh and the Miramar Naval Air Station, the center that was controlling the flight of the Cessna. Miramar reported to PSA: "Traffic, 12 o'clock [directly ahead], one mile, northbound." PSA replied, "We're looking." Miramar then reported, "Additional traffic, 12 o'clock, three miles north of field, northeast-bound Cessna 172, climbing out of 1400 [altitude]." PSA replied, "O.K., we got that one." Miramar then reported, "Traffic, 12 o'clock, three miles out of 1700." And PSA replied, "Traffic in sight." Although it is not clear what plane the PSA pilot had "in sight," what seems probable is that it was not the Cessna beneath him.

The Miramar center then reported to the Cessna: "Traffic, 6 o'clock [directly to the rear], two miles, eastbound. PSA jet inbound to Lindbergh out of 3200. Has you in sight." But the Cessna reply was unintelligible. Lindbergh then reported to the PSA flight, "Traffic, 12 o'clock, one mile, Cessna." And PSA replied "O.K. We had him a minute ago," and then, "I think he passed off to our right." Miramar reported to the Cessna, "Traffic in your vicinity is a PSA jet. Has you in sight. He is descending toward Lindbergh."

The recording of the cockpit conversation on the airliner, recovered from the wreckage, revealed that there was confusion among the crew about the Cessna. The PSA copilot apparently did finally see the Cessna beneath them—saying, "There is one underneath"—but four seconds later the two planes collided, the Cessna tearing into the right wing of the Boeing 727 and bursting into flames. The PSA's wing was on fire, and both craft plummeted toward the ground. Captain McFeron's last communication was "Tower, we're going down."

The two planes fell in a residential neighborhood, completely destroying a dozen homes and severely damaging others. There were many witnesses to the crash, and one photographer captured the falling jet on film. As the disintegrating jet rained fiery metal and dismembered bodies from the sky, it was a horrifying experience for those on the ground. One resident reported that "It felt like 200 degrees for a second, then there was a mushroom cloud of smoke and then I saw bodies and pieces of the plane flying through the air." Another said, "I saw my apples and oranges bake on the trees. I walked into the alley to look at the house in back and I saw a human leg."

Father Jim Clifford of nearby St. Augustine School reported: "I happened to look up and I saw the jet and a small plane near it. I said, 'They're too close,' just as the jet started to bank slightly. Then the small plane hit the wing of the jet and there was an explosion. The jet's wing burst into flames and the jet turned right toward the school. It looked like it was going to hit us so I started yelling 'Run, run,' but it went down about six blocks from here. It was a sight I'll never forget."

After colliding with a single engine aircraft, a PSA jetliner plunges into a residential neighborhood in San Diego, California, on September 25, 1978.

Bill O'Shaunghnessy, a teacher at the school, said: "I saw about a dozen of our kids over there. They were running up into the flames with little garden hoses, showing no regard for their own lives. I had to keep chasing them back to where they would be safe."

It was reported that thousands of people came to the scene —some to try to help, others to search for valuables. "While there were no arrests for looting," Deputy Police Chief Veon Nyhus said later, "we did make forty-seven arrests for failure to disperse or for refusing to follow a police order." He also commented that "Several vivid impressions remain—one was all the shoes, everywhere you looked were shoes. Another was the sight of a man's necktie, blue and white stripes, fluttering from the guy wire of a phone pole." The gymnasium of St. Augustine was turned into a morgue where the charred and dismembered bodies were taken. The tragedy killed 144

A dozen homes in the vicinity of St. Augustine School were destroyed, others were severely damaged, and the entire area was strewn with wreckage from the San Diego crash.

persons—the 135 passengers and crew members of the PSA jet, both men in the Cessna, and 7 residents of the neighborhood where the planes fell.

The San Diego crash focused attention once again on the question of the safety of the U.S. skies. The number of aircraft now in use in the United States approaches 200,000 (with only about 2,500 of these being planes used by commercial airlines) in addition to military aircraft. The number of planes concentrated near the busiest airfields has increased the threat of collisions. In 1977 nearly 400 near-misses were reported, but the number probably represents only a small percentage of the near-misses that actually occurred. John J. O'Donnell, president of the Air Line Pilots Association, has testified that the FAA relies on outmoded techniques—essentially pilots' vision—to avoid collisions. O'Donnell and others advocate the installation of automatic collision-avoidance systems to warn of such dangers. Many FAA officials and others, however, have argued that such systems are impractical, particularly in congested areas where collisions are most likely to occur. A more sophisticated, more reliable automatic system would take several years to perfect.

The collision in San Diego seems to have been the result of a number of factors that no single person, neither the pilots nor those in control on the ground, could have avoided. Although the PSA flight recording revealed that at least one off-duty pilot was riding in the cockpit and that there was personal conversation unrelated to the flight, there was no indication of negligence on the part of the PSA crew. Traffic is heavy at Lindbergh, but the airport does not have a "conflict alert" system, the most sophisticated warning system now in use. Although Miramar does have such a system and did have a warning of the impending collision, the division of control between Lindbergh and Miramar meant that the center was not in direct contact with the PSA jetliner. The rising Cessna and the descending jetliner—their pilots properly warned but their visions of one another obscured—led to a tragic accident.

In December 1978 the FAA acknowledged, however, that it had been somewhat lax in guarding against air collisions and announced changes in the control of air traffic. The new program included increasing radar service at many airports and putting most of the busiest air routes in the United States above 10,000 feet under the direct supervision of air controllers.

Colombo, Sri Lanka

During a heavy thunderstorm a half hour before midnight on November 15, 1978, a chartered Icelandic Airlines DC-8 jetliner crashed in a coconut plantation a mile away from its destination, killing 183 passengers and crew members. Filled with Indonesian Muslims returning from a pilgrimage to the holy city of Mecca in Saudi Arabia, the plane was making its final landing approach for a refueling stop at Colombo, the capital city of Sri Lanka, the island country formerly known as Ceylon.

Plowing through 400 yards of coconut trees, the plane broke into three separate sections and burst into flames. Miraculously, there were 79 survivors, some of whom were treated at local hospitals and released, but others were critically injured and hospitalized under intensive care. A civil aviation official at the crash scene said, "It passes all understanding how anybody at all could have come out alive after a wreck like that."

The rear section of the huge four-engine jet sustained the least damage, and officials speculated that most of the survivors were in that part of the plane. Amir Hussain, a clerk for the Indonesian government, escaped through a broken window. "People were wailing," he said. "I was dragging my wife out when I saw the cockpit go up in flames."

Maasabi Karsa, editor of the *Banjaraasi Post* in Surabaja, Indonesia, said, "We were coming in to land when suddenly the plane was crashing through trees and started to break up. When it stopped I tore myself out of my seat belt and walked out of the wreckage." Karsa's wife was also among the survivors, many of whom crawled from the broken fuselage of the plane and walked away without aid.

"The plane came down like a ball of fire from the sky," eyewitnesses reported. The crash site was strewn with colorful Muslim prayer rugs, clothing, and jewelry among the charred bodies and twisted metal. The plane burned for hours before fire fighters were able to extinguish the flames.

The prime minister of Sri Lanka, Ranasinga Premadas, accompanied workers who later searched through the debris identifying victims, salvaging their belongings, and looking for the black flight recorder box that was eventually retrieved from the rubble. Flight recorder data was examined by investigators in an effort to reconstruct the events leading to the fatal crash.

The airport control tower had tracked the incoming jet from ninety miles away as it flew through the storm on instruments. Landing clearance was transmitted to the plane, and the pilot was instructed to maintain an altitude of 650 feet as it approached the airport. Radar indicated that the aircraft was flying too low, however, and air controllers told the pilot to climb. Contact with the jetliner was abruptly lost, and then a fiery explosion seen from the control tower indicated that the plane had gone down.

Charges that the instrument system at Colombo's airport was not functioning properly and had caused planes to have landing difficulties had been recently reported in newspapers. A government official, however, said the instrument-guidance system had been in operation on the night of the crash "as far as we know." Just prior to the disaster four landings and takeoffs had occurred without incident. The airport approach lights, however, had not been working.

The accident duplicated almost exactly the circumstances of a previous crash at the Colombo airport on December 4, 1974, in which 191 Indonesian Muslims returning from Mecca

On November 15, 1978, a jetliner transporting pilgrims from the holy city of Mecca in Saudi Arabia crashed in a Colombo coconut plantation in Sri Lanka. One of the 79 survivors is carried on a stretcher to a nearby hospital for treatment.

were killed. The incidents were two of the worst chartered airline disasters ever.

Other Aviation Disasters, 1959–78

1959
Jan. 8
Near Kingsport, Tennessee. A commercial airliner crashed during heavy fog, killing 10 persons.
Jan. 11
Rio de Janeiro, Brazil. A West German airliner crashed and burned on the marshy edge of Guanabara Bay; 29 passengers and 7 crew members were killed.
Jan. 17
Mar del Plata, Argentina. An Argentine airliner crashed in attempting to land; 51 persons were killed.
Feb. 3
New York, New York. An airliner coming in for a landing plunged into the East River; 65 persons died.

Feb. 17
London, England. A Turkish airliner crashed during landing; 15 passengers and crew members were killed.

March 10
Near Belem, Brazil. A Brazilian Air Force plane crashed; 28 men were killed.

March 29
Near Hailakandi, India. An Indian commercial airliner crashed, killing all 24 persons aboard.

April 17
Hermosillo, Mexico. A Mexican commercial airliner crashed, killing all 26 aboard, including a child born on the plane 1½ hours earlier.

April 29
Madrid, Spain. A Spanish airliner crashed en route to Madrid from Barcelona; 28 persons were killed.

May 12
Baltimore, Maryland. A U.S. commercial airliner disintegrated in the air during a thunderstorm, killing 31 persons.

May 15
Near Lima, Peru. A Peruvian airliner crashed in the jungle; 12 persons perished.

May 15
Mar del Plata, Argentina. An Argentine airliner crashed into the ocean; all 10 persons aboard were presumed dead.

June 26
Near Milan, Italy. A U.S. commercial airliner crashed in a thunderstorm, killing 68 persons.

June 30
Naha, Okinawa. A burning U.S. jet fighter plunged into a school after the pilot had parachuted to safety; 16 persons were killed, and 118 others were injured.

July 1
Near Marion, Ohio. The crash of a Continental Can Company plane killed 10 company executives.

Aug. 19
Barcelona, Spain. A British airliner crashed into a mountainside, killing all 32 persons aboard.

Sept. 23
Villa Facchini, Brazil. A Brazilian commercial airliner exploded in midair, killing 20 persons.

Sept. 24
Bordeaux, France. A French airliner crashed, killing 54 persons and injuring 12 others.

Sept. 25
Great Sitkin Island, Alaska. An airliner hit a mountain, killing 16 persons.
Sept. 29
Near Buffalo, Texas. A commercial airliner exploded in mid-air, killing 34 persons.
Oct. 29
Tanaga, Greece. A Greek airliner caught fire in midair and crashed; 18 persons died.
Oct. 30
Waynesboro, Virginia. An airliner crash in the Blue Ridge Mountains killed 26 persons.
Nov. 16
Gulf of Mexico. A U.S. airliner plunged into the Gulf, killing 42 persons.
Nov. 21
Beirut, Lebanon. An Afghan airliner smashed into a mountain, killing a reported 24 persons.

Firemen search for missing persons in a residential area near Midway Airport in Chicago, Illinois, where a cargo plane crashed on November 24.

Nov. 24
Chicago, Illinois. A cargo plane crashed into homes near Midway Airport; the crew of 3 and 8 residents perished.
Dec. 1
Montoursville, Pennsylvania. An airliner rammed into a mountain; 25 persons perished.
Dec. 8
San Blás Mountains, Panama. A Colombian airliner crash killed 46 persons.
Dec. 13
Tashkent, U.S.S.R. A Soviet plane crashed with 29 persons aboard; there were no survivors.
Dec. 22
Ramos, Brazil. A commercial airliner and an air force trainer collided in midair; 38 persons were killed.

1960
Jan. 6
Bolivia, North Carolina. An airliner disintegrated in midair, killing all 34 persons aboard.
Jan. 18
Holdcroft, Virginia. An airliner crashed in fog, killing all 50 persons aboard.
Jan. 19
Ankara, Turkey. A Scandinavian airliner crashed into a hilltop; 41 persons died.
Jan. 19
Adana, Turkey. A U.S. Navy plane crashed on Karanfil Dag (Pink Mountain), killing 16 persons.
Jan. 21
Montego Bay, Jamaica. A Colombian airliner exploded and burned upon landing; 37 persons perished.
Feb. 5
Cochabamba, Bolivia. A Bolivian airliner crashed into a lagoon, killing 59 persons.
Feb. 25
Rio de Janeiro, Brazil. A U.S. Navy plane collided with a Brazilian airliner and fell into the bay; among the 61 persons killed were 19 members of the U.S. Navy band.
Feb. 25
Shannon, Ireland. An Italian airliner crashed and exploded after takeoff, killing 33 of 52 persons aboard.
March 17
Tell City, Indiana. A U.S. commercial airliner exploded in

midair; 63 persons died.

April 14

Taipei, Formosa. A Thai Air Force plane crashed shortly after takeoff; 18 lives were lost.

April 19

Bogotá, Colombia. A Colombian airliner crashed while attempting to land; 33 persons were killed.

April 22

Bunia, Western Congo. A Belgian airliner hit a mountain, killing all 35 persons aboard.

May 15

Near El Fasher, Sudan. A Swiss commercial airliner struck a mountainside; all 12 persons aboard were killed.

June 10

Mackay, Queensland, Australia. U.S. Consul John O'Grady and 28 others were reported dead in the crash of an Australian commercial airliner.

June 14

Anchorage, Alaska. A U.S. airliner with 14 persons aboard crashed into Mount Gannett; there were no survivors.

June 24

Rio de Janeiro, Brazil. A Brazilian airliner carrying 51 persons crashed into Guanabara Bay; no survivors were found.

July 6

Off the New Jersey coast. A Navy blimp crashed into the Atlantic Ocean, killing 18 crewmen.

July 11

Near Quito, Ecuador. A U.S. Air Force transport plane carrying 18 persons crashed into Mount Pichincha; there were no survivors.

July 20

Near Lake Kivu, Republic of Congo. A Belgian army transport plane crashed, killing 34 Belgian soldiers.

July 27

Near Chicago, Illinois. A helicopter crashed into a suburban cemetery; all 13 persons aboard were killed.

Aug. 17

Near Kiev, U.S.S.R. Included among the 27 victims of a plane crash were members of the first Algerian diplomatic mission to Communist China.

Aug. 18

Near Casablanca, Morocco. A French naval bomber caught fire and exploded in flight; all 27 persons aboard were killed.

Aug. 29

Near Dakar, Senegal. A French commercial plane plunged into the Atlantic Ocean; all 63 persons aboard were killed.

Sept. 7

Northern Uruguay. An Argentine airliner exploded and crashed, killing 25 passengers and 6 crew members.

Sept. 8

Near Tokyo, Japan. A U.S. Air Force weather reconnaissance plane crashed into the side of a mountain; 10 crewmen were killed, and one was missing and believed dead.

Sept. 19

Guam. An airliner carrying U.S. military personnel and their dependents exploded and crashed, killing 78 persons; 16 others survived the crash.

Sept. 22

South of Okinawa. A U.S. Marine Corps transport plane crashed into the sea, killing all 29 marines aboard.

Preparations are made to transport a streetcar containing charred victims to the morgue after a U.S. military plane struck a church spire and crashed into the streetcar in downtown Munich, Germany, on December 17.

Sept. 26
Near Moscow, U.S.S.R. An Austrian airliner crashed on its approach to a landing; 31 of 37 persons aboard were killed.

Sept. 29
Near Elba. An Egyptian airliner carrying 23 persons was reported missing; it was presumed down at sea, with the loss of all aboard.

Oct. 4
Winthrop, Massachusetts. A commercial airliner fell into Boston Harbor, after exploding in midair shortly after take-off; 61 persons were killed, and 11 others survived the crash.

Oct. 28
Near Frenchtown, Montana. A commercial airliner crashed and burned in the Cayuse Hills; all 12 persons aboard were killed.

Oct. 29
Toledo, Ohio. A chartered plane crashed shortly after take-off, killing 22 persons and injuring 26 others; among the dead were 16 members of the California State Polytechnic college football team.

Nov. 7
Near Quito, Ecuador. An airliner crashed into an extinct volcano; 41 persons were killed.

Nov. 23
Philippines. A commercial airliner crashed into a jungle mountainside; all 33 persons aboard were killed.

Dec. 11
Near San Andrés de Giles, Argentina. An Argentine air ministry airliner exploded and crashed; 32 persons were killed.

Dec. 17
Munich, Germany. A U.S. Air Force plane crashed onto a streetcar in downtown Munich; 53 persons were killed, 20 aboard the plane and 33 streetcar riders or pedestrians.

1961

Jan. 3
Near Vaasa, Finland. A Finnish commercial airliner crashed minutes before a scheduled landing, killing all 25 persons aboard.

Feb. 15
Near Brussels, Belgium. A Belgian commercial airliner, coming in for a landing, crashed near the airport, killing 73 persons; the dead included 18 members of the U.S. figure-skating team and a farmer working in a field at the crash scene.

March 28
Near Ruesselbach, West Germany. A Czech airliner crashed and burned in a wooded area while attempting a forced landing; all 52 persons aboard were killed.

April 3
Near Santiago, Chile. A commercial airliner crashed in an inaccessible spot in the Andes Mountains; all 28 persons aboard were presumed dead, including 8 members of the Santiago soccer team.

May 10
Edjele, Algeria. A French commercial airliner crashed in the Sahara; all 79 persons aboard were killed.

May 24
Tacoma, Washington. A U.S. C-124 Air Force transport plane crashed and burned near McChord Field; 18 persons were killed and 4 others were injured.

May 30
Lisbon, Portugal. A Venezuelan airliner crashed on takeoff, killing all 62 persons aboard.

June 12
Cairo, Egypt. A Dutch commercial airliner crashed while landing; 21 of the 37 persons aboard were killed.

July 1
Buenos Aires, Argentina. An Argentine airliner crashed and burned near an airport landing strip; 23 persons were killed, and 12 others were injured.

July 11
Denver, Colorado. A U.S. DC-8 commercial jetliner, coming in for a landing with 122 persons aboard, careened off the runway and crashed into a parked truck; 16 passengers and an airport worker in the truck were killed.

July 12
Near Casablanca, Morocco. A Czech airliner struck a high-tension cable in a heavy fog and crashed at the Camp Cazes Airport; all 72 persons aboard died.

July 19
Azul, Argentina. An Argentine DC-6 airliner crashed and burned in attempting an emergency landing; all 67 persons aboard were killed.

Aug. 6
Near Budapest, Hungary. A Hungarian commercial aircraft crashed in a suburb while flying sightseers over the city; all 24 persons aboard died.

Aug. 9

Near Stavanger, Norway. A British airliner, chartered for a schoolboys' holiday, crashed on a mountaintop; all 34 boys, 2 teachers, and 3 crewmen were killed.

Sept. 1

Clarendon Hills, Illinois. A U.S. Constellation jetliner crashed in a cornfield minutes after takeoff from Chicago's Midway Airport; all 78 persons aboard were killed.

Sept. 10

Shannon, Ireland. A chartered U.S. DC-6 transport plane plunged into the estuary mudbanks shortly after takeoff; all 84 persons aboard were killed.

Sept 12

Rabat, Morocco. A French Caravelle jetliner fell into a ravine and burned; all 72 persons aboard were killed.

Sept. 17

Chicago, Illinois. A U.S. Electra II jetliner, out of control seconds after takeoff from O'Hare Airport, smashed into a tomato field and exploded; all 37 persons aboard were killed.

Sept. 18

Ndola, Northern Rhodesia. A Swedish DC-6B aircraft, flying an 8-member UN peace mission to the Congo, crashed and burned; all 16 persons aboard died, including UN Secretary-General Dag Hammarskjöld.

Sept. 23

Ankara, Turkey. A Turkish twin-engine airliner, nearing Esendoga Airport, hit a mountain during a torrential downpour; 28 persons were killed, and one survivor was seriously injured.

Oct. 7

Near Prades, France. A British DC-3 airliner, buffeted by high winds, crashed in the eastern Pyrenees; all 34 persons aboard were killed.

Nov. 1

Recife, Brazil. A Brazilian DC-7 airliner, making a landing approach, struck a tree, smashed into a hillside, and exploded; 57 of the 88 persons aboard were killed.

Nov. 8

Richmond, Virginia. A chartered Constellation transport plane, carrying 74 U.S. Army recruits and 5 crewmen, developed engine trouble, made a forced landing in a thicket, and burst into flames; 77 persons died, 2 crewmen survived.

Nov. 23

São Paulo, Brazil. An Argentine Comet IV airliner exploded shortly after takeoff and burned; all 52 persons aboard were

killed.
Dec. 19
Seville, Spain. A plane chartered by a Madrid news photographer, reporting on a convoy of supplies for flood victims, hit a high-tension wire and plunged into a crowd of spectators; 30 persons were killed, including the pilot and newsman, and 120 others were injured.
Dec. 21
Ankara, Turkey. A British Comet IVB jetliner exploded and crashed moments after takeoff in a snowstorm; 28 persons were killed, and 6 passengers survived.

1962
Feb. 4
Tingo Maria, Peru. A Peruvian DC-3 airliner crashed in the mountains of central Peru about 125 miles from Lima; all 18 persons aboard were killed.
Feb. 25
Margarita Island, Caribbean Sea. A Venezuelan twin-engine airliner, on a landing approach, hit a cloud-covered mountain, killing all 22 persons aboard.
March 1
New York, New York. A U.S. Boeing 707 Astrojet crashed into Jamaica Bay seconds after takeoff from Idlewild Airport; all 95 persons aboard were killed.
March 4
Douala, Cameroon. A British DC-7C airliner plunged into a jungle swamp minutes after takeoff from Douala Airport; all 111 persons aboard perished.
March 16
Island of Guam. A U.S. Super Constellation plane disappeared in the Pacific during a flight from Guam to Manila; all 107 persons, including 93 U.S. servicemen, were presumed dead.
March 28
Santiago Bay, Cuba. A Cuban commercial airliner crashed into the sea near the bay entrance, killing all 22 persons aboard.
April 8
Near Villavicencio, Colombia. A Colombian Air Force C-47 crashed into a mountain in the eastern Llanos region; all 31 persons aboard were killed.
April 22
Northwest Colombia. A Colombian DC-3 airliner crashed in

the mountainous jungle; all 38 persons aboard were killed, including 2 U.S. Peace Corps members.

May 9

Vitoria, Brazil. A Brazilian Convair 440 exploded after a landing crash; 24 of the 27 persons aboard were killed.

May 10

Northern Burma. A Burmese Air Force plane plunged into a ravine, killing all 29 persons aboard.

May 12

Godthaab, Greenland. A Canadian amphibious plane chartered by the Danish government crashed on landing; 15 of the 21 persons aboard were killed.

May 17

Nairobi, Kenya. A U.S. Air Force C-130 transport crashed in hilly country 20 miles west of the city; all 13 men aboard were killed.

May 22

Near Munich, Germany. A U.S. Navy Constellation exploded in midair; all 26 persons aboard were killed.

May 22

Near Centerville, Iowa. A U.S. 707 jetliner disintegrated in flight, following an explosion (caused by a bomb planted in the tail section); all 45 persons aboard died.

June 3

Paris, France. A French 707 jetliner bound for New York burned after failure to become airborne at takeoff from Orly Airport; 130 of the 132 persons aboard were killed.

June 22

Basse-Terre Island, Guadeloupe. A French 707 jetliner bound for Santiago, Chile, crashed as it approached Le Raizet Airport on Grande-Terre Island; all 113 persons aboard were killed.

July 7

Bombay, India. An Italian DC-8 jetliner, within minutes of Santa Cruz Airport, crashed in the Nimgiri hills; all 94 persons aboard were killed.

July 19

Near Bangkok, Thailand. A U.A.R. Comet 4-C airliner, making a landing approach, crashed in a forest and burned; all 26 persons aboard were killed.

July 22

Honolulu, Hawaii. A Canadian turboprop airliner, attempting an emergency landing, missed the runway and crashed into some parked bulldozers; of the 40 persons aboard, 27 were killed.

Aug. 20

Rio de Janeiro, Brazil. A Brazilian DC-8 jetliner taking off from Galeâo International Airport plunged into Guanabara Bay; of the 104 persons aboard, at least 15 were killed.

Aug. 23

Barrancabermeja, Colombia. A Colombian DC-3 passenger plane crashed on takeoff and burst into flames; 18 of the 31 persons aboard were killed.

Sept. 4

Ravenna, Ohio. A twin-engine Lockheed, transporting oil company executives, crashed and exploded; all 13 persons aboard were killed.

Sept. 10

Near Spokane, Washington. A U.S. Air Force KC-135 tanker crashed on Mount Kit Carson in a landing attempt through thick fog; all 44 persons aboard were killed.

Sept. 23

Atlantic Ocean. A U.S. Constellation airliner crashed into the sea 500 miles off the Irish coast; 48 of the 76 persons aboard were rescued; 28 persons were killed, 21 others were seriously injured.

Oct. 12

Carmona, Spain. A Spanish airliner crashed into a hill because of poor visibility; all 18 persons aboard were killed.

Nov. 10

South Vietnam. A Vietnamese DC-3 airliner crashed near the summit of 6,000-foot Mount Hai Van; all 26 persons aboard were killed.

Nov. 23

Paris, France. A Soviet-built Ilyushin-18 Hungarian airliner, making an approach to Le Bourget Airport through fog, crashed into a beet field and burned; all 21 persons aboard were killed.

Nov. 23

São Tomé Island. A Portuguese C-54 military transport exploded after takeoff from a refueling stop; of the 32 persons aboard, 19 died.

Nov. 23

Ellicott City, Maryland. A U.S. Viscount airliner collided with a large bird and plummeted into a woods, killing all 17 persons aboard.

Nov. 26

Near Paraibuna, Brazil. A twin-engine Brazilian airliner with

23 persons aboard collided with a private cabin plane carrying 4; both aircraft fell into rugged mountain terrain, killing all 27 persons.

Nov. 27

Near Lima, Peru. A Brazilian 707 airliner on a flight to Los Angeles, California, crashed on a hilltop and burned; all 97 persons aboard were killed.

Nov. 30

New York, New York. A U.S. DC-7B airliner, approaching Idlewild Airport through thick fog, crashed and burned; of the 51 persons aboard, 25 were killed.

Dec. 14

Near Manaus, Brazil. A Brazilian Constellation airliner went down over the Amazon jungles; all 50 persons aboard were killed.

Dec. 19

Warsaw, Poland. A Polish Viscount airliner crashed and exploded at the end of a runway at the Warsaw Airport; all 33 persons aboard were killed.

Dec. 29

Ajaccio, Corsica. A four-engine, propeller-driven stratoliner crashed and burned on a mountaintop; all 24 persons aboard perished.

1963

Feb. 1

Ankara, Turkey. A Lebanese Viscount airliner and a Turkish Air Force C-47 transport plane collided in a dense cloud at 6,500 feet; flaming wreckage fell into the central part of the city, killing a total of 95 persons in the planes and on the ground and injuring at least 150 others.

Feb. 12

Florida Everglades. A U.S. 720-B jetliner en route to Chicago, Illinois, plunged into the swamplands 10 minutes after takeoff from Miami International Airport; all 43 persons aboard were killed.

March 2

Mindanao Island, Philippines. A Philippine DC-3 airliner crashed on a mountain slope, killing all 27 persons aboard.

March 15

Charaña, Bolivia. A Bolivian DC-6 airliner plunged into the side of a volcanic peak near the Chilean-Bolivian frontier; all 40 persons aboard perished.

March 20

Near Cuneo, Italy. A Comet IV jetliner, private plane of King Saud of Saudi Arabia, off course in heavy fog and clouds, crashed in the snow-covered Alps; no wreckage and no trace of the 18 persons aboard could be found.

May 3

São Paulo, Brazil. A Brazilian twin-engine airliner caught fire moments after takeoff and crashed into a residential area; of the 49 persons aboard, 41 were killed and 8 others were injured.

May 5

Near Douala, Cameroon. An Air Afrique DC-6 plane crashed into the side of 13,000-foot Mount Cameroon, killing 54 of the 55 persons aboard.

May 12

Near Cairo, Egypt. An Egyptian DC-3 airliner en route to Alexandria exploded in the air minutes after takeoff from Cairo Airport; all 34 persons aboard were killed.

June 3

Near Pathankot, India. An Indian passenger plane on a short run from Amritsar to Srinagar crashed, killing all 29 persons aboard.

June 3

Off Queen Charlotte Island, British Columbia. A U.S. military-chartered DC-7 airliner en route to Elmendorf Air Force Base, Anchorage, plunged into the North Pacific Ocean; all 101 persons aboard, mostly military personnel and dependents, were killed.

June 16

Near Tókomlós, Hungary. A Romanian twin-engine Ilyushin-14 airliner, en route from Munich, Germany, to Bucharest, crashed and killed all 31 persons aboard.

June 26

Detmold, Germany. A Belgian C-119 military transport caught fire and crashed near the Sennelager army training camp, killing 38 persons; 9 others parachuted to safety.

July 28

Bombay, India. A U.A.R. jetliner, swept by monsoon rains, crashed into the Arabian Sea about nine miles west of Bombay Airport; all 62 persons aboard were killed.

Aug. 12

Lyons, France. A French Viscount airliner crashed into a farmhouse during a violent rainstorm; 16 persons died and 4 others were injured, including one dead and 3 who were injured in the house.

Sept. 4

Zürich, Switzerland. A Swiss Caravelle airliner, carrying a party of 43 farmers from the village of Humlikon for a visit to Geneva, crashed and burned moments after takeoff from Kloten Airport; all 80 persons aboard died.

Sept. 12

Perpignan, France. A French Viking airliner crashed into a mountainside during a violent thunderstorm; all 40 persons aboard were killed.

Nov. 8

Aland Island, Finland. A Finnair DC-3 airliner missed the runway on its letdown at Mariehamn Airport; 21 of the 24 persons aboard were killed.

Nov. 29

Near St. Thérèse de Blainville, Quebec, Canada. A Canadian DC-8F jetliner crashed and burned a few minutes after a bad weather takeoff from Montreal International Airport; all 118 persons aboard were killed.

Dec. 8

Elkton, Maryland. A U.S. Boeing 707 Puerto Rico–Philadelphia jetliner was struck by lightning and exploded during a thunderstorm, moments after taking off from Baltimore Airport where 71 passengers had been discharged; all of the remaining 81 persons aboard were killed.

1964

Jan. 9

Zárate, Argentina. An Argentine DC-3 on a flight from Santa Fe to Buenos Aires burst into flames, plunged to the ground, and burned; 29 of the 31 persons aboard were killed.

Feb. 21

Mindanao Island, Philippines. A Philippine DC-3 crashed in mountainous terrain near Marawi; 31 persons aboard died.

Feb. 25

Lake Pontchartrain, Louisiana. A U.S. DC-8 on a flight from Mexico City, Mexico, to New York, New York, plummeted into the murky waters of the lake moments after takeoff, following a scheduled stop at New Orleans; all 58 of the passengers and crew perished.

Feb. 27

Oita, Japan. A Japanese twin-engine Convair CV-240 overshot the runway, rammed into a retaining wall, and burst into flames; 20 of the 42 persons aboard were killed.

Feb. 29

Near Innsbruck, Austria. A British Bristol Britannia four-engine turboprop, loaded with vacationing skiers from London, hit the side of Mount Glungezer during a snowstorm and slid into an Alpine gorge; all 83 persons aboard died.

March 1

Tahoe Valley, California. A U.S. four-engine Constellation on a local flight encountered a blinding snowstorm and smashed into an 8,700-foot ridge in the Sierra Nevadas; all 85 passengers and crew were killed.

March 8

Bogotá, Colombia. A Colombian DC-3 crashed about 60 miles west of the city, killing all 33 persons aboard.

March 28

Naples, Italy. An Italian four-engine Viscount jetliner, flying through fog and rain on a Turin–Rome–Naples run, struck a lava hump on Mount Vesuvius, broke apart, and burned; all 45 persons aboard were killed.

April 17

Dhahran, Saudi Arabia. A Middle East Airlines Caravelle jetliner, on a flight from Beirut, Lebanon, was driven off course in a severe sandstorm and fell into the Persian Gulf about 10 miles from shore; all 49 persons aboard were presumed dead.

April 18

Wilmington, Ohio. Two U.S. Air Force C-119 flying boxcars collided while maneuvering in formation, killing 17 of the 19 men aboard.

May 7

Concord, California. A U.S. twin-engine F-27 propjet airliner, on a flight from Reno, Nevada, to San Francisco, dived into a hilltop, possibly as a result of injury to the pilot; all 44 persons aboard were killed.

May 8

Lima, Peru. An Argentine Air Force DC-4, on a passenger flight from Buenos Aires, encountered fog in approaching the airport and plowed through a sand dune to become lost in the sea; 3 persons were rescued, and 46 were presumed dead.

May 11

Clark Air Force Base, Philippines. A U.S. Air Force Stratolifter C-135, on a flight from Travis Air Force Base, California, landed short of the runway in a rainstorm, struck a radio tower and a taxicab, flipped over, and broke up into flaming debris; 78 of the 83 persons aboard died, as well as a passenger in the cab.

June 20
T'ai-chung, Formosa. A Nationalist Chinese C-46 transport plunged into a rice paddy shortly after takeoff for Taipei; all 57 persons aboard were killed.

July 9
Newport, Tennessee. A U.S. Viscount airliner, en route from Philadelphia, Pennsylvania, to Knoxville, crashed in the mountainous area of the Great Smokies; all 39 persons aboard were killed.

Sept. 4
Nova Friburgo, Brazil. A Brazilian Viscount turboprop, flying through rain and fog, crashed on Nova Caledonia Mountain, only 60 miles short of its Rio de Janeiro destination; all 39 persons aboard were killed.

Sept. 4
Ubol, Thailand. A Thailand Royal Air Force C-47 transport came in too low for a landing at Ubol Airport, struck some trees, and was wrecked; 26 airmen were killed, and 8 others were injured.

Oct. 2
Near Trevelez, Spain. A chartered French DC-6 struck El Goteron Peak in the Sierra Nevada and scattered in pieces in the valley below; all 80 persons aboard were killed.

Oct. 19
Near Belgrade, Yugoslavia. A U.S.S.R. Ilyushin 18 four-engine turboprop airliner, in making a landing approach during a heavy fog, crashed into 1,700-foot Mount Ayala and burned; all 18 persons aboard died, including 7 high-ranking Soviet military officers.

Nov. 15
Near Las Vegas, Nevada. A U.S. F-27 twin-engine turboprop, en route from Phoenix, Arizona, in a blinding snowstorm, flew into a 1,110-foot rocky butte just nine miles short of McCarran Field; all 29 persons aboard were killed.

Nov. 20
Angelholm, Sweden. A Swedish Convair airliner struck a maze of power lines in its approach to the airport and fell to the ground; 31 of the 43 persons aboard perished.

Nov. 23
Rome, Italy. A U.S. Boeing 707 bound for Athens, Greece, veering from the runway as the pilot attempted to brake to a stop during takeoff when an engine failed, struck a steamroller and burst into flames; 48 (including 28 Americans) of the 73 persons aboard died.

1965

Jan. 16

Wichita, Kansas. A U.S. Air Force KC-135 stratotanker crashed in a residential area, killing all 7 crewmen and 23 persons on the ground.

Feb. 6

Santiago, Chile. A Chilean DC-6B airliner, flying through a cloud-filled pass, crashed into the snowy Andean slopes and burst into flames; all 88 persons aboard were killed.

Feb. 8

Off Long Island, New York. A U.S. DC-7B commercial airliner, taking off from Kennedy Airport, fell into the ocean; all 84 persons aboard perished.

March 22

Near Bucaramanga, Colombia. A Colombian DC-3 commercial airliner came down on an Andean mountainside, killing all 29 persons aboard.

March 26

Near Peshawar, Pakistan. A Pakistani DC-3 transport, in flight from Peshawar to Chitral, crashed in mountainous terrain; 22 of the 26 persons aboard died.

March 31

Off Cape Spartel, Morocco. A Spanish twin-engine Convair plunged into the Strait of Gibraltar, killing 50 of the 53 persons aboard.

April 10

Near Damascus, Syria. A Jordanian airliner caught fire and plummeted into Kanisa Mountain; all 54 passengers and crewmen were killed.

April 14

Jersey, Channel Islands. A British DC-3 airliner, attempting to land in thick fog, crashed and killed 26 of the 27 persons aboard.

May 5

Los Rodeos Airport, Canary Islands. A Spanish four-engine Constellation ran off the runway on a landing approach; 32 of the 49 persons aboard died.

May 20

Cairo, Egypt. A Pakistani Boeing 720-B jetliner, on a Karachi–London route inauguration flight, crashed on approaching Cairo Airport and burst into flames; 121 of the 127 persons aboard were killed.

June 15

Fort Benning, Georgia. Two U.S. Army assault helicopters on a training flight collided in midair, killing all 18 servicemen aboard.

June 25

Los Angeles, California. A U.S. Air Force C-135 jet transport bound for Okinawa struck a low hill moments after takeoff from El Toro Marine Air Station; all 72 marines and the 12 crewmen were killed.

July 6

Oxfordshire, England. A Royal Air Force four-engine transport exploded in midair, killing all 41 servicemen aboard.

July 7

Near Cairo, Egypt. A Soviet-built AN-12 troop transport en route to Yemen crashed and killed all 22 Egyptian soldiers and 8 of the 9 crewmen aboard.

July 8

Near 100 Mile House, British Columbia, Canada. A Canadian DC-6B commercial airliner exploded in midair and crashed; all 52 persons aboard were killed.

July 25

Panay Island, Philippines. A Philippine Air Force C-47 transport plunged into a mountainside, killing all 36 persons aboard.

Aug. 16

Near Chicago, Illinois. A U.S. Boeing 727 commercial airliner disappeared with a burst of flame into Lake Michigan; all 30 persons aboard died.

Aug. 24

Hong Kong. A U.S. Air Force C-120 transport plane, taking off from Kaitak Airport for the Da Nang Air Base in Vietnam, veered suddenly and slid into the shallow waters of the bay; 58 of the 71 servicemen aboard died.

Sept. 16

Quang Ngai, Vietnam. A Vietnamese C-47 commercial airliner crashed into a rice paddy, killing 39 of the 40 persons aboard.

Sept. 17

Near Plymouth, Montserrat. A U.S. Boeing 707 jetliner, en route from Martinique to New York, New York, hit a mist-shrouded mountain peak; all 30 persons aboard were killed.

Oct. 17

Bucaramanga, Colombia. A Colombian DC-3 airliner collided with a small private plane; 16 persons died, including the pilot of the smaller plane.

On November 11 a commercial jetliner burst into flames while landing at the municipal airport in Salt Lake City, Utah.

Oct. 27

London, England. A British Vanguard turboprop, landing in heavy fog at London Airport, hit the runway, broke up, and burned; all 36 persons aboard died.

Nov. 2

Obock, French Somaliland. A French DC-3 military plane, carrying an army sports team, crashed at the Obock Airport; all 30 persons aboard, including crewmen and French soldiers, were killed.

Nov. 3

Off Limón, Costa Rica. An Argentine Air Force C-54 transport on a training mission caught fire and fell into the Caribbean Sea; 68 crewmen, officers, and cadets were killed.

Nov. 8

Constance, Kentucky. A U.S. Boeing 727 Astrojet, attempting to land during a thunderstorm, rammed into a hillside and exploded about 1½ miles short of its runway at Greater Cincinnati Airport; 58 of the 62 persons aboard perished.

Nov. 11

Salt Lake City, Utah. A U.S. Boeing 727 jetliner made a hard landing at the municipal airport, skidded several thousand feet, and suddenly burst into flames; 42 of the 89 persons aboard burned to death.

Dec. 7

Santa Cruz de Tenerife, Canary Islands. A Spanish DC-3, chartered by Scandinavian tourists, faltered on takeoff in a rainstorm, plunged into a house, and burned; all 32 persons aboard died.

1966

Jan. 14

Off Cartagena, Colombia. A Colombian DC-4 passenger plane crashed in the shark-infested waters of the bay moments after takeoff for Barranquilla; 56 of the 61 persons aboard perished.

Jan. 20

Sanghar, Thailand. A crippled U.S. F-105 jet fighter fell into a small village and killed 16 Thai civilians.

Jan. 22

Duchiti area, Haiti. A Haitian DC-3 commercial airliner crashed near the southwest coast, killing 30 of the 35 persons aboard.

Jan. 24

Near Chamonix, France. An Indian 707 jetliner, on a flight from Bombay to Geneva, Switzerland, rammed into a fog-obscured ridge about 45 feet below the summit of Mont Blanc; all 117 persons aboard died.

Jan. 25

Ankhe, South Vietnam. A U.S. Air Force C-123 transport, taking off in bad weather, plunged to the ground and burst into flames; 46 U.S. infantrymen and crewmen were killed.

Jan. 28

Bremen, Germany. A twin-engine German airliner overshot the Bremen Airport landing strip, exploded, and burned in a nearby field; all 46 persons aboard died, including 7 members of an Italian swimming team.

Feb. 2

Faridpur, Pakistan. A Pakistani S-61 helicopter, en route from Dacca, fell to the ground in flames when a vulture flew into the rotor blades; 23 persons died, and one survived.

Feb. 4

Tokyo, Japan. A Japanese 727 jetliner, completing a flight from Chitose, and only moments away from the airport, plunged into Tokyo Bay amid a pillar of flame; all 133 persons aboard perished.

Feb. 7

Banihal Pass, Kashmir. An Indian F-27 propjet, on a Srina-gar–New Delhi flight, disappeared in the Himalayas during a storm; all 37 persons aboard died.

Feb. 17

Moscow, U.S.S.R. A Soviet TU-114 airliner, scheduled to inaugurate a service to Brazzaville in the Congo Republic, skidded in wet snow at takeoff and split in two; 48 of the 70 persons aboard were reported killed.

March 4

Tokyo, Japan. A Canadian DC-8 jetliner, en route from Hong Kong to Buenos Aires, Argentina, in making a landing in fog at Tokyo's International Airport, snagged the ap-proach lights, struck a breakwater wall, and careened down the runway in flames; 64 of the 72 persons aboard were killed.

March 5

Near Tokyo, Japan. A British 707 Tokyo–London airliner caught fire moments after takeoff about 3,000 feet above the summit of Mount Fuji and crashed on the eastern slopes; all 124 persons aboard were killed.

March 18

Cairo, Egypt. A Soviet-built AN-24 plane, en route from Cyprus, crashed and burned while attempting a landing at Cairo Airport during a sandstorm; at least 30 persons per-ished.

April 22

Near Ardmore, Oklahoma. A U.S. Electra propjet, chartered to transport a group of U.S. Army recruits from Fort Ord, California, to Fort Benning, Georgia, crashed when it missed the Gene Autry Airport runway, while making a fuel stop during a rainstorm; 76 recruits and 6 crewmen perished, but 16 of the servicemen survived.

April 27

Coclococha, Peru. A Peruvian Constellation airliner, en route from Lima to Cuzco, crashed in the Andes; all 49 persons aboard were killed.

Aug. 6

Falls City, Nebraska. A U.S. BAC-111 New Orleans–Min-neapolis jetliner plunged in flames and exploded in a muddy soybean field; all 42 persons aboard were killed.

Aug. 11

Near Bucharest, Romania. A Romanian airliner, en route from Cluj to Bucharest, crashed and killed all 24 persons aboard.

Aug. 17

Danang, South Vietnam. A U.S. Marine F-8E Crusader jet suffered engine failure moments after takeoff, plunged into a small village, and killed 26 Vietnamese civilians; 15 others were injured.

Sept. 1

Ljubljana, Yugoslavia. A British-chartered Britannia 102 turboprop, carrying vacationing Britons from London to Ljubljana, struck some treetops as it approached the airport runway, hit the ground, and burst into flames; 97 of the 117 persons aboard died.

Sept. 22

Queensland, Australia. An Australian Viscount airliner on a flight from Mount Isa to Longreach, Queensland, crashed and killed 24 persons aboard.

Oct. 1

Near Squaw Mountain, Oregon. A U.S. DC-9 jet en route from San Francisco, California, to Seattle, Washington, plunged into a mountain ravine and burned; all 18 persons aboard died.

Nov. 11

Off Nantucket, Massachusetts. A U.S. Air Force radar picket plane plunged into rough seas and sank with 19 crewmen aboard; all were presumed dead.

Nov. 13

Near Matsuyama, Japan. A Japanese YS-11 turboprop, on a scheduled flight from Osaka to Shikoku Island, overshot the runway and then, as it circled for a second try, plummeted into the Inland Sea; all 50 persons aboard, including 11 honeymooning couples, were killed.

Nov. 22

South Arabia. An Aden DC-3 commercial plane, flying from the Wahidi Desert area, crashed moments after taking off for Aden; all 28 persons aboard died.

Nov. 24

Bratislava, Czechoslovakia. A Bulgarian IL-18 turboprop, resuming flight after an unscheduled foul-weather landing, crashed in the nearby Carpathian Mountains; all 82 passengers and crewmen were killed.

Nov. 26

Tan Son Nhut, South Vietnam. A U.S. Air Force C-47 transport, attempting an emergency landing immediately after takeoff, nose-dived into a rice paddy and exploded; all 27 Americans aboard perished.

Dec. 18

Bogotá, Colombia. A Colombian Super Constellation, en route from Miami, Florida, missed the runway and crashed as dense fog closed in on El Dorado Airport; 18 of the 59 persons aboard were killed, and at least 10 others were hospitalized.

Dec. 24

Binh Thai, South Vietnam. A U.S. CL-44 cargo-transport, en route from Tachikawa, Japan, to the Da Nang Air Base, crash-landed in a heavy rainstorm, smashed into a small village, and burned; 125 Vietnamese civilians and the 4 U.S. crewmen were killed, and 42 civilians were injured.

1967

Feb. 16

Manado, Indonesia. An Indonesian Electra propjet exploded and burned a few seconds after landing at the Manado Airport in northern Celebes; 21 persons were killed, and 9 others were injured.

March 5

Monrovia, Liberia. A Brazilian DC-8 airliner, en route from Beirut, Lebanon, to Rio de Janeiro, attempted to land in heavy fog but crashed in a native village two miles short of the airport runway; 48 plane passengers and 5 villagers were killed.

March 5

Kenton, Ohio. A U.S. twin-engine Convair 580 on its way from Columbus to Toledo, Ohio, went down in a sleet and snow storm; all 38 passengers and crewmen were killed.

March 9

Urbana, Ohio. A U.S. DC-9 jetliner and a twin-engine Beechcraft collided in midair; all 26 persons aboard the planes died.

March 10

Near Phan Rang, Vietnam. A U.S. Navy C-47 transport crashed and exploded, killing all 25 persons aboard.

March 13

Near East London, South Africa. A South African airliner plunged into the ocean; all 29 persons aboard were lost.

March 30

New Orleans, Louisiana. A U.S. DC-8 jet, on a training flight, sideslipped into a cluster of houses and a motel at the edge of the airport, killing 9 teenage girls from Juda, Wisconsin, who were staying at the motel while on their "Senior Trip" to New Orleans, along with 3 other persons on the ground and all 6 crewmen aboard the plane; 40 others were injured.

April 8
Near Yoido Air Base, South Korea. A Korean Air Force C-47, taking off in drizzling rain, struck a church steeple, fell into a slum area, and exploded; 14 persons aboard the plane and 41 others on the ground perished, while 30 others were injured and 6 were missing.

April 11
Tamanrasset, Algeria. An Algerian DC-4 airliner, coming in for a landing, crashed and killed 35 of the 39 persons aboard.

April 17
Saveh, Iran. An Iranian Air Force C-130 was struck by lightning and exploded in the air; 22 persons were killed.

April 20
Nicosia, Cyprus. A Swiss four-engine Britannia turboprop, homeward-bound from a chartered tour of the Orient, rammed into a small hill in attempting a bad-weather landing; 126 passengers and crewmen perished, and 4 persons survived.

June 3
Near Perpignan, France. A British DC-4 chartered airliner, en route to a seaside resort at Costa Brava, Spain, smashed into the slopes of 9,137-foot Mont Canigou; all 88 persons aboard died.

June 4
Stockport, England. A British four-engine Argonaut chartered airliner, returning with a tour group from Palma, Majorca, dived low over the city, hit a power station, fell into a small park, and burst into flames; 72 of the 84 persons aboard were killed.

June 23
Blossburg, Pennsylvania. A U.S. BAC-111 twinjet en route to Washington, D.C., crashed and burned in a wooded area; all 34 persons aboard died.

June 24
Near Camp Le Jeune, North Carolina. Two U.S. Marine helicopters, a small Huey HU-1B and a large CH-53A Sea Stallion troop carrier, collided in midair over the New River Marine Air Facility; 22 Marines were killed, and 14 were injured.

June 30
Hong Kong. A Thai twinjet Caravelle, on a flight from Japan, was attempting a bad-weather instrument landing when it suddenly dived into Kowloon Bay; 24 of the 80 persons aboard died; 35 others were hospitalized.

July 6

Negros Island, Philippines. A Philippine Fokker turboprop, on an interisland hop, struck a mountaintop; all 21 persons aboard were killed.

July 19

Hendersonville, North Carolina. A U.S. Boeing 727 airliner, bound from Atlanta, Georgia, to Washington, D.C., collided with an off-course Cessna 310 and spiraled to the ground; all 82 persons aboard the planes, including 3 in the small craft, were killed.

July 19

Tananarive, Malagasy, A Malagasy DC-4, en route to Diego-Suarez in the north, crashed moments after takeoff from the airport; 40 persons died, and 35 others were injured.

Sept. 5

Gander, Newfoundland, Canada. A Czechoslovak Ilyushin-18 taking off for Havana, Cuba, after a refueling stop plunged into a swamp and burst into flames; 36 persons perished, and the remaining 33 were injured.

Oct. 11

South Vietnam. A U.S. C-130 military transport crashed into a mountain along the north coast, killing all 23 persons aboard.

Oct. 12

Off southwestern coast of Turkey. A British-Cypriot Mark IV Comet jetliner, on a flight from London, England, to Nicosia, Cyprus, plunged into the sea near the Greek island of Kastellorizon, killing all 66 persons aboard.

Nov. 3

Southeastern Brazil. A Brazilian twin-engine airliner crashed in the Marombas Mountain Range, killing 25 persons.

Nov. 4

Haslemere, England. A Spanish Caravelle jetliner en route from Málaga, Spain, went down suddenly as it approached the London Airport; all 37 persons aboard were killed.

Nov. 20

Boone County, Kentucky. A U.S. Convair 880 from Los Angeles, California, coming in for a landing through snow squalls, crashed just short of the Greater Cincinnati Airport; 68 of the 82 persons aboard perished.

Nov. 21

Near Sverdlovsk, U.S.S.R. A Soviet Il-18 turboprop struck a mountain when its radar failed; an estimated 70 to 100 persons were reported to have died.

Dec. 8

Near Huánuco, Peru. A Peruvian DC-6, flying from Lima to the interior, went down between Huánuco and Tingo María; all 66 persons aboard were killed.

1968

Jan. 10

Near Battle Mountain, Nevada. A U.S. Marine Corps C-54 transport plane, caught in a blizzard, crashed into 9,978-foot Mount Tobin; all 19 Marines aboard were killed.

Feb. 7

In the Himalayas, India. An Indian Air Force AN-12 transport plane was lost in the mountains; all 98 persons aboard were presumed dead.

Feb. 8

Amazon region, Brazil. A Brazilian Air Force Catalina seaplane went down in dense jungle; all 27 men aboard were missing and presumed dead.

Feb. 16

Taipei, Taiwan. A Nationalist Chinese Boeing 727 transport jet failed to make a proper landing at Taipei International Airport and fell into a tea plantation; 21 of the 63 passengers were killed, as well as a villager on the ground.

March 5

Saint-Claude, Guadeloupe. A French Boeing 707 jetliner en route from Santiago, Chile, to Paris, France, slammed into a mountainside and burst into flames; all 63 persons aboard perished.

March 9

Réunion Island. A French DC-6, taking off in a rainstorm, veered to the right and plowed into a hill; 19 persons died, and one survived.

March 24

Off Southwestern Wales. An Irish Viscount turboprop en route from Cork, Ireland, to London, England, plunged into the Irish Sea after going into a spin; all 61 persons aboard were killed.

April 8

Southern Chile. A Chilean DC-3 airliner, flying from Santiago to Chihaigue, dived into a mountainside and burst into flames; all 36 persons aboard were killed.

April 20

Windhoek, South West Africa. A South African Boeing 707, bound for London, England, from Johannesburg, South

Africa, crashed on takeoff from J. G. Strijdom Airport; 122 passengers and crewmen were killed, and 6 persons survived.

April 30

West Pakistan. A Pakistani Air Force transport crashed in the northern hills, killing all 22 crewmen aboard.

May 3

Dawson, Texas. A U.S. Electra turboprop exploded while heading through a rainstorm; all 85 passengers and crewmen perished.

May 23

Paramount, California. A U.S. S-61L passenger helicopter, loaded with Disneyland visitors, disintegrated in flight, fell, and burst into flames; all 23 persons aboard were killed.

June 25

Near Saigon, South Vietnam. Two U.S. Army helicopters collided in midair and exploded, knocking down a third copter; 29 men were killed.

Aug. 9

Pfaffenhofen, West Germany. A British Viscount en route from London to Innsbruck, Austria, fell onto the grassy bank along an autobahn, presumably while attempting an emergency landing; all 48 persons aboard the plane died in the blazing wreckage.

Aug. 10

Charleston, West Virginia. A U.S. FH-227 turboprop, in making an instrument approach to Kanawha Airport, crashed and burned; 35 of the 37 persons aboard died.

Aug. 14

Compton, California. A U.S. S-61L helicopter broke apart in midair, fell into a playground, and caught fire; all 21 persons aboard were killed.

Aug. 18

Off the south coast of Cyprus. A U.A.R. AN-20 airliner en route from Cairo, Egypt, to Damascus, Syria, plunged into the Mediterranean; all 40 passengers and crew were presumed dead.

Sept. 3

Near Burgas, Bulgaria. A Bulgarian Il-18 turboprop crashed on its way from Dresden, East Germany, to the Black Sea coast; 50 of the 89 persons aboard were killed.

Sept. 11

Off the French Riviera. A French Caravelle jetliner caught fire in midair and plunged into the sea just ten minutes from Nice, its destination; all 95 persons aboard perished.

Sept. 28

Lagos, Nigeria. A Red Cross-chartered DC-4 transport plane, ferrying Nigerian troops to Port Harcourt, crashed as it approached the runway; all 57 persons aboard were killed.

Oct. 4

Near Hue, South Vietnam. A U.S. Army CH-47 Chinook helicopter and a U.S. Air Force Caribou cargo plane collided in midair; 24 men were killed (11 aboard the copter and 13 on the plane).

Oct. 21

Near Ban Me Thout, South Vietnam. A U.S. Air Force C-47 plane en route from Saigon to Da Nang crashed in the Central Highlands when one engine failed; 24 men died in the wreckage.

Oct. 25

Near Hanover, New Hampshire. A U.S. twin-engine propjet, on a scheduled flight from Boston, Massachusetts, to Lebanon, New Hampshire, rammed into fog-covered Moose Mountain; 32 of the 42 persons aboard died in the burning plane.

Nov. 25

Savannakhet, Laos. A U.S. C-46 transport, chartered for a flight to Vientiane, cracked up when an engine failed; at least 20 persons were killed.

Dec. 2

Near Iliamna, Alaska. A U.S. F-27 twin-engine propjet, en route to Anchorage in fog and sub-zero weather, fell onto the marshy shore of Spotsy Lake; all 39 persons aboard died.

Dec. 12

Off Caracas, Venezuela. A U.S. Boeing 707 jetliner fell into the shark-infested waters of the Caribbean as it started its approach, one minute from Maiquetia Airport; all 51 persons aboard the plane perished.

Dec. 24

Bradford, Pennsylvania. A U.S. twin-engine Convair 580, on a routine flight from Detroit, Michigan, to Washington, D.C., made a too-short landing approach at the snow-obscured Bradford-McKean Airport and crashed into wooded, marshy terrain; of the 47 persons aboard, 20 were killed and the other 27 were hospitalized.

Dec. 27

Chicago, Illinois. A U.S. turboprop Convair 580, about to touch down on a fog-covered runway at O'Hare Airport, veered suddenly to the left, ripped through the closed door of a hangar, and burst into flames; 27 of the 53 persons aboard the plane were killed, as was one of the eight young members of a drum and bugle corps practicing in the hangar.

Dec. 31

Port Hedland, Western Australia, Australia. An Australian Viscount propjet, ending a flight from Perth and coming in for an apparently normal landing, suddenly burst into flames and crashed; all 26 persons aboard perished.

1969

Jan. 5

Gatwick, England. An Afghan Boeing 727 commercial airliner, en route from Kabul to London, came into Gatwick Airport through dense fog and just short of the runway rammed into a brick house; 50 persons, including 2 in the house, were killed, and 13 others were injured.

Jan. 6

Bradford, Pennsylvania. A U.S. Convair 580 propjet, flying 1,000 feet below the regular approach altitude into Bradford Regional Airport, plowed into a snow-covered golf course (the second plane to crash in the same area within a two-week period); of the 27 persons aboard, 11 were killed.

Jan. 13

Santa Monica Bay, California. A Scandinavian DC-8 jetliner, on a trip from Copenhagen, Denmark, to Los Angeles, developed landing gear trouble in making its descent into Los Angeles International Airport and nosed into the bay; 15 of those aboard drowned, and 30 were rescued.

Jan. 18

Off Los Angeles, California. A U.S. Boeing 727 jet, scheduled for Denver, Colorado, and Milwaukee, Wisconsin, was shattered by a violent explosion moments after takeoff and fell into the water; all 38 persons aboard perished.

Feb. 5

Off southern Taiwan. A U.S. Air Force Hercules rescue plane, on a search mission for eight missing crewmen of the Japanese freighter *Shoka Maru*, crashed into the icy sea; 11 airmen were lost and presumed dead, and one survived.

Feb. 11

South of Manila, Philippines. A Philippine C-47 plane was reported missing; an air and sea search failed to find any sign of the craft or its 20 passengers and crew members.

Feb. 18

Hawthorne, Nevada. A U.S. DC-3 "gamblers' flight" bound

for southern California disappeared over the Sierra Nevada; all 35 persons aboard were presumed dead.

Feb. 24

Near Kaohsiung, Taiwan. A Nationalist Chinese twin-engine transport propjet, on a regular flight from Kaohsiung to Taipei, reported engine trouble and crashed in a sugarcane field; all 36 passengers and crewmen died.

March 16

Maracaibo, Venezuela. A Venezuelan DC-9 jetliner, en route from Caracas to Miami, Florida, at takeoff from Grano de Oro Airport plunged to earth and exploded in a residential area; known dead were 155 persons—74 passengers and the 10 crew members, and at least 71 on the ground.

March 20

New Orleans, Louisiana. A U.S. DC-3, chartered by 24 sportsmen from Memphis, Tennessee, for a hunting trip to British Honduras, in making an approach to New Orleans International Airport crashed in heavy fog and burned; 13 hunters and 3 crewmen were killed, and 11 others survived.

March 20

Aswan, Egypt. A special flight of an Egyptian Ilyushin 18 ended in disaster when the plane crashed at Aswan Airport on its return trip from Mecca to Jiddah, Saudi Arabia; most of the 87 persons who perished were Muslim pilgrims.

April 2

Near Cracow, Poland. A Polish AN-24 en route from Warsaw to Cracow plunged to the ground, killing all 51 persons aboard.

April 16

Near Kinshasa, Congo (Zaire). A Congolese Air Force plane dived into the Congo River in attempting a landing at Ndjili Military Airport; 45 soldiers and members of their families died.

April 23

Near Saigon, South Vietnam. Two U.S. Army helicopter gunships collided in midair, crashed, and killed 16 U.S. and Vietnamese soldiers.

June 4

Near Monterrey, Mexico. A Mexican Boeing 727 jet bound for Monterrey from Mexico City rammed into Monk's Peak, a rain-soaked Sierra Madre mountainside, and killed all 79 passengers and crewmen aboard.

June 5

Western Aleutian Islands, Alaska. A U.S. Air Force RC-135

reconnaissance plane, on a routine mission from Shemya to Eielson Air Force Base near Fairbanks, was reported missing about 250 miles east of Shemya; the 19 men aboard were presumed dead.

July 6

Near Winder, Georgia. A small U.S. feeder-line Beechcraft 99 on a flight from Atlanta to Greer, South Carolina, crashed into a pasture 50 miles east of Atlanta; all 14 persons aboard were killed.

July 12

Near Simra, Nepal. A Nepalese DC-3 aircraft, on a flight from Katmandu to Simra, lost contact and was believed to be down near the Indian border; all 35 persons aboard were presumed dead.

July 26

Biskra, Algeria. An Algerian twin-jet Caravelle, chartered in Paris, France, and bound for the oil field of Hassi Messaoud, crashed in the Sahara and burned; of the 30 technicians and 7 crewmen aboard, 35 died.

Aug. 4

Valparaiso, Chile. A U.S. Navy C-47 transport, en route from Santiago to Mendoza, Argentina, with U.S. Navy and Air Force personnel aboard, was reported to have been forced down in the Andes Mountains during a storm; all 16 persons aboard were presumed dead.

Aug. 26

Moscow, U.S.S.R. A Soviet Ilyushin Il-18 with 112 passengers aboard, flying from Sochi to Moscow's Vnukovo Airport, crash-landed and burned after an apparent landing gear malfunction; an unofficial report listed 15 deaths.

Sept. 8

Eastern Colombia. A Colombian C-47 military transport on a village-to-village hop went down in the mountainous countryside and killed all 32 persons aboard.

Sept. 9

Shelbyville, Indiana. A U.S. twin-engine DC-9, letting down over Weir-Cook Municipal Airport, Indianapolis, collided with a small Piper Cherokee flown by a student pilot; the two aircraft plummeted into a soybean field, killing all 82 persons aboard the DC-9, as well as the small plane's pilot.

Sept. 12

Antipolo, Philippines. A Philippine 111 twinjet, in approaching Manila International Airport, struck a hillside in a housing subdivision; 45 persons aboard the aircraft died, and 2 others survived.

Sept. 20

Da Nang Air Base, South Vietnam. A Vietnamese DC-4 commercial jetliner en route from Pleiku collided with a U.S. Air Force F-4 Phantom jet as both planes were making final landing approaches to the airport; the F-4 crewmen were unhurt, but when the DC-4 fell into a field all 75 Vietnamese aboard, as well as 2 persons on the ground, were killed.

Sept. 21

Mexico City, Mexico. A Mexican Boeing 727 on a flight from Chicago, Illinois, with U.S. tourists bound for Mexico City and Acapulco, plowed into swampy ground at the end of a runway at the International Airport; 29 of the 118 persons aboard died.

Sept. 26

Central Bolivia. On a one-hour flight between Santa Cruz and Cochabamba, a Bolivian DC-6 disappeared somewhere in the snowcapped Andes; all 71 persons aboard, including members of Bolivia's leading soccer team, were presumed dead.

Oct. 2

Gulf of Tonkin. A U.S. Navy C-2A Greyhound cargo plane on a routine flight from Cobi Point, Philippines, to the carrier *Constellation* went down for undetermined reasons; all 26 U.S. servicemen drowned.

Nov. 19

Lake George, New York. A U.S. 227-B twin-engine turbo-prop nearing its destination at Warren County Airport slammed into an Adirondack peak and burst into flames; all 14 persons aboard were killed.

Nov. 20

Iju, Nigeria. A Nigerian VC-10 jet bound for Lagos from London, England, and three minutes away from a scheduled landing at Ikeja Airport, crashed into a thickly wooded area, burst into flames, and killed all 87 persons aboard.

Dec. 3

Off La Guaira, Venezuela. A French Boeing 707 jetliner on its way to Paris fell into the Caribbean and exploded minutes after taking off from Caracas; all 62 passengers and crew members died.

Dec. 8

Keratea, Greece. A Greek DC-6 airliner, flying from Crete to Athens, encountered driving rain and hurricane winds that slapped it against a 2,000-foot mountain 25 miles southeast of Athens Airport, killing all 90 persons aboard.

Dec. 22

Nha Trang, South Vietnam. A South Vietnamese DC-6B passenger liner exploded and crashed into a group of homes and a school; 22 persons died, and 14 others were unaccounted for.

Dec. 22

San Diego, California. A U.S. Navy F-8 Crusader jet fighter slammed into a hangar, burst into flames, and set off explosions that destroyed eight other jets; 15 men were killed, and at least 20 were injured.

1970

Jan. 13

Western Samoa. A Samoan DC-3 airliner taking off from the Faleolo Airport in a heavy rainstorm plunged into a lagoon, killing all 30 persons aboard.

Jan. 25

Poza Rica, Mexico. A chartered Mexican twin-engine Convair 300, carrying newsmen assigned to cover the Mexican presidential elections, crashed in heavy fog and burned on the side of Mesón Hill; of the 20 persons on board, 19 were killed.

Feb. 15

Off Santo Domingo, Dominican Republic. A Dominican DC-9 jetliner, taking off from the International Airport and bound for San Juan, Puerto Rico, fell into the Caribbean Sea, killing all 102 persons aboard.

Feb. 21

Near Wüenlingen, Switzerland. A Swiss Convair Coronado jet, 15 minutes out of Zürich en route to Israel, crashed after an explosion on board; all 47 persons aboard were killed.

March 14

Off Belém, Brazil. A Brazilian twin turboprop Fairchild Hiller 227B on an approach to Belém International Airport ditched in the sea near the mouth of the Amazon River; of the 40 persons aboard, 37 died.

April 1

Casablanca, Morocco. A Moroccan twin-engine Caravelle jetliner en route to Paris, France, crashed as it approached Nouaseur Airport; of the 82 persons aboard, 61 were killed.

April 21

Nueva Ecija, Philippines. A Philippine two-engine Hawker Siddeley, ripped by an explosion in the tail section, fell near the village of Pant Bangan; all 36 persons aboard died.

May 2

Off St. Croix, Virgin Islands. A Dutch chartered DC-9 jetliner en route to the Netherlands Antilles ran out of fuel and ditched in the Caribbean Sea, killing 23 of the 60 persons aboard.

July 4

Near Arbucias, Spain. A British Comet airliner carrying English vacationers crashed in mountainous terrain as it was coming in for a landing at Barcelona Airport; all 112 passengers and crewmen aboard were killed.

July 5

Toronto, Ontario, Canada. A Canadian DC-8 jetliner, scheduled from Montreal to Los Angeles, California, lost two engines on its landing approach to Toronto International Airport and plunged into a cornfield north of the airport, killing all 109 persons aboard.

July 18

Off Keflavik, Iceland. A Soviet turboprop Antonov-22 cargo plane on a mercy mission to Peru failed to make a scheduled stop at Halifax, Nova Scotia, Canada, and was believed lost in the North Atlantic with all 23 persons on board.

Aug. 6

Islamabad, Pakistan. A Pakistani airliner crashed minutes after taking off from the airport, killing all 30 persons aboard.

Aug. 9

Near Cuzco, Peru. A Peruvian Lockheed Electra turboprop, en route from Cuzco to Lima, developed engine trouble soon after takeoff from Cuzco Airport and, attempting a return to the airport, plunged into a hillside and exploded; 99 passengers and crewmen died, and the copilot survived.

Aug. 29

Assam State, India. An Indian Fokker Friendship aircraft went down with 39 persons aboard; all were killed.

Oct. 2

Near Taipei, Taiwan. A U.S. Air Force C-130 transport plane crashed into a mountain, killing all 43 persons aboard.

Oct. 2

Silver Plume, Colorado. A chartered U.S. Martin 440, carrying members of the Wichita State University football team, lost power and, in attempting to land on a highway, smashed into Mount Bethel; of the 40 persons aboard 31 died, including 14 team members.

Nov. 14

Huntington, West Virginia. A U.S. DC-9 jet, chartered for the Marshall University football squad, exploded in a wooded

A fireman battles the flaming wreckage of a plane that exploded and crashed during takeoff on November 27 at the International Airport at Anchorage, Alaska.

hollow as it approached the foggy rain-bound Tri-State Airport; all 75 persons aboard died, including 43 players and coaches of the Marshall team.

Nov. 27

Anchorage, Alaska. A U.S. DC-8 airliner, attempting to halt at takeoff, fell back onto the icy runway, exploded, and burned; of the 230 persons aboard, 48 were killed.

Nov. 27

Central South Vietnam. A U.S. Army C-123 transport went down in monsoon rains and heavy fog; all 79 persons aboard died.

Nov. 29

Central South Vietnam. A U.S. Army C-123 transport, second plane in two days to crash in the same area, brought death to 44 of the 46 persons on board.

Dec. 7

Constanta, Romania. A Romanian airliner en route from Tel Aviv, Israel, crashed near the landing site at Lydda Airport, killing 18 of the 27 persons on board.

1971

Jan. 18

Zürich, Switzerland. A Bulgarian Ilyushin-18 turboprop passenger plane crashed and burned in attempting an instrument landing at the fogbound Zürich Airport; 35 of the 37 persons aboard were killed.

Jan. 20

Near Lima, Peru. A Peruvian Air Force transport plane crashed into a mountain; all 31 persons aboard were presumed dead.

Jan. 21

Near Privas, France. A French Air Force Nord 262 turboprop transport went down in the mountainous Massif Central region; all 21 persons aboard died, including the crewmen and several high-ranking members of the French armed forces and of the French Atomic Energy Commission.

Jan. 25

Mérida, Venezuela. A Venezuelan Viscount turboprop en route from Mérida to Caracas developed engine trouble and crashed in the Andes Mountains; at least 36 persons were killed.

April 15

Near Manila, Philippines. A Philippine Air Force plane faltered at takeoff from Basa Air Field, hit a creek embankment, and split apart; 39 persons died, and a small child survived.

May 23

Rijeka, Yugoslavia. A Yugoslav Tu-134 twin-jet charter plane, carrying British tourists from London, England, crashed and burned at the airport, killing 78 persons.

June 6

Near Azusa, California. A U.S. Marine Phantom F-4 fighter jet collided with a DC-9 commercial airliner 12,000 feet above the San Gabriel Mountains; both planes plunged into a mountain ravine, killing 50 persons—49 aboard the liner and the F-4 pilot.

June 7

New Haven, Connecticut. A U.S. Convair 580 propjet, attempting to land in low visibility at Tweed-New Haven Airport, crashed through three empty beach cottages, caught fire, and fell into a swamp; 28 of the 31 persons aboard the plane died.

July 3

Hakodate, Japan. A Japanese YS-11 turboprop airliner approaching Hakodate Airport in fog and rain struck a mountainside, broke up, and killed all 68 persons aboard.

July 30

Morioka, Honshu, Japan. A Japanese Air Force F-86 jet

fighter smashed into a Japanese Boeing 727 passenger plane 26,000 feet over Morioka; all 162 persons aboard the airliner died; the student pilot of the F-86, however, was able to parachute to safety.

July 30

Pau, France. A French military transport on a paratrooper training flight over the air base fell to the ground when an engine caught fire; 34 paratroopers and 3 aircrewmen were killed.

Mid-August

Irkutsk, U.S.S.R. A Soviet Tu-104 twin-jet commercial airliner en route from Odessa to Vladivostok crashed and exploded on takeoff from Irkutsk Airport, killing all 97 persons aboard.

Aug. 18

Pegnitz, West Germany. A U.S. Army Ch-47 Chinook twin-engine helicopter exploded in midair, plunged into a hayfield, and killed all 37 U.S. servicemen aboard.

Sept. 6

Hamburg, West Germany. A West German BAC 111 charter plane flying vacationers to Spain developed engine trouble at takeoff and, in attempting an emergency landing on a super-highway, struck an overpass bridge; 22 of the 120 persons aboard died, and 42 others were hospitalized.

Mid-September

Kiev, U.S.S.R. A Hungarian Tu-134 airliner on a scheduled flight from Budapest to Kiev crashed near the Kiev Airport, killing all 49 persons aboard.

Oct. 2

Ghent, Belgium. A British Vanguard turboprop airliner en route from London to Salzburg, Austria, went out of control when an engine exploded and fell in flames to the ground; all 63 persons aboard died.

Nov. 29

Near Phu Bai, South Vietnam. A U.S. Army CH-47 Chinook helicopter disappeared along the storm-swept north coast of South Vietnam; all 34 crewmen and military passengers were killed.

Dec. 24

Near Pucallpa, Peru. A Peruvian Lockheed Electra turoprop passenger plane flying from Lima to Iquitos went down in a mountainous jungle area; all 92 persons aboard were believed dead.

1972

Jan. 7

Valencia, Spain. A Spanish Iberia Airlines Caravelle commercial passenger jet en route from Valencia to the Mediterranean island of Ibiza crashed into a mist-covered rocky peak as it made an approach to the Ibiza Airport; all 164 persons aboard were killed instantly.

Jan. 21

Northern Colombia. A Colombian Satena Airlines DC-3 crashed and burned in the Andes, killing 35 persons.

Jan. 21

Bogotá, Colombia. A Colombian Airlines turboprop failed to gain altitude after taking off in a rainstorm and fell to the ground, killing 20 persons.

Jan. 26

Northwestern Czechoslovakia. A Yugoslav Airlines DC-9 jetliner en route from Stockholm, Sweden, to Belgrade exploded in midair and plunged into a snow-covered mountain slope; 27 of the 28 persons aboard perished, but a stewardess survived the 31,000-foot fall.

March 14

Near Kalba, United Arab Emirates. A Danish Sterling Airways Super-Caravelle jet on a charter vacation flight returning from Ceylon to Copenhagen crashed in an attempted landing in torrential rain at Dubai Airport; all 112 persons aboard the plane died.

March 19

Near Aden, People's Democratic Republic of Yemen. A Yugoslav Airlines DC-9 chartered by Egyptian Airways smashed into the side of Shamsan Mountain, killing all 30 persons aboard.

April 18

Addis Ababa, Ethiopia. An East African Airways VC-10 en route from Nairobi to London, England, and taking off from its first stop at Addis Ababa, hurtled from the end of the runway into a farmhouse; of the 107 persons aboard (many of them British children on vacation) 41 were killed, and about 40 others were injured.

May 5

Palermo, Sicily. An Alitalia DC-8 jetliner en route from Rome encountered bad weather as it neared Punta Raisi Airport and slammed into a 2,250-foot mountainside; all 117 persons aboard perished.

May 18
Kharkov, U.S.S.R. A Soviet Aeroflot Antonov-10 turboprop went down near Kharkov, taking the lives of 108 persons.

May 21
Lobito, Angola. An Angola Airlines twin-engine turboprop plunged into the sea in an attempted landing at the fogbound Lobito Airport; 20 of the 23 persons on board were killed.

June 14
New Delhi, India. A Japan Air Lines DC-8 jetliner on a flight from Tokyo to London, England, crashed moments after getting clearance to land at Palam International Airport; 83 of the 89 persons aboard and 2 on the ground were killed.

June 15
Pleiku, South Vietnam. A British Cathay Pacific Airlines Convair 880 jetliner on a scheduled flight from Bangkok, Thailand, to Hong Kong broke up at a high altitude and went down in the Central Highlands, killing all 81 persons aboard.

June 18
London, England. A British European Airways Trident-1 aircraft went into a stall and plunged to the ground shortly after taking off in rainy weather from Heathrow Airport; all 118 crewmen and passengers perished.

Rescue workers search the wreckage of a Japanese jetliner in a desert village southeast of New Delhi, India, after the plane exploded and crashed on approach to the Palam International Airport on June 14.

July 29
Villavicencio, Colombia. A midair collision between two Colombian Avianca Airlines planes ended in tangled wreckage deep in the Las Palomas Mountains and the deaths of 37 persons.

Aug. 14
Königs Wusterhausen, East Germany. An East German state airline (Interflug) Soviet-built Ilyushin-62 on a charter flight to a Black Sea resort crashed at Königs Wusterhausen moments after taking off from Schönefeld Airport in East Berlin; all 156 persons aboard were killed.

Aug. 27
Southeastern Venezuela. A Linea Aeropostal Venezolana DC-3 twin-engine plane flying between Canaima and Ciudad Bolívar suffered engine failure and went down in deep jungle; all 24 persons aboard perished.

Aug. 28
Papua New Guinea. A Royal Australian Air Force Caribou transport plane carrying a group of Papua New Guinea Army school cadets plunged into the thickly jungled slopes of Mount Kulama; 24 persons were killed, but 5 cadets were rescued.

Sept. 13
Dhulikhel, Nepal. A Royal Nepalese DC-3 on a training flight came in low between two rocky heights, struck one, spun into a high-tension cable, and exploded; all 31 servicemen (including 27 student paratroopers) aboard were killed.

Sept. 24
Sacramento, California. An 18-year-old U.S. surplus F-86 Sabrejet, converted for use in air shows, failed in a takeoff attempt, bounced across a road hitting three cars, and smashed into an ice cream parlor; 22 persons (12 children and 10 parents) died in the flaming ice cream parlor, and 16 others were injured.

Oct. 3
Sochi, U.S.S.R. A Soviet Aeroflot Ilyushin-18 airliner exploded moments after takeoff from the Black Sea resort city of Sochi, bringing death to all 100 persons aboard the aircraft.

Oct. 13
Krasnaya Polyana, U.S.S.R. Chartered by Intourist, a Soviet Aeroflot Ilyushin-62 passenger jet en route from Paris, France, crashed and exploded as it attempted to land in rain and fog at Moscow's Sheremetyevo International Airport; a reported 176 persons perished.

Oct. 21

Athens, Greece. A Greek Olympic Airways plane on a flight from the island of Corfu in a heavy rainstorm undershot the Athens Airport and plunged into the sea; 37 persons died, but 16 others were rescued.

Oct. 30

Bari, Italy. An Aero Trasporti Italiani domestic airliner crashed en route from Naples to Taranto, killing all 27 persons on board.

Nov. 28

Moscow, U.S.S.R. A Japan Air Lines DC-8 jet en route from Copenhagen, Denmark, to Tokyo burst into flames and fell to the ground moments after taking off from Sheremetyevo International Airport; 66 of the 76 persons aboard the plane were reportedly killed.

Dec. 3

Santa Cruz de Tenerife, Canary Islands. A Spanish Convair 990-A Coronado, chartered from Spantax Airlines by a group of predominantly German tourists, fell from a height of about 500 feet as it left the runway at Las Rodeos Airport en route to Munich, Germany; all 155 passengers and crewmen died.

Dec. 8

Chicago, Illinois. A United Air Lines Boeing 737 flying from Washington, D.C., to Midway Airport failed in an attempt to pull up from its landing pattern and plowed into a cluster of houses; 45 persons, including 2 in a destroyed home, perished in the inferno.

Dec. 20

Chicago, Illinois. Two passenger planes collided on intersecting runways at O'Hare Airport; 10 persons were killed, and 15 others were injured.

Dec. 23

Oslo, Norway. A Norwegian Braathens S.A.F.E. Fokker Fellowship airliner flying through rain and fog crashed in a forest near the outskirts of the city, bringing death to 39 of the 45 persons aboard.

Dec. 29

Florida Everglades. An Eastern Airlines L-1011 TriStar superjet came in too low on its approach to the Miami International Airport and crashed into the swampy terrain of the Everglades, strewing wreckage over a 1,520-foot area; 101 persons aboard the 350,000-pound jumbo aircraft died, and most of the 75 survivors received injuries.

1973

Jan. 22

Kano, Nigeria. A Royal Jordanian Airways Boeing 707 jetliner, chartered by Nigeria Airways and carrying Muslim pilgrims home from a trip to Mecca, Saudi Arabia, crashed and burst into flames as it landed in dense fog at the Kano Airport; of the 205 passengers and crew members aboard, 176 perished.

Jan. 29

Northern Cyprus. An Egyptian Soviet-built Ilyushin-18 turboprop airliner, en route to Nicosia, Cyprus, from Cairo, struck the side of a rocky mountain peak and killed all of the 38 persons aboard.

Feb. 19

Prague, Czechoslovakia. A Soviet national airline Aeroflot Tupolev-154 trijet, completing the regular morning flight from Moscow, smashed into the ground and burst into flames as it came into the Prague International Airport; 66 of the 100 persons aboard were killed.

Feb. 28

Szczecin, Poland. A Polish Air Force Soviet-built Antonov-24 turboprop carrying several top Polish and Czechoslovak security officials crashed near the Szczecin Airport and killed all 15 persons aboard.

March 3

Moscow, U.S.S.R. A Bulgarian Balkan Airlines Ilyushin-18 turboprop flying from Sofia to Moscow plunged into a deep snowbank and burned near the village of Skhodyna as it came in for a landing at Moscow's Sheremetyevo Airport; all 25 persons aboard died.

March 5

Nantes, France. Two Spanish jetliners, an Iberian twin-engine DC-9 and a Spantax Convair 990 charter plane, collided in the sky 29,000 feet over Nantes; the DC-9 fell in flames, killing all 68 persons aboard; the Convair 990 made a landing with all its 108 passengers and crew members safe.

March 19

Central Highlands, South Vietnam. A South Vietnamese national airline Air Vietnam four-engine DC-4 prop plane, en route from Saigon, crashed as it approached the Ban Me Thuot airport; at least 58 persons died.

April 10

Hochwald, Switzerland. A British Invicta charter plane, a four-engine Vanguard turboprop, en route from Bristol with a group of women on a one-day holiday trip to Switzerland, cracked up when a wing hit a tree as it approached the Basel airport during a heavy snowstorm; 107 of the 145 persons on board the plane perished.

April 12

Sunnyvale, California. A U.S. Space Agency Convair 990 laboratory aircraft collided with a U.S. Navy P-3 Orion antisubmarine patrol plane in midair about 300 feet above a golf course, and both plunged to the ground in flames; 16 men died, but a Navy crewman survived.

May 31

New Delhi, India. An Indian Airlines Boeing 737 jetliner, en route from Madras, burst into flames and crashed into a residential area moments before a scheduled landing at Palam Airport; 48 persons aboard the plane were killed, and 17 were injured.

June 2

São Luis, Brazil. A Brazilian Cruzeiro do Sul airlines Caravelle jet crashed in a landing attempt at the São Luis Airport, killing all 23 persons aboard.

June 3

Paris, France. A Soviet Tupolev-144 civilian supersonic airliner exploded in midair during a demonstration flight at the Paris International Air Show at Le Bourget Airport, with the flaming wreckage falling on the town of Goussainville; 7 villagers on the ground perished, as did all 6 crewmen aboard the plane.

June 20

Puerto Vallarta, Mexico. An Aeromexico DC-9 jet, on a flight from Houston, Texas, to Mexico City, smashed into a mountainside, killing all 27 persons aboard.

July 11

Saulx-les-Chartreux, France. A Brazilian Varig Airlines Boeing 707, nearing the end of a 6,000-mile flight from Rio de Janeiro, caught fire and fell into a vegetable patch just short of Paris's Orly Airport; 122 of the 134 persons aboard the plane died in the smoke and fire, and 12 survived.

July 22

Papeete, Tahiti. A Pan American Boeing 707 heading for Los Angeles, California, plunged into the sea moments after its takeoff from the Papeete Airport; only one person of the 79 passengers and crew members aboard the plane survived.

July 23

St. Louis, Missouri. A U.S. Ozark Air Lines twin-engine Fairchild 227 turbojet slammed into a St. Louis suburban area as it approached the runway in a thunderstorm at Lambert Airport; 37 of the 45 persons aboard were killed.

July 31

Boston, Massachusetts. A Delta Air Lines jetliner on a flight from Burlington, Vermont, crashed while landing in a dense fog at Boston's Logan International Airport; of the 89 persons aboard, only one survived.

Aug. 13

La Coruña, Spain. A Spanish Caravelle airliner arriving from Madrid exploded and crashed into several houses after striking treetops near the fogbound La Coruña Airport; none of the 85 passengers and crew survived.

Aug. 27

Bogotá, Colombia. A Colombian Lockheed Electra turbo-prop airliner crashed into a hill and burned shortly after taking off from Bogotá; none of the 40 persons aboard survived.

Aug. 28

Madrid, Spain. A. U.S. Air Force C-141 StarLifter cargo jet on a flight from Athens, Greece, to an air base near Madrid hit a low hill during its landing approach and exploded in flames as it struck the ground; of the 24 persons who died, some were children and military wives.

Sept. 11

Titograd, Yugoslavia. A French-built Caravelle aircraft belonging to Yugoslav Airlines crashed into a mountain as it was approaching the Titograd Airport after a flight from Skoplje, Macedonia; all 42 persons aboard were killed.

Oct. 12

Near Requena, Peru. A Sikorsky helicopter carrying 15 geologists and technicians in search of oil reserves crashed in the Peruvian jungle; 4 survivors were rescued two days later.

Oct. 13

Moscow, U.S.S.R. A Soviet airliner crashed at a Moscow airport after completing a flight from Tbilisi; 28 persons were reported killed.

Dec. 11

Mount Sitkin Island, Alaska. A C-118 U.S. Navy Reserve transport plane crashed into a mountain about 25 miles from Adak Naval Air Station; all 10 persons aboard died.

Dec. 22

Near Tangier, Morocco. A French-built Caravelle twin-jet airliner, under charter by the Belgium Sabena Airlines and flying from Paris to Casablanca via Tangier, crashed into a mountain in stormy weather near the coastal town of Tetuán, 30 miles southeast of Tangier; none of the 99 passengers and 7 crewmen survived.

1974
Jan. 1
Near Turin, Italy. An Italian twin-engine Fokker F-28 jetliner, on a flight from Cagliari, Sardinia, to Geneva, Switzerland, crashed in bad weather while approaching Turin Airport for a stopover; only 4 of the 42 persons aboard were rescued from the flaming wreckage.
Jan. 6
Johnstown, Pennsylvania. A Beechcraft 99 twin-engine commuter turboprop struck a bank of runway lights at the Johnstown-Cambria County Airport, flipped over, and broke almost in half; 11 persons died, and 6 were critically injured.
Jan. 26
Izmir, Turkey. A Fokker F-28, taking off from Izmir's military airport on a domestic flight to Istanbul, crashed and burst into flames; 65 of the 73 persons aboard died.
Jan. 30
Pago Pago, American Samoa. A Pan American Boeing 707, arriving from Auckland, New Zealand, crashed during heavy rains about one mile short of the Pago Pago Airport runway; with its wings severed and fuselage torn apart, the plane burst into flames, killing 96 of the 101 persons aboard.
March 8
Hanoi, North Vietnam. A Soviet-made North Vietnamese airplane crashed as it attempted to land at Hanoi's military airport; 13 Algerian journalists and 3 radio reporters were killed.
March 14
Bishop, California. A chartered twin-engine Convair, taking a television crew from location in Bishop back to Burbank, crashed into a mountain ridge shortly after takeoff; 31 cast and film crew members and 5 members of the plane's crew were killed.
March 15
Tehran, Iran. A chartered Danish airliner, returning vacationers to Copenhagen after a tour of the Far East, burst into flames as it taxied into position for a takeoff from Tehran Airport; of the almost 100 persons aboard, at least 16 died, and many were hospitalized.

April 4

Francistown, Botswana. A DC-4, transporting gold miners home to Malawi after work in South Africa, caught fire shortly after takeoff and crashed as it attempted to return to the Francistown Airport; 77 persons lost their lives, but 7 others, thrown clear by the crash, survived.

April 11

Near Hilo, Hawaii. A twin-engine Beechcraft, flying tourists from Hilo to the island of Maui, crashed into a mountain 31 miles from the Hilo Airport; a rescue team recovered all 11 bodies.

April 22

Bali. A Pan American Boeing 707, carrying an international group of passengers from Hong Kong to Sydney, Australia, by way of Bali, crashed into a precipitous mountain as it began its approach to the international airport at Denpasar; rescue teams eventually recovered all 107 bodies.

April 27

Leningrad, U.S.S.R. A four-engine turboprop Ilyushin-18, departing on an Aeroflot flight to Krasnodar, crashed shortly after leaving the runway at Leningrad Airport; 118 persons reportedly died in the flaming wreckage.

May 2

Andes Mountains, Ecuador. A twin-engine DC-3 owned by the local Ecuadorean airline, Atesa, crashed in the Andes Mountains east of Quito on a flight from Pastaza to Ambato; 22 persons were killed.

May 26

Celebes, Indonesia. An Indonesian Air Force aircraft crashed into a mountain, killing all 10 crew members.

June 8

Colombia. A Colombian airliner crashed and burned in a jungle area near the Venezuelan border; all 43 persons on board were killed.

June 28

Battambang, Cambodia. A Cambodia Air Commercial plane, piloted by a Taiwanese crew, crashed on takeoff; 20 of the 25 persons aboard were reported killed.

Aug. 12

Near Linoghin, Upper Volta. An Air Mali Ilyushin turboprop, on a flight from Saudi Arabia to Mali, crashed during a violent storm as the Soviet pilot apparently attempted an emergency landing when his plane ran out of fuel; although 13 persons survived, at least 47 others perished.

Aug. 14
Margarita Island, Venezuela. A four-engine turboprop of the government-owned Aeropostal airline was driven into a hill by hurricane-strength winds while on a flight from Caracas; the 49 casualties included two "stowaway" teenage girls who had been allowed to board by a stewardess friend.

Aug. 18
Near Kisangani, Zaire. A C-130 Zaire Air Force transport crashed with the loss of all 31 persons aboard.

Sept. 7
Near Telukbetung, Indonesia. An Indonesian Airways Fokker F-27, on a flight from Jakarta, was driven off course by a thunderstorm as it neared Telukbetung Airport and crashed into an abandoned house and burned; 28 persons were reported killed, 7 hospitalized, and 3 missing.

Sept. 8
Ionian Sea. A TWA Boeing 707, on a flight from Tel Aviv, Israel, to New York, New York, by way of Athens, Greece, and Rome, Italy, crashed into the sea after flying westward across Greece; all 88 persons aboard died on impact or were drowned.

Sept. 11
Near Charlotte, North Carolina. An Eastern Airlines DC-9 flying to Charlotte from Charleston, South Carolina, burst into flames and disintegrated when it crashed into a wooded area more than two miles from the Charlotte runway; 72 of the 82 persons aboard were killed.

Sept. 18
Ponta Pora, Brazil. A Brazilian Air Force transport exploded and crashed shortly after taking off from Ponta Pora; 2 generals and an army base commander were among the 23 officers killed; one survived.

Oct. 30
Near Melville Island, Northwest Territories, Canada. A four-engine Lockheed Electra, operated by Panarctic Oils Ltd., crashed into Byam Channel while on a flight from Edmonton; only 2 of the 34 persons aboard survived when the plane hit the ice-covered channel.

Nov. 20
Nairobi, Kenya. A West German Lufthansa airliner, probably impaired by malfunctioning wing flaps, plunged into a muddy field and burned moments after taking off from the Nairobi Airport; of the 157 persons involved in the first fatal crash

of a Boeing 747 aircraft, 59 died and 23 were hospitalized.

Dec. 1

Upperville, Virginia. A TWA Boeing 727, battling heavy rains, crashed into a wooded slope near a secret U.S. government installation while approaching Dulles International Airport near Washington, D.C., on a flight from Columbus, Ohio; all 92 persons aboard the jetliner were killed.

Dec. 22

Near Maturín, Venezuela. An Avensa Airlines DC-9, on a domestic flight to Caracas, exploded and crashed shortly after taking off from Maturín Airport; 77 persons died.

Dec. 28

Near Tikal, Guatemala. A chartered Lockheed Lodestar airliner, carrying a group of U.S. tourists back to Guatemala City after a visit to Mayan ruins in the north, crashed shortly after taking off from the Tikal Airport; all 21 passengers were killed, as were the 3 Guatemalan crew members.

1975

Jan. 4

Lotru Mountain, Romania. A Romanian airliner on a domestic flight crashed into a mountainous area, killing 33 persons.

Jan. 6

Near Tucumán, Argentina. A two-engine military plane crashed during a storm and burst into flames; 2 of the 13 officers who died were army generals.

Jan. 8

Near Neiva, Colombia. A C-47 Satena airliner crashed and burned shortly after taking off from the Neiva Airport; none of the 20 persons aboard survived.

Jan. 9

Near Whittier, California. A Golden West Airliner commuter plane was hit by a single-engine Cessna 150 carrying a student pilot and his instructor; all 14 persons aboard the two planes lost their lives.

Jan. 30

Near Istanbul, Turkey. A Turkish Airlines F-28 carrying 37 passengers and 4 crew members crashed into the Sea of Marmara when a citywide power failure blacked out the landing strip lights at Yesilkoy Airport; there were no survivors.

Feb. 3

Near Manila, Philippines. The engine of a Philippine airliner burst into flames shortly after the pilot took off from the

Manila Airport; 31 of the 32 persons aboard died in a crash landing.

Feb. 9

Crete. A West German military plane heading for a military base crashed on the Greek island of Crete in the Mediterranean Sea, killing all 42 persons aboard.

Feb. 27

Congonhas, Brazil. A VASP airliner scheduled to fly into the interior crashed while taking off from the Municipal Airport; 15 persons died.

Feb. 28

Near Natal, Brazil. A helicopter carrying petroleum workers to a drilling platform exploded near Natal; 12 persons lost their lives.

March 16

Near San Carlos de Bariloche, Argentina. A Fokker 26, operated as a passenger plane by the Argentine Air Force, smashed into a mountain; there were at least 52 fatalities.

March 20

Near Quilcene, Washington. A U.S. military C-141 Starlifter, nearing the end of a flight from Japan, crashed inside Olympic National Park when the pilot followed landing directives intended for another plane; all 16 persons aboard perished.

April 4

Near Saigon, South Vietnam. A U.S. Air Force Galaxy C-5A, carrying 243 Vietnamese orphans and their adult escorts on the first leg of a flight to the United States, crashed and broke apart in a soggy paddy before the pilot was able to return safely to Saigon's Tan Son Nhut Airport; improperly closed rear hatches were blamed for the disaster, which claimed the lives of 172 persons, most of them tiny children.

Mid-July

Near Batumi, U.S.S.R. A Soviet Yak-40 airliner operating out of Armenia crashed near Batumi, killing at least 28 persons.

July 31

Taipei, Taiwan. A Far Eastern Air Transport turboprop on a routine domestic flight from Hualien skidded off the Taipei Airport runway during a sudden rainstorm and broke into three pieces; at least 27 persons were killed, and 48 were injured.

Aug. 3

Near Imzizen, Morocco. A Boeing 707, carrying workers home from France for a summer vacation, crashed into a fog-shrouded mountain and burned as it approached the

Agadir Airport; none of the 188 persons aboard survived.
  Aug. 20
Near Damascus, Syria. A four-engine Soviet-made Ilyushin 62 jetliner that was operated by Czechoslovakia crashed into a hill and burst into flames as it approached the Damascus Airport; there were only 2 survivors among the 128 persons aboard.
  Aug. 30
St. Lawrence Island, Alaska. A Wien Air Alaska F-27B turbo-prop crashed into a fog-veiled hillside at Gambell while on a routine flight from Nome; 10 persons died, but 23 others were rescued by Eskimos living in a nearby village.
  Aug. 31
Leipzig, East Germany. A Tu-134 jetliner operated by the Interflug Airline of East Germany crashed just short of the Leipzig Airport runway at the completion of a flight from Stuttgart, West Germany; 26 persons died in the flaming wreckage.
  Sept. 24
Palembang, Indonesia. A Garuda Indonesian Airways Fokker 28 on a routine flight from Jakarta overshot the Palembang runway, struck coconut trees, and burst into flames; 29 persons were killed, including a woman farm worker who was burned to death.
  Sept. 30
Mediterranean Sea. A Soviet-built Tu-154, operated by the Hungarian Malev Airlines, crashed into the sea and sank as it was preparing to land at the Beirut Airport in Lebanon; none of the 60 persons aboard survived.
  Oct. 25
Bolivia. A Bolivian Air Force Convair 440 that was transporting military personnel and their relatives to La Paz crashed into a mountain shortly after taking off from a resort at Tomonoco; all 70 persons aboard were presumed dead.
  Oct. 30
Prague, Czechoslovakia. A twin-jet DC-9 airliner chartered by Yugoslavia crashed on the outskirts of Prague as it came in for a landing at the fog-shrouded airport; 68 of the 120 persons aboard were killed.
  Nov. 25
Sinai Peninsula. An Israeli C-130E Hercules transport, on a night training flight over the Sinai Desert, crashed into the summit of 2,900-foot Jebel Halal; all 20 persons aboard were killed.

1976

Jan. 1

Saudi Arabia. A Lebanese Middle East Airlines Boeing 707, on a flight from Beirut to the Persian Gulf states, crashed in a desert area of Saudi Arabia; all 82 persons aboard lost their lives.

Jan. 21

Southern China. A Soviet-built An-24 airliner, with a capacity of 44 passengers, went down in southern China; in its first public announcement of a local air disaster, the Chinese government reported that one American and two Danish businessmen were among the undisclosed number of fatalities.

March 5

Near Yerevan, U.S.S.R. A Soviet Il-18 turboprop airliner crashed as it neared the end of a flight from Moscow to Yerevan; unofficial sources placed the death toll at about 120 persons.

April 14

Neuquén Province, Argentina. A British-made Avro 748 belonging to Yacimientos Petroliferos Fiscales, a government-owned oil company, crashed in west-central Argentina with the loss of 37 lives.

April 23

Gulf of Mexico. A Bell 205 helicopter, on a routine morning flight to an offshore drilling rig, went down in the Gulf of Mexico; the bodies of 7 victims were recovered, and 5 other persons aboard were presumed dead.

April 27

Charlotte Amalie, Virgin Islands. An American Airlines Boeing 727 jetliner, on a flight from Rhode Island to St. Thomas, overran the runway at the Harry S. Truman Airport, knocked down two fences, swept across an embankment, and burst into flames when it smashed into several buildings; 37 of the 88 persons aboard were killed, and many survivors were seriously injured.

May 3

Monze, Zambia. A Twin Otter aircraft manufactured by de Havilland Aircraft of Canada crashed in south-central Zambia while the Canadian pilot was demonstrating the aircraft to Zambian Air Force officers; of the 13 persons aboard, only 2 survived.

May 9

Near Huete, Spain. A Boeing 747 cargo plane belonging to the Iranian Air Force caught fire and crashed during a storm as it was heading for a stopover in Madrid; all 17 persons aboard the aircraft were killed.

June 1

Malabo Island, Equatorial Guinea. A Soviet Aeroflot Tu-154 crashed on a flight from Luanda, Angola, to Moscow; 46 bodies were recovered after the wreckage was located in mid-June.

June 4

Guam. An Air Manila Lockheed Electra, after taking off from Guam International Airport, crashed into a hill, bounced over a highway, struck a small truck, and burst into flames; the truck driver and all 45 persons aboard the aircraft were killed.

July 28

Near Bratislava, Czechoslovakia. A Soviet-made Il-18 turbo-prop aircraft belonging to Czechoslovakia caught fire and crashed into Zlate Pisky Lake as it neared the end of a domestic flight from Prague; only 6 of the 76 persons aboard survived.

Aug. 28

Near Peterborough, England. A U.S. Air Force C-141 jet transport, en route from New Jersey to a military base at Mildenhall, England, crashed near Peterborough; all 18 persons aboard were killed.

Aug. 28

Søndre Strømfjord, Greenland. A U.S. Air Force C-141 Star-Lifter transport burst into flames after landing at Søndre Strømfjord; 21 of the 27 persons who had made the flight from Thule, Greenland, were killed.

Sept. 4

Near Cochrane, Ontario, Canada. A single-engine DHC-3 Otter aircraft, on an intraprovince flight from Moosonee to Timmins, hit three transmission lines before crashing into a hill and burning; 10 persons were killed.

Sept. 6

Near Sochi, U.S.S.R. According to unofficial reports, two Soviet airliners collided in midair near the Black Sea resort town of Sochi; at least 90 persons were believed to have died.

Sept. 9

Managua, Nicaragua. A military helicopter, carrying 8 survivors of a plane crash to a hospital in the nation's capital, crashed; all 13 persons aboard were killed.

Sept. 10

Near Zagreb, Yugoslavia. A British Airways Trident jet, flying from London to Istanbul, Turkey, collided at 33,000 feet with a Yugoslav Inex-Adria DC-9 flying to Cologne, West Germany; the 176 fatalities included all 63 persons aboard the British plane and all 113 on the Yugoslav aircraft.

Sept. 19

Near Isparta, Turkey. A Turkish Airlines Boeing 727, on a flight from Italy to Antalya, Turkey, via Istanbul, crashed into the 7,220-foot Karakaya Mountain some 50 miles short of its destination; a pilot's miscalculation was blamed for the crash, which killed all 155 persons aboard.

Sept. 26

Near Alpena, Michigan. A U.S. Air Force KC-135 Stratotanker crashed and burned in rugged terrain some 12 miles from Alpena; 5 persons survived the crash that took 15 lives.

Oct. 12

Bombay, India. An Indian Airlines Caravelle jet, scheduled to fly to Madras, crashed and burned shortly after taking off from Bombay's Santa Cruz Airport; none of the 95 persons aboard survived the crash.

Oct. 13

Santa Cruz, Bolivia. An American-owned Boeing 707 cargo plane crashed through the downtown area of Santa Cruz shortly after leaving El Trompillo Airport; of the estimated 100 persons who were killed, many were children attending classes in a primary school that was partly destroyed by one of the plane's wings.

Oct. 25

Villavicencio, Colombia. A DC-3 crashed in flames soon after taking off from Yopal Airport in Villavicencio; there were 32 fatalities.

Oct. 26

Near Hot Springs, Virginia. A Grumman Gulfstream II jet aircraft owned by the Johnson & Johnson Corporation crashed about 500 feet short of the Blue Ridge Airport runway when the pilot attempted an instrument landing; the 3-man crew together with 4 company executives and their wives were killed.

Nov. 6

Northern Peru. A Peruvian Air Force helicopter crashed in the Andes; officials listed all 11 persons aboard as missing and presumed dead.

Nov. 23

Greece. An Olympic Airways YS-11A two-engine plane, on a domestic flight from Athens to Kozani, crashed and burned about 250 miles north of Athens; none of the 50 persons aboard the plane survived.

Nov. 28

Near Moscow, U.S.S.R. A Soviet Tu-104 crashed shortly after taking off from Sheremetyevo Airport on a flight to Leningrad; unconfirmed reports said there were no survivors among the 72 persons aboard the aircraft.

Dec. 25

Near Bangkok, Thailand. An Egyptian Boeing 707 crashed into a textile factory on the outskirts of Bangkok as it prepared to land; all 55 persons aboard the aircraft were killed, and 18 factory workers were listed as dead or missing.

1977

Jan. 13

Alma-Ata, U.S.S.R. A Soviet Tu-104 airliner exploded at an altitude of 3,200 feet and crashed into an open field when the aircraft attempted to land at Alma-Ata; at least 90 passengers and crewmen were reported dead.

Jan. 14

Terrace, British Columbia, Canada. A Twin Otter passenger airplane crashed into a hillside known as Little Herman Mountain during a flight from Prince George to Prince Rupert; 9 passengers and 3 crewmen were killed.

Jan. 19

Near Valencia, Spain. A Spanish Air Force transport plane crashed in a mountainous area southwest of Valencia; all 11 occupants of the aircraft were killed.

March 3

Near Pisa, Italy. An Italian Air Force Hercules C-130 transport plane slammed into the side of a mountain 10 miles east of Pisa during a training flight; 38 cadets, a naval officer, and the crew of 5 air force officers lost their lives in the crash.

April 4

New Hope, Georgia. A Southern Airways DC-9 twin-engine jet flying from Huntsville, Alabama, to Atlanta crashed onto a roadway and crushed automobiles and buildings in its path when heavy hail apparently knocked out both engines; more than 70 persons were killed, and 25 others were injured.

May 10

Near Jericho, Jordan. A U.S.-built CH-53 Sikorsky helicopter crashed and burst into flames minutes after takeoff during a military training exercise; none of the 54 Israelis aboard survived the crash, which was attributed to pilot negligence.

May 27

Havana, Cuba. An Aeroflot Il-62 airliner en route from Moscow to Cuba slammed into a row of trees shortly before its final approach and crashed at José Martí Airport; of the 68 persons aboard, only 2 survived.

June 21

Near Wake Island. A C-130 four-engine U.S. Navy reconnaissance plane crashed into the Pacific Ocean shortly after takeoff from Wake Island, where it had refueled for its return to Guam; all 16 persons aboard were believed dead.

July 24

Puerto Montt, Chile. A Chilean DC-6 military transport plane crashed in southern Chile; 38 persons survived the crash that killed 38 others.

July 25

Yoro, Honduras. A Honduran Air Force DC-3 transport plane carrying civil servants from the justice and interior ministries to Tegucigalpa, the Honduran capital, crashed on takeoff; 22 persons were killed, and 12 others were injured.

Sept. 4

Near Cuenca, Ecuador. A Viscount airliner flying from Guayaquil to Cuenca crashed into a peak in the Cajas Mountains; all 33 persons aboard were killed.

Sept. 15

Near Albuquerque, New Mexico. A U.S. Air Force EC-135 communications aircraft struck a mountainside and exploded three minutes after takeoff from Kirtland Air Force Base; the 20 military personnel aboard were killed.

Sept. 22

Near Urziceni, Romania. A Hungarian Tu-134 jet, traveling from Istanbul, Turkey, to Budapest, crashed and burned 40 miles east of Bucharest when the pilot attempted an emergency landing; 24 passengers jumped to safety when nearby farmers rushed to the scene and helped them escape the burning wreckage, but 29 persons, including the 8-member Hungarian crew, were killed.

Sept. 27

Near Kuala Lumpur, Malaysia. A Japan Air Lines DC-8 jet, flying from Tokyo to Singapore via Hong Kong and Kuala Lumpur, crashed in a rubber plantation north of Kuala Lumpur during a thunderstorm; of the 79 persons aboard, 34 were killed and 45 were seriously injured.

Oct. 21

Mindoro Island, Philippines. A U.S. Marine Corps CH-53

helicopter carrying 39 servicemen crashed and burned while taking part in an amphibious exercise; serious injuries and at least 10 deaths were reported.

Nov. 19

Near Funchal, Madeira Islands. A Portuguese Boeing 727 airliner attempting to land during a rainstorm crashed and burned at the Madeira Airport; 130 of the 164 passengers and crew members aboard were killed.

Nov. 21

Near Bariloche, Argentina. A twin-engine BAC-111 jet, traveling from Buenos Aires to the resort of Bariloche, crashed after making several attempts to position its landing gear; 45 of the 79 persons aboard were killed.

Dec. 2

Northeastern Libya. A chartered Bulgarian jetliner, carrying Muslims home from a pilgrimage to Mecca, Saudi Arabia, crashed while attempting to make an emergency landing; at least 56 of the 159 passengers were believed dead.

Dec. 8

Off the coast of Louisiana. A helicopter attempting to land on the deck of an offshore oil rig during high winds crashed into the rig and dropped some 130 feet into rough seas; 2 oil workers were injured, and the 17 others aboard were killed.

Dec. 11

Hierro, Canary Islands. A U.S. military plane flying at 1,200 feet in clouds and rain crashed into a 4,200-foot mountain peak and exploded; all 12 servicemen aboard were killed.

Dec. 13

Evansville, Indiana. A chartered DC-3 transporting the University of Evansville basketball team to Nashville, Tennessee, crashed and burned within two minutes of takeoff; 29 persons were killed, including all 14 members of the Evansville basketball team and its coach.

Dec. 18

Near Funchal, Madeira Islands. A chartered Swiss airliner plunged into the sea on its approach landing at the Madeira Airport; 19 of the 57 persons aboard were killed; another 17 were missing and believed dead.

1978

Jan. 1

Arabian Sea. A total of 213 persons died when an Air India Boeing 747 jumbo jet exploded in midair, cracked in two, and plunged into the Arabian Sea shortly after taking off from

Rescue workers stand near the wreckage of a tail section of a passenger jet that crashed in a snowstorm on February 11 in Cranbrook, British Columbia. Six passengers and a flight attendant survived.

Santa Cruz International Airport in Bombay; three days before the crash the International Proutist Organization, the political arm of a Hindu sect known as Ananda Marga, threatened to blow up Indian airliners.

Feb. 10

Artigas, Uruguay. A DC-13 twin-engine Air Force transport plane, returning to the airport at Artigas because of engine trouble, exploded and burst into flames about 350 yards short of the runway; all 31 persons aboard were killed.

Feb. 11

Cranbrook, British Columbia, Canada. A Pacific Western Airlines Boeing 737 crashed and exploded while dodging a snowblower that blocked its landing path; the 7 survivors of the crash that claimed 40 lives were seated in the tail section, which dropped off the second time the airplane touched down on the runway.

Feb. 24

Guatemala. A twin-engine Piper Comanche airplane, carrying 14 Seventh-Day Adventist missionaries, crashed in a hospital garden as it attempted to make an emergency landing; all aboard the plane were killed, and 6 pedestrians and 2 persons traveling in automobiles near the site of the crash suffered minor burns.

March 1

Near Kano, Nigeria. A Nigerian Airways F-28 passenger airplane, traveling from Sokoto to Kano, collided in midair with an Air Force plane conducting a training flight; 18 persons were killed, including all 16 civilians on the passenger plane and 2 crewmen on the military plane.

March 3

Near Caracas, Venezuela. A twin-engine 748 Hawker-Siddeley passenger airplane, en route to Cumana, crashed into the Caribbean Sea moments after takeoff; 47 persons were killed, including 43 passengers and 4 crew members.

March 16

Near Sofia, Bulgaria. A Tupelov 134 Bulgarian airliner, en route to Warsaw, Poland, exploded and plunged to the ground 35 miles northeast of the capital shortly after takeoff; all 73 persons aboard were killed.

March 25

Near Rangoon, Burma. A Burmese airliner headed for Mandalay exploded shortly after takeoff; all 48 persons aboard were killed.

June 23

Near St. John's, Newfoundland, Canada. A twin-engine chartered Beechcraft 80 crashed shortly after takeoff from St. John's Airport; 10 persons were killed, including 8 members of the Historic Sites and Monuments Board of Canada.

June 26

Off the coast of Norway. A Sikorsky helicopter, en route to the Stasfjord oil rig in the North Sea, crashed about 100 miles northwest of Bergen; 13 persons were killed, and 5 others were missing and believed dead.

Aug. 30

North Las Vegas, Nevada. A twin-engine Piper Navajo airplane, carrying 10 persons, crashed moments after takeoff from the North Las Vegas air terminal; there were no survivors.

Early September

Near Mexico City, Mexico. A twin-engine charter airplane crashed and exploded in a mountainous region on the outskirts of Mexico City; 19 of the 23 passengers aboard were killed.

Sept. 2

Vancouver, British Columbia, Canada. A twin-engine Otter

airplane, making its final approach before landing, crashed into the yacht basin of the Royal Vancouver Yacht Club; 11 of the 13 passengers aboard the aircraft died in the crash.

Sept. 3

Near Kariba, Rhodesia. An Air Rhodesia Viscount aircraft was shot down by guerrillas of the Patriotic Front who claimed they thought the airplane carried military personnel; 38 passengers were killed when the plane crashed 35 miles from the Kariba Airport, and, later, 10 of the 18 survivors were massacred by guerrillas.

Sept. 14

Near Manila, Philippines. A Philippine presidential airplane, trying to land during a torrential monsoon rain, smashed through trees and houses and exploded in a fishpond one mile short of the runway; 15 villagers on the ground and 18 of the 24 persons aboard the plane were killed.

Oct. 4

Kuopio, Finland. A DC-3 turboprop Finnish Army airplane carrying 15 persons caught fire, exploded, and crashed into a lake moments after takeoff from Kuopio Airport in central Finland; the disaster claimed the lives of all aboard, including three members of the Finnish Parliament.

Bodies are recovered from a presidential plane that crashed in a fishpond near Manila in the Philippines on September 14.

Oct. 6

Near Santiago, Chile. A U.S. Navy C-118 airplane crashed into a hill during heavy fog and burst into flames; all 18 persons aboard were killed.

Nov. 19

Leh, India. An Indian Air Force AN-12 transport plane crashed while attempting to land on a mountain airfield in the northern state of Kashmir; 78 persons were killed, including all 77 persons aboard the aircraft and one person on the ground.

Dec. 23

Palermo, Sicily. An Alitalia DC-9 jetliner crashed into the Tyrrhenian Sea, two miles short of the runway on its final approach to Palermo's Punta Raisi Airport; 103 of the 129 persons aboard were missing and presumed dead.

Dec. 28

Portland, Oregon. A disabled United Airlines DC-8 jetliner, carrying 185 persons, crash-landed in a sparsely populated residential area southeast of Portland International Airport; at least 10 persons died, and more than 69 others were injured.

2.
Fires and Explosions

Fire has always played an important role in human activities. The discovery of ways of controlling and using fire was probably the most decisive development in the early cultural evolution of mankind. When controlled, fire for heating and cooking greatly improved the quality of life; uncontrolled, it remained a terrible danger to life and property. The fact that hell has been thought of as a place of eternal fire in many of the world's religions is an indication of the horror fire has inspired in people's imaginations.

Fire still poses a considerable threat to human safety. Throughout the world an average of about 6,500 deaths a year result from accidents involving fire. Some of the worst fires have occurred in rural forested areas. In November 1825, for example, 4 million acres were destroyed in the province of New Brunswick, Canada, and in October 1871, for example, four million acres of forest and prairie land were burned by a fire in and around Peshtigo, Wisconsin. But the most devastating fires have been those that destroyed great urban centers. In past centuries, when fire-fighting methods were not very effective, the closely packed houses that filled the poorer quarters of most cities were extremely vulnerable. Once a fire got started, it frequently spread from house to house, and it was not uncommon for whole cities to be leveled by such blazes.

The fabled city of Babylon, Mesopotamia, site of Nebuchadrezzar's hanging gardens (later called one of the seven wonders of the world), was destroyed by fire in 538 B.C., and the entire ancient city of Carthage on the coast of northern Africa burned in 146 B.C. In A.D. 1212 about 3,000 persons perished when a fire swept through London, England, and in 1570 an estimated 200,000 persons died when Moscow, Russia, was reduced to blackened rubble. Other massive man-made urban conflagrations, killing thousands of persons, occurred in Constantinople, Turkey (1729); Cairo, Egypt (1824); and Hakodate, Japan (1934). The two city fires that most captured the interest of the Western world, however, took place in London, England, in 1666, and in Chicago, Illinois, in 1871—though both had relatively small death tolls.

The Great Fire of London

Early in the reign of Charles II, London—with a population of around half a million persons—was probably the largest city in Europe. Despite its growth, London still looked much as it had in the Middle Ages. Its narrow, crooked streets were lined with tall houses built of timber and plaster, the upper stories extending beyond the lower ones so that they almost touched the buildings opposite them. People emptied their garbage into the open sewers that ran down the middle of the streets. Overcrowded and unsanitary conditions made epidemics a constant danger. One of the worst of these occurred in 1664 and 1665, when 75,000 Londoners died of bubonic plague. The plague had hardly abated when a new calamity hit the city.

On Sept. 1, 1666, a fire started in the house of the king's baker in Pudding Lane near London Bridge. There had been no rain for weeks, and a strong east wind quickly spread the flames. Efforts to contain the fire by means of bucket brigades were ineffectual, and by the morning of the second, 300 houses had burned down. Samuel Pepys, the secretary to the

The Great Fire of London—beginning on September 1, 1666, near London Bridge—spread rapidly through the narrow streets, destroying most of the civic buildings and leaving hundreds of thousands of people homeless.

Navy Board, whose famous diary gives one of the best accounts of the fire, went to the Tower of London to get a view of what was happening. The whole area north of London Bridge was in flames, and the fire was spreading to the bridge itself, which was lined with houses. Pepys hurried to Whitehall, where he saw the king and reported on the situation.

Meanwhile, panic reigned in the city. The bells of the churches were ringing the alarm, and the streets were choked with people trying to escape with their household possessions. Those who lived near the Thames River got into boats if they could. Some of those who could not find boats threw their possessions into the river. The chaos was increased by country people coming into town to see the fire or to make money by hiring their carts out to fleeing Londoners.

The king gave orders that all buildings in the path of the fire be pulled down to stop its advance. The demolition was accomplished by attaching hooks to the ridge beams of houses and pulling them loose with teams of men or horses so that the buildings collapsed. The lord mayor called out the militia, or "trained bands," to assist in the work, but the progress was too slow. Before the workers could create a gap wide enough to have any effect, the fire was already on top of them. After touring the affected areas on Monday, September 3, King Charles realized that the situation was rapidly getting worse. The flames were spreading unchecked west from London Bridge in the direction of St. Paul's Cathedral. Charles, known as the Merry Monarch because of his extravagant and pleasure-loving ways, showed a real concern for the welfare of his subjects in this crisis. Placing his brother James, the Duke of York, in charge of the fire-fighting operations, he arranged for fire posts to be set up around the perimeter of the blaze. Troops and civilian volunteers under the supervision of army officers and justices of the peace were assigned to each post.

Rumors were already circulating that the fire had been set deliberately. At the time England was at war with Holland, and many thought that Dutch agents were responsible. Others blamed the French or even England's own Roman Catholic minority, always likely scapegoats when anything went wrong. A number of foreigners were attacked by angry mobs. The Duke of York came across one such crowd threatening a Dutch baker and had the man committed to prison for his own safety.

On the morning of Tuesday, September 4, the wind that

had been fanning the flames was stronger than ever. By this time half of London was in ruins; in some places the fire had advanced from the river almost as far as the old city wall. The king and his brother rode from post to post on horseback, dismounting from time to time to lend a hand with the work. People told of seeing Charles standing ankle-deep in mud, his face covered with dirt, passing water buckets to the fire fighters. To save time, houses were being blown up with gunpowder, leading some people to think that the city was under bombardment. One report was that 50,000 French troops had landed on the coast.

When London burst into flames, chaos reigned as the residents of the city attempted to escape with their household belongings.

The flow of refugees continued, many of them camping in the fields outside the gates of the city. The cost of hiring a cart had risen until the cartmen were asking for payment amounting to half the value of the goods transported. Pepys removed everything from his house for safekeeping, depositing the Admiralty records in a pit in his neighbor's garden. Then he dug a pit of his own where he buried a store of wine and "Parmazan cheese."

After many of the city's old parish churches had been gutted, St. Paul's Cathedral itself was threatened. People found it difficult to believe that the cathedral was really in danger. Originally erected in the seventh century, it had been rebuilt and added to several times. Its massive Gothic central tower rising above the roofs of their city had been a familiar sight to generations of Londoners, but in recent years the condition of the cathedral had deteriorated. During the English Civil War of 1642–51, Oliver Cromwell had quartered his troops in St. Paul's, and subsequently booksellers had been allowed to set up shop in the cathedral yard. Charles II had planned to restore the building, and scaffolding for the repair work had been set up only a week before the fire began. On the evening of September 4, sparks ignited the wooden beams that supported the roof of the cathedral, and the heat of the flames began to melt its outer covering of lead. As the roof gave way, pieces of masonry came crashing down into the nave and through the floor into the crypt below, where great stacks of stored books were set on fire. After the walls had collapsed, the ruins of the cathedral burned for days.

As the fire edged closer to the Tower of London, the large quantities of gunpowder stored there were removed to prevent an explosion. As it turned out, however, the Tower was spared. Before morning, the wind died down; from then on, the fire, although it continued to burn, was gradually brought under control.

When the fire was over, barely one-fifth of London was left standing. In addition to St. Paul's, the Royal Exchange, the Custom House, Guildhall (the center of the city's administration), and nearly all of the other civic buildings were destroyed, along with more than 13,000 private dwellings. Surprisingly, the death toll was negligible. Only six people are known to have died as a direct result of the fire. But in its wake, food, water, and fuel were in short supply, and hundreds of thousands of people were homeless. The king issued a proclamation directing nearby towns to give shelter to the refugees, giving his word that they would not become a permanent burden on the communities that received them. He rode out to the Moorfields, where many of the refugees were encamped, and addressed them personally—explaining the measures that were being taken for their relief, assuring them that the fire had not been the result of a plot, and urging them to remain calm.

Nevertheless, many witnesses came forward to tell of having seen strangers throw firebombs into houses and run off before they could be captured. Others claimed that saboteurs had posed as fire fighters, throwing "water" on burning buildings that only made them burn more fiercely. Robert Hubert, a demented French watchmaker who was arrested trying to leave the country, confessed to having set the fire and was hanged. Later it was found that Hubert had not even been in England when the fire started.

Christopher Wren and other architects submitted detailed plans for the reconstruction of the burned-out area. They called for a system of wide, straight avenues and spacious squares. Factories and workshops that gave off offensive odors or made excessive noise would be banned from residential areas. Instead of warehouses, stately homes and gardens would line the Thames. King Charles incorporated many of their suggestions in a plan he sent to Parliament, emphasizing above all that wooden houses should no longer be permitted. "No man whatsoever," he said, "shall presume to erect any house or building, great or small, but of brick or stone." After seeing the plan, people objected that it would be too costly to implement such radical changes and opposed the elimination of London's traditional streets and landmarks.

Wren and his colleagues on the Royal Building Commission came up with a compromise: the city would be rebuilt on the old plan, but with streets of uniform width, strict zoning regulations, and all-new construction in brick or stone. The reconstruction was to be financed by a tax on coal. These proposals were embodied in a series of bills that were approved by Parliament in February 1667.

Progress in rebuilding London was slow at first. By the spring of 1668, 800 houses had been rebuilt, but the city still looked like a vast ruin, with heaps of rubble piled everywhere. Most of the work on private dwellings and civic buildings was completed by 1671; rebuilding the churches took longer. Wren, who had been appointed surveyor general by the king, began work on more than fifty new parish churches in the early 1670s. Most of them are still standing today and have become familiar landmarks of modern London. Wren's greatest achievement was the new St. Paul's Cathedral, which he worked on from 1673 until 1711. Deciding that the old cathedral was beyond repair, he built an entirely new edifice that combined traditional English features with others drawn from French and Italian baroque models. The great dome of Wren's cathedral dominates the skyline of London today just as the tower of the old cathedral did before the fire.

The disaster of 1666 remained vivid in the memory of Londoners long after the event. Every September for nearly two hundred years, an annual religious service was held to commemorate the event. Equally persistent was the belief that the fire had been caused by sabotage. In 1677 a 200-foot column was erected near the place where the fire had started. Known simply as The Monument, it originally bore an inscription (since removed) that laid the blame for the fire on a Roman Catholic conspiracy.

The Great Chicago Fire

In 1871 Chicago was less than forty years old, but in the short period of its existence it had become one of the great cities of the United States. Chicago had grown in importance as a rail center during the period before the Civil War, when it emerged as the main port through which midwestern agricultural products were shipped to the East. The war brought a tremendous increase in the grain trade, and Chicago's prosperity increased along with the new commerce. As one of the gateways to the West, the city's importance grew still further with the great burst of westward expansion in the postwar years.

Bounded on the east by Lake Michigan, Chicago covered an area six miles long and three miles wide. It had more than five hundred miles of streets, only seventy miles of which were paved. Two branches of the Chicago River, one flowing from the north and the other from the south, met like the arms of a Y near the center of the city and flowed eastward into the lake. Above the Y was the North Side, or North Division, and below it the South Side. Beyond the fork of the Y was the West Side. Except for commercial buildings in the downtown business district and the homes of the wealthy, Chicago was largely a city of wood. Even the sidewalks were made of wooden planks.

The summer and early fall of 1871 had been unusually dry, and there had been a large number of fires in the first week of October. The worst of them, on Saturday, October 7, destroyed four square blocks on the city's West Side. Chicago's fire department, organized in 1858, was one of the best in the country. There were 185 firemen, commanded by Chief Marshal Robert Williams; their equipment consisted of seventeen horse-drawn fire engines, four hook and ladder wagons, and twenty-three hose carts. Telegraph alarm boxes were located in various parts of the city, and a fire watch was always stationed on top of the courthouse, where there was a good view for miles around. Being one of America's best fire departments in 1871, however, didn't mean very much, because most fire departments were inadequate. The Chicago department was too small for a city of 300,000, and for lack of money its equipment was usually in a bad state of repair. Fire prevention regulations were on the books but were seldom enforced.

After battling the fire on October 7 for hours, Chicago's fire fighters were exhausted; according to some reports, they did a little too much celebrating after putting out the fire. In any case, they probably were not in top form when another West Side fire broke out on De Koven Street the next day. De Koven Street was in a neighborhood of small wooden cottages inhabited by Irish and Bohemian immigrants. The fire apparently started in a barn owned by a Mrs. Catherine O'Leary, either because her cow kicked over a lantern, as was popularly believed, or from some other cause. As was the case with the fire of London, a strong wind spread the flames, and soon several houses were burning. Someone did try to use one of the fire alarm boxes to get help, but the signal never reached headquarters. The lookout in the courthouse tower did not spot the fire until it had been burning for half an hour or more. When he did report it, he gave the fire company the wrong location. He tried to correct the mistake a few minutes later, but the telegraph operator refused to send the message, saying that it would confuse the fire fighters.

The fire had started at around nine in the evening. When the first fire engines finally reached De Koven Street an hour later, the blaze was still confined to a single block. But in a very short time, windblown sparks started fires in the next street; by midnight, despite the fact that all the resources of the fire department were being used to combat the blaze, twenty blocks were burning. In the darkness, panic spread among people and animals, and the police were unable to maintain order.

In the early morning hours of October 9, the fire leaped the South Branch of the Chicago River, where the crowded slum dwellings, bordellos, and dance halls in the neighborhood of Franklin and Jackson streets went up like matchwood. Chief Williams, whose forces were already overwhelmed by the fire on the West Side, was forced to send some of his men to try to contain the new outbreak. But there were too few of them, and the crowds of frightened people running through the streets made their job more difficult. In the red-light district known as Conley's Patch, the fire fighters had to fight the fear- and drink-crazed inhabitants as well as the fire. Reform-

The terrified populace began to panic as the blazing fire roared through the streets of Chicago in 1871.

ers and police had been trying to close down Conley's Patch for years without success; now the entire area was leveled in a few minutes.

The fire rapidly moved northward into the main business district. The marble courthouse on Randolph Street, where the mayor's office and the police and fire department headquarters were located, was thought to be fireproof, but the building burned along with everything else, its great fire alarm bell falling with a crash that was heard over the roar of the flames for blocks around. By dawn on Monday, the flames had spread between the river junction and the lake, where it destroyed many ships. The opera house and all of the down-

The Great Chicago Fire spread between the river junction and the lake, destroying ships in the harbor and leveling buildings along the shore.

town hotels and stores were completely gutted. Among the casualties was John B. Drake's hotel, the Tremont House, which had burned down four times since he had first opened it. Undaunted, Drake bought out another hotel on Michigan Avenue while the fire was still raging, renaming it the Tremont House. The hotel escaped destruction in 1871 but burned down three years later.

James Hildreth, a former Chicago alderman, went to Mayor Roswell B. Mason and demanded permission to blow up buildings in the path of the fire. The harried mayor reluctantly gave his assent, and Hildreth went off with 3,000 pounds of explosives he and some policemen had removed from one of the city's armories. Their first venture, an attempt to blow up the Union National Bank, miscarried. They succeeded only in shattering the windows and blowing out one of the walls, which made the building even more vulnerable to fire. One of Hildreth's lieutenants, Police Sergeant Edward Mahoney, was directing similar operations on Michigan Avenue when the Civil War hero General Philip H. Sheridan, then the commander of the regional military district, came riding through the crowd on horseback. Sheridan ordered Mahoney to turn the gunpowder over to him. The sergeant, having been warned by Hildreth not to give up the explosives to anyone, refused. When Sheridan insisted, Mahoney drew his revolver and told him to move on. "Do you know who I am?" the general sputtered. "I do not care a damn who you are!" Mahoney replied. "No powder!" Sheridan rode away in disgust.

When the steeple of the Wabash Avenue Methodist Church caught fire, Hildreth, who was nearby, realized that the church formed a natural barrier to the flames and that if it burned, the whole area to the south of it would be lost. As the firemen were unable to raise enough pressure to spray the steeple with their hoses, a gymnast named William Haskell volunteered to climb up to the roof. He and others formed a chain, and managed to put out the flames by passing water buckets up from one man to the next. By doing so, they probably saved the far South Side from destruction.

Most people thought that the North Side would be spared too. The area was mostly a middle- and upper-class residential area with solid, well-built homes set in spacious surroundings—markedly different from the crowded commercial and industrial zones of the west and south sides. In actuality, the north side was to suffer worse damage than any other section.

Early on the morning of the ninth, a burning plank carried by the wind landed atop the engine house of the North Side waterworks, which supplied all of the city's water. The roof caught fire immediately, and before long the entire building was destroyed, and water supplies to all of the fire-fighting units were cut off. Despite the fact that the buildings in the vicinity were widely spaced, the wind carried sparks from the waterworks in all directions, making an inferno of the North Division. Chief Williams, unable to spare men or equipment from the other fires, was forced simply to let it burn. Many of its 75,000 inhabitants fled to the Sands, an area along the lake, or to Government Pier, which extended far out into the water. Some persons were drowned trying to reach boats offshore as the flames crept closer. Others were killed by the intense heat, which rose to 3,000° in places. One man buried his wife and children in the sand, leaving air holes for them facing away from the fire. He himself stood in the lake up to his neck in water for seven hours. All were eventually rescued by a passing tug.

The fire did not stop until it reached Fullerton Avenue, the city's northern boundary. Except for the Chicago Water Tower and one or two houses, the area between North Avenue and the East Branch of the Chicago River was completely leveled.

In the aftermath of the Chicago fire, four square miles of the city lay in ruin. The city was rapidly rebuilt, however, with buildings that conformed to newly revised fire regulations.

Late on Monday night, a light rain began to fall in some areas of the city, and although fires continued to burn in places until the next day, the rain helped make them easier to extinguish. A section of Chicago four miles long and a mile wide had been almost completely razed. Nearly 18,000 buildings had been destroyed, and between 250 and 300 persons had been killed. The mayor declared martial law to put an end to the looting that had been going on for two days, and a number of looters were shot by General Sheridan's troops. When the newspapers began to propagate the story of Mrs. O'Leary's cow, angry citizens claimed that her husband was responsible and ought to be lynched. The O'Leary family—whose house, ironically, was still standing—hid in their attic for days, and Patrick O'Leary finally had to leave town in disguise.

The city government acted quickly to provide for the destitute and to safeguard the general interests of the community. The price of bread was fixed; and Mayor Mason pledged the city's credit to pay for necessities, opened public buildings as places of refuge and distribution centers, ordered saloons to close at 9:00 P.M., and invited volunteers to help the army restore order. Aid came from many places, organizations, and individuals throughout the country. Although the fire was calamitous, it left the sources of Chicago's commercial prowess unharmed. The city had not lost its strategic location in relation to rivers, lakes, and canals and could, therefore, preserve its leadership in water-borne traffic. The railroads still provided contact with the main sources of its commerce and trade. In about a year the business district was largely rebuilt, and prosperity was rapidly restored. The lessons of the fire were not forgotten in Chicago and other U.S. cities, which began to give more serious attention to fire prevention and effective fire-fighting facilities.

Certain less damaging fires—because of their circumstances, location, time, and gruesomeness—loom large in having changed building codes, fire laws, prevention procedures, and general safety from fire. Two such fires in the United States were the Iroquois Theater fire in 1903 and the Triangle Shirtwaist Factory fire in 1911.

The Iroquois Theater Fire, 1903. The worst theater fire in U.S. history blazed into world headlines on the wintry afternoon of December 30, 1903, when—during a matinee performance of the musical stage farce, *Mr. Bluebeard*—the elegant, new Iroquois Theater in Chicago, Illinois, caught fire. Within fifteen minutes, the fast-spreading flames left the theater a burned-out shell and took 602 lives, mostly women and children.

Flames first erupted when sparks from the carbons of an improperly enclosed electric arc lamp, being used as a floodlight, ignited the cloth borders of several stage scenery backdrops. As cast members and stagehands fled through an emergency backstage exit, the open door created a billowing draft, forcing a massive tongue of flame under the partially lowered, nonasbestos stage curtain, and into the auditorium. Panic erupted as hysterical audience members shoved and clawed their way toward the exits; hundreds were trampled underfoot in the frenzied attempt to escape.

Although the thirty-eight-day-old theater had been advertised as being "absolutely fireproof," it was—in truth—anything but that. Everything in the theater was flammable, including the carpeting, the hemp-stuffed plush covered seats, and the heavy plush drapes that hung in front of all thirty-five exits (of which all but three were blocked). Neither the ventilating system nor the sprinkler system was in working order, and the theater staff had had no instructions or practice in what to do in the eventuality of fire or panic. Nor had there been any attempt made to limit the number of patrons to the actual 1,602 seats in the Iroquois. A tally of tickets sold for that particular matinee performance showed that 1,830 persons were in attendance, with many of the audience standing in aisles and in front of exits.

Staircases throughout the theater were poorly designed, with both the main balcony and gallery exits feeding into one corridor and one series of staircases. It was in this passage that most of the victims died, though countless others died in grotesquely twisted heaps, piled in front of locked exit doors, and yet others leaped to their death from flame-engulfed fire escapes. Scores of children were knocked down and trampled to death; hundreds of others were found dead in their seats where they had remained, choking to death on smoke. When the flames were finally out, firemen and policemen shouldered the grisly task of removing victims from the devastated theater, at the rate of three to four bodies every minute for almost three hours.

Subsequent investigation proved, without doubt, that the theater was indeed unsafe and woefully lacking in protective fire devices. Although various persons were held responsible by the findings of a coroner's jury, none were ever brought to trial. Eventually, however, this disaster did lead to stricter fire codes.

Tragic though the fatality figure in the Iroquois Theater fire might seem, other catastrophic conflagrations—likewise in theaters—have produced even greater numbers of victims. About 700 persons died in the Lehman's theater fire in St. Petersburg, Russia, on December 30, 1836—coincidentally enough, sixty-seven years earlier, on the exact date of the Iroquois Theater tragedy. And in Canton, China, in 1845, a theater fire claimed a stupefying total of 1,670 lives. In Vienna, Austria, on the night of December 8, 1881, the Ring Theater caught fire on stage a few minutes before the evening's performance of Jacques Offenbach's opera *Les Contes de Hoffmann* was to start. The blaze, ignited when a stage lamplighter carelessly brushed his torch against some low-hanging scenery behind the drawn curtain, trapped hundreds of theatergoers in the balconies; of these, 850 perished.

Triangle Shirtwaist Factory Fire, 1911. Among the more horror-provoking building fires in history, the burning of the Triangle Shirtwaist Factory in New York, New York, on March 25, 1911, remains one of the most gruesome. The factory was gutted in eighteen minutes, but in that relatively short span of time, 146 employees, mostly young women, were killed. Of the victims, more than 50 leaped to their deaths—hair and clothing ablaze, as they plummeted downward before smashing into the pavement below.

Occupying the eighth, ninth, and tenth floors of the Asch Building on the corner of Washington Place and Greene Street, the Triangle factory's operation was typical of the prevailing "sweatshop" conditions of that day—when mostly foreign-born employees labored long hours at low wages, crammed together under unsanitary conditions, and with safety regulations virtually nonexistent. The Asch Building itself, whose planners had skimped on construction codes, had no sprinkler system and only one complete roof-to-street stairway on the Greene Street side. A second stairway on Washington Place ran only to the tenth floor. At the rear of the building, a fire escape reached down only to the second floor—ending hazardously over an open concrete courtyard. In addition, the Triangle owners had installed especially narrow exits on their premises, so that homeward-bound employees would be forced to file out singly, while being scrutinized, as a precaution against pilferage.

Against this backdrop, the tragedy began unfolding—on that sunny Saturday in March—when, at 4:45 P.M. and close to quitting time, a flash of flame darted suddenly through a bin of fabric remnants in the cutting department on the eighth floor. When the firm's production manager tried to douse the flames with a rotting fire hose, he got no pressure and, in fact, no water at all. The flames spread rapidly throughout the eighth-floor area, and a general panic ensued.

Scores of women raced into the halls and stumbled down staircases. Workers on the tenth floor, alerted to the danger by telephone, either joined in the headlong crush downward or dashed up the stairs to the roof. When flames erupted on the ninth floor, where no warning had been given, the work force there—about 250 persons in all—bolted for the single door leading to the stairway. It was locked, and most then fled to the windows, screaming for help. For many of these, there would be no way out other than through those same windows.

Some of the ninth-floor employees, when they did manage to reach the hallway, crammed themselves into the building's single elevator. Other panic-stricken women threw themselves upon the roof of the descending elevator, only to be pounded into unconsciousness, or killed, by the tumbling bodies of others who fell or leaped on top of them.

By the time the first fire units responded to the fire, the flames had spread so rapidly that the blaze was beyond control. Bodies were already falling through space, as girls began leaping from windows and ledges, many with hair and clothing aflame. Horrified onlookers cried out in disbelief, and firemen cursed their ladders that reached only to the sixth floor and their hoses whose streams of water did not reach the already smoldering figures they could discern climbing onto window ledges.

Employees who sought to flee down the lone fire escape at the back of the Asch Building fared little better. Those who managed to reach the bottom held back, afraid to jump the final two stories into the courtyard below. Finally, many did and died; others were shoved to their death by the continuing crush of people piling up from behind. Meanwhile, the fire escape's bolts began to pop and the metal to melt in places, so intense was the heat. Eventually, the overloaded structure pulled loose from the wall, ballooning outward, and shaking dozens of shrieking victims from their sizzling perches.

Firemen tried desperately to catch or at least break the fall of the jumpers, but most bodies tore straight through the firemen's canvas nets, tearing them apart. In time, even the fire hoses were so densely covered with bodies that their collective weight interfered with the water flow.

Ironically, many of the fire's victims were the same young ladies who had gone out on strike a year earlier, in protest against their working conditions and their employers' notorious neglect in matters of employee safety. Public outrage, following the tragedy, and a persistent clamor in the press, resulted in the factory owners being indicted on manslaughter charges. They were acquitted. Eventually, however, much good came from this terrible calamity—though it would take years before stricter safety regulations and proper fire-fighting devices were made mandatory on commercial premises. (Fifty seamstresses died when trapped in a similar sweatshop fire that raged through the four-story Binghamton Clothing Company in Binghamton, New York, on July 22, 1913.) As yet another direct result of the Triangle fire, the then-fledgling International Ladies Garment Workers Union was considerably strengthened; it, in turn, played a decisive role in bringing about the needed changes.

Major Explosions
San Antonio, Texas, 1912. On March 18, 1912, mechanics for

the Southern Pacific Railroad were repairing a locomotive in the line's yards at San Antonio. As the steam pressure was being raised in the locomotive's boiler, it exploded. Pieces of metal were hurled for long distances.

One large piece of the locomotive weighing about 900 pounds was thrown nearly 2,000 feet; it smashed into a house, fatally injuring everyone inside. The explosion killed a total of 26 workers and residents of the area and caused serious injuries to 32 others.

Chester, Pennsylvania, 1917. During World War I, on April 10, 1917, an explosion occurred at the Eddystone Ammunition Corporation near Chester. The 133 persons killed were mostly women working on the factory's assembly line. Determining the cause of the explosion was delayed by the remark of a plant official to the effect that it had been a plot. The basis for his statement was apparently a note found in a railroad station in Philadelphia, Pennsylvania, which read, "Am ready to blow up Eddystone. Send us help, N. K." The saboteur, of course, was thought to be German.

Many persons were arrested, detained, and questioned as suspects. One man was arrested because of a pro-German remark he made; "diagrams" in his boardinghouse room turned out to be plans the man had drawn of a farm he owned. Another suspect, a man who had come to the factory to apply for work, was not released until a hospital certified his sanity. Eventually a far simpler explanation for the explosion was accepted. Survivors explained that vibrators, which shook the explosive powder into the shrapnel shells, had been malfunctioning for weeks. The vibrators probably short-circuited, which accounted for a blinding flash of light that the assembly workers had seen.

Port Chicago, California, 1944. During World War II, Port Chicago was a small but busy seaport on San Francisco Bay. It was one of the centers for Liberty ships and one of the important ports on the West Coast for ammunition shipped to the Pacific fronts.

On July 17, 1944, two ships in the port were being loaded with TNT and cordite, both powerful explosives. Late in the evening an explosion virtually annihilated the ships and the wharves. People throughout the Bay Area felt tremors, and flames could be seen for fifty miles. Every house in Port Chicago was damaged, and buildings twenty miles away suffered broken windows. All of the 321 men on the ships and the dock were killed; only pieces of their bodies remained. Al-

During World War II a munitions explosion at Port Chicago, California, destroyed the dock area, killing 321 persons, and sent tremors throughout the San Francisco Bay area.

though no cause of the explosion was definitely established, one explanation was that the ammunition—which had been manufactured more than twenty-five years earlier during World War I—was simply unsafe for handling.

Cleveland, Ohio, 1944. Three storage tanks were constructed in 1940 by the East Ohio Gas Company in Cleveland to hold 240 million cubic feet of natural gas. The tanks had occasionally leaked, but each time they had malfunctioned it had been possible to shut off the escaping gas before an explosion occurred. On October 20, 1944, however, all three tanks exploded, producing darting, intensely hot flames that destroyed several blocks of houses in the city. Manhole covers were blown high into the air, and a cloud of black smoke formed over the city. The flames raged into the following day, until the escaping gas could be shut off and the fires put out.

Those working on the tanks were, of course, killed instantly. Tragically, however, residents of the area ran *toward* the burning, exploding tanks to get a better look, and they also became victims. In all, 121 persons were pronounced dead and another 82 were missing. It was estimated that a thousand persons were left homeless by the fires.

Texas City, Texas, 1947. In 1947, Europe was just beginning to recover from the devastation of World War II. Its ruined economy was largely dependent on aid from the United States, which had been spared the effects of invasion. European countries were being introduced to a variety of American products, such as chemical fertilizer like that produced at the large Monsanto plant in the Gulf Coast port of Texas City, Texas.

On the morning of April 16, 1947, the French vessel *Grandcamp*, actually one of the American "Liberty ships" built during the war, was berthed alongside the Texas City plant, taking on a load of fertilizer to be transported to France. The fertilizer contained ammonium nitrate, a highly explosive substance used in the manufacture of TNT, and was packed in dangerously inflammable plastic containers.

Around eight in the morning, the ship's carpenter, Julien Gueril, discovered that a small fire had started in the hold where the cargo was being stored. He and some others tried to put the flames out with water and fire extinguishers, but the fire continued to spread among the bags of fertilizer. Becoming alarmed, Capt. Charles de Guillebon tried to suffocate the fire by using steam jets, a standard shipboard procedure, but this just seemed to make things worse. Smoke began pouring out of the hold, and it became obvious that the fire was getting out of control. The captain ordered his crew ashore, and the Texas City Fire Department took over. Their efforts were equally unsuccessful, and a crowd of onlookers began to gather on the dock.

At 9:12 A.M. the *Grandcamp* and everything around it went up in an enormous explosion. Some witnesses compared the effect to that of a low-yield nuclear bomb. More than 200 people on the dock were killed instantly. Fragments of the ship were blown three miles into the air, and two airplanes flying overhead were incinerated by the blast. Windows were shattered for miles around; the noise of the explosion was heard 160 miles away. The Monsanto plant and the adjoining oil storage tanks were engulfed in flames, and ruptured water mains crippled all attempts to fight the fire. By midday the entire city was ablaze. Medical assistance was sent from the surrounding communities, and National Guard units were ordered into the area to maintain order.

Storage tanks (above) at the East Ohio Gas Company in Cleveland exploded and burst into flames on October 20, 1944. The flames spread rapidly (below)—destroying several city blocks, killing 121 persons, and injuring scores more (left).

On April 16, 1947, in Texas City, Texas, the Monsanto chemical plant was set ablaze after a French vessel loaded with ammonium nitrate fertilizer exploded in the harbor.

The *Highflyer*, another cargo vessel that had been berthed near the *Grandcamp*, was also carrying ammonium nitrate. It was left relatively undamaged by the blast, but it collided with another ship, the *Wilson B. Keene*, and the two could not be separated. On the following morning, the *Highflyer* caught fire. An attempt was made to have the ship pulled away from the wharf by tugs. The attempt was unsuccessful—some said because the *Highflyer* was locked fast to the *Keene*; others, because the tugboat operators thought that the ship was carrying munitions and refused to tow her. At any rate, the *Highflyer* remained in its berth, and at 1:10 P.M. on the seventeenth there was a second disastrous explosion that destroyed the *Highflyer* and the *Keene*, ignited a nearby sulfur warehouse, and added new fuel to the fires that wiped out one-third of Texas City. With 561 persons dead and 3,000 injured, and property damage exceeding $100 million, this explosion and fire rank as the worst in the history of the United States.

Ludwigshafen, West Germany, 1948. The I. G. Farben Works, an enormous industrial complex manufacturing chemicals and related products, had repeatedly been the site

Smoke continues to rise from the I. G. Farben Works chemical manufacturing plant in West Germany the day after a devastating explosion on July 28, 1948, killed 184 persons and injured more than 6,000 others.

of death. An explosion in 1921 killed more than 550 persons, and another during World War II killed more than 70. In addition, the complex was bombed several times during World War II by the Allies in raids that killed hundreds of people. The Farben Works was a Nazi center for the development of propulsion fuel for rockets, and following the war the occupying French forces continued the work on fuels.

The Allied governments saw the Farben Works as a key industry in the rebuilding of Germany. By 1948 the complex was again a major chemical manufacturing center. On July 28 of that year, however, another explosion ripped through the works. Containers of chemicals and rocket fuels exploded first, followed by other explosions as highly combustible materials ignited. Of the 22,000 persons working in the complex at the time, a total of 184 were killed, 70 were missing, and more than 6,000 others were treated for injuries. Recovery of the bodies and first aid for the wounded required a

A fireman inspects the steam boiler that exploded at a New York Telephone Company office building and crashed into the company cafeteria on October 3, 1962, killing 23 occupants.

mass effort by medical personnel and by French and U.S. troops. Although there were rumors of sabotage, the incident was officially listed as an accident.

New York, New York, 1962. On October 3, 1962, a steam boiler in a two-story office building of the New York Telephone Company exploded. The boiler crashed through a wall into the building's cafeteria where more than a hundred workers were having lunch, knocked a hole in the cafeteria ceiling, and then smashed through another wall into a filing office.

Some of the workers on the second floor fell through into

the cafeteria. Others jumped out of second-story windows, and some formed a human chain and groped their way through the steam-filled building to safety. Hundreds of police and firemen worked to rescue the occupants and to put out the fires in the building, but twenty-three persons lost their lives in the explosion, and nearly a hundred others were treated in hospitals for their injuries.

Abadan, Iran, 1978. Even in an age when terrorism became commonplace, the Rex movie house fire in southern Iran was recognized as one of the most horrifying terrorist deeds of modern times. Yet it may in fact have been a bungled attempt to generate only enough smoke, fire, and confusion to register a symbolic but nonlethal protest.

In the summer of 1978 antagonism to the Shah of Iran, Mohammed Reza Pahlavi, was gathering from both the religious right and the political left. Conservative Shiite Muslim leaders were determined to halt his efforts to modernize the country, wishing to return it to a land of the veil for women and strict Muslim law for everyone. Leftist students simultaneously assailed the shah for not moving Iran rapidly enough toward Western-style civil rights and liberties. Sometimes these mutually hostile interests appeared to merge, as in the "Islamic Marxists," a small band of which police said confessed later to setting the tragic fire.

Abadan, Iran's major oil port on the Persian Gulf, has long been exposed to Western influence. Such influence led to the establishment of the Rex, where Western and other movies were shown, to the profound distaste of Muslim extremists. During the holy month of Ramadan, when Islamic teachings call for fasting and abstinence, extremist leaders had urged mass rallies throughout the country to shun movies, television, and restaurants and to turn instead to their mosques for prayer.

Late on Saturday, August 19, the 11th day of Ramadan, about 450 persons were in the second-floor cinema watching the Iranian-made family film *Reindeer*, when smoke, then cries of fire and fingers of flame, appeared along the left and rear walls. These were the only walls containing exits—one centered at the rear and three along the left-hand wall.

Terrorists—whether their motive was death or panic, or merely discomfort for moviegoers—had poured gasoline along the corridors at left and rear, touched off a blaze, and escaped probably down the rear stairs and out of the building. Instantly the L-shaped corridor was aflame along its entire

In Abadan, Iran, policemen inspect the charred interior of the Rex, where 430 moviegoers were killed on the 11th day of Ramadan. The fire was allegedly set by Islamic extremists.

length. A few patrons managed to dash out either the left front or right rear doors and down front or back stairs to safety in the few seconds before the heat became unbearable. All the others backed away as the blaze penetrated the wooden corridor walls and licked across the acoustic ceiling, forced to the windowless wall on the right side of the building, where there was no corridor.

Undoubtedly virtually all the victims were killed within a few minutes by lack of oxygen, rather than by actually burning. When the ruins were cool enough, rescue workers labored for ten hours to separate and remove the charred remains of the victims, two hundred of whom were never identified. In all, 430 persons died.

The shah promised families of the victims that the arsonists would face severe punishment, and before long ten suspects were arrested, and Abadan's police chief said that five "Islamic Marxists" had confessed. Among investigators sent to the scene by the national government was the chief of the fire safety unit at Tehran, the capital. After studying the ruins and interviewing witnesses, Behzal Zamani stated his opinion that the arsonists "wanted to cause some smoke and fire but did not realize that the wooden walls and acoustic ceiling would burn immediately. I don't think they intended to kill all those people."

Whatever their intent, the arsonists appeared to have no place to turn for sympathy. The chief priest of Shiite Muslims, the Ayatollah Shariat Madhari, decried the deed and said it was done by "hotheaded people with whom we have no links whatsoever." Other opposition leaders condemned the act in the strongest terms. Karim Sanjabi, a longtime dissident leader and antagonist of the shah's government, called it "really an abominable act." Abadan went into mourning, and city merchants donated yards of white cloth to make shrouds for the dead. Bulldozers were permitted to scoop out mass graves, ordinarily strictly forbidden by Muslim custom.

If the objective of the terrorists was indeed killing, it appeared to be overkill, for it alienated even the regime's staunchest foes. If the aim was merely enough smoke and flame to frighten and harass, the culprits made an enormous, indeed murderous, miscalculation. Whatever its motivation, the Abadan incident took its place as one of history's most gruesome man-made disasters, its shocking dimensions evidently created by accident.

Other Fires and Explosions, 1959–78

1959
Jan. 6
Istanbul, Turkey. Dynamite stored in a mining company office exploded, wrecking several buildings and killing 33 persons.
Feb. 14
Ashland, Kentucky. An apartment house fire killed 11 persons and injured 8 others.
March 5
Little Rock, Arkansas. A fire at the Arkansas Negro Boys Industrial School killed 21 boys.
March 18
Belford Roxo, Brazil. A fireworks factory explosion killed 13 persons.
April 11
Dagupan, Luzon. Newly uncovered World War II bombs exploded, killing 38 persons.

May 12
Port Moresby, New Guinea. When a ship loaded with gasoline exploded, 12 crewmen were killed.

June 2
Schuylkill, Pennsylvania. A gasoline truck exploded after collision with a tractor-trailer; 11 persons were killed.

June 5
Bombay, India. A warehouse explosion killed 11 persons and injured 7 others.

June 23
Stalheim, Norway. A fire that destroyed a resort hotel killed 24 persons.

June 28
Meldrim, Georgia. Two butane-filled tank cars exploded as a train was crossing a trestle, killing 22 persons in the vicinity.

July 2
Near Pori, Finland. A prison fire killed 16 persons.

July 3
Near Bernet, Mexico. An oil pipeline exploded, killing 12 persons and injuring 25.

July 9
Haderslev, Denmark. An excursion boat exploded, killing 55 persons.

Aug. 2
Augres Mountains, Algeria. Forest fires killed 48 soldiers.

Aug. 7
Roseburg, Oregon. A truck explosion in the center of town killed 13 persons.

Nov. 20
Yokohama, Japan. An explosives plant blew up, killing 78 persons and injuring 1,000 others.

Nov. 29
Jamuri Bazar, India. An explosives shop blew up, killing 46 persons.

Dec. 13
Dortmund, Germany. Explosions in two apartment houses killed 26 persons.

1960
Jan. 7
Yokosuka, Japan. A hospital fire killed 8 adults and 8 newborn infants.

March 3
Pusan, South Korea. A chemical plant fire killed 63 persons.

March 4

Havana, Cuba. A munitions ship exploded at dock, killing 75 persons.

March 19

Kurume, Japan. A fire in a mental hospital killed 11 patients.

March 28

Glasgow, Scotland. A fire and explosion in a whiskey warehouse killed 20 firemen.

July 14

Guatemala City, Guatemala. Fire swept the Guatemala City hospital for the insane; 225 persons perished.

Aug. 18

Belo Horizonte, Brazil. A boiler at an iron foundry exploded, killing 17 persons.

Sept. 2

Grafenwoehr, Germany. An artillery shell exploded during a U.S. Army training exercise, killing 16 soldiers.

Oct. 19

Jolo, Philippines. A fire that razed the city's business center killed at least 10 persons; nearly 10,000 others were left homeless.

Oct. 25

Windsor, Ontario, Canada. An explosion shattered a department store, killing at least 10 persons and injuring nearly 100 others.

Nov. 13

Amude, U.A.R. Fire, following an explosion in the projection room, swept through a movie house; 152 children were killed, and at least 20 others were injured.

Dec. 19

New York, New York. Fire swept the aircraft carrier *Constellation*, which was under construction at the naval shipyard in Brooklyn; 50 men were killed, and at least 150 others were injured.

1961

Jan. 6

San Francisco, California. Fire swept through a five-story hotel, killing 20 persons; 38 others were injured.

March 17

Jalgaon, India. A factory fire killed 23 persons.

May 1

Bolton, England. A fire destroyed a private club; 19 persons died.

May 3

Caracas, Venezuela. An explosion in a fireworks factory killed 38 persons and injured more than 50 others.

May 15

Hong Kong. An explosion and fire destroyed a tenement in the Kowloon district; at least 25 persons died.

Aug. 15

Taubaté, Brazil. A prison dormitory was set ablaze by inmates attempting an escape; 40 prisoners died in the flames.

Nov. 28

Mexico City, Mexico. An explosion in a nursery and training school killed 15 persons and injured 54 others.

Dec. 8

Hartford, Connecticut. A fire on the ninth floor of a thirteen-story hospital killed 16 persons; more than 100 patients were rescued.

Dec. 13

Gdansk, Poland. A newly commissioned Polish freighter, the 10,000-ton *Maria Konopnicka*, caught fire in a shipyard; at least 22 workmen died, and an undetermined number of others were injured.

Dec. 17

Niteroi, Brazil. A blazing circus tent collapsed on about 2,500 spectators; 323 persons were killed, and more than 800 were injured.

Dec. 24

Buga, Colombia. A bomb exploded among a crowd of 500 persons during a Christmas Eve celebration being held in an army barracks; 51 persons were killed, and more than 110 were injured.

1962

Jan. 15

Center Ridge, Arkansas. When their farm home burned to the ground, all 10 members of the north-central Arkansas "farm family of 1960" perished.

Jan. 17

Nürnberg, Germany. Fire destroyed a downtown warehouse; 17 persons died, and 10 others were injured.

March 4

Tehran, Iran. Fireworks in a basement store exploded and killed 19 persons, and 17 others were injured.

April 9

St. Just d'Ardeche, France. A series of explosions ripped

through a munitions factory; at least 18 persons were killed, and 27 others were injured.

April 29

São Paulo, Brazil. An explosion in a fireworks factory killed 20 persons.

June 4

Salvador, Brazil. An explosion in a fireworks warehouse killed 13 persons and injured 60 others.

Aug. 1

Hong Kong. A Kowloon tenement building was gutted by fire; 33 persons were burned to death.

Aug. 29

Guayaquil, Ecuador. A square-block area of homes was destroyed by fire; 20 persons were killed, 30 were injured, and more than 700 were left homeless.

Sept. 24

Damascus, Syria. A blazing house trapped a group of women and children preparing for a wedding; 25 persons perished, and 14 others were severely burned.

1963

Jan. 2

Terre Haute, Indiana. An explosion ripped through a meat-packing plant, killing 16 persons and injuring more than 50 others.

Jan. 29

Chandler, Quebec, Canada. An oil stove explosion set fire to a home; a mother and 10 of her children perished.

Feb. 10

Manila, Philippines. A government hospital was destroyed by fire; 35 persons were reported dead.

Feb. 23

Morehouse, Missouri. Fire destroyed a home, burning to death all 10 members of the family.

March 9

Modderfontein, South Africa. Four blasts ripped through the world's largest dynamite factory, killing an estimated 45 workers; 27 others were injured.

March 9

Belecke, Germany. An explosion in the air-pressure system of a large foundry damaged five buildings and destroyed another; 19 persons were killed, and at least 40 others were injured.

March 21

Saigon, Vietnam. A four-hour fire raged through a waterfront district leaving more than 40,000 persons homeless; about 300 children were reported missing and presumed dead, and more than 100 other persons were injured.

May 4

Diourbel, Senegal. A movie house jammed with a holiday crowd was swept by fire; 64 persons died, and another 18 were severely burned.

May 16

Alexandria, Egypt. A fire destroyed the nearby village of Abyadeya; 17 persons burned to death, 150 others were injured, and about 4,000 were left homeless.

Aug. 13

Gauhati, India. An explosives dump near the edge of town exploded and killed 32 persons.

Sept. 7

Paraná state, Brazil. Forest fires burned unchecked for ten days, destroying acres of pine forests and coffee plantations; 146 persons died, and at least another 400 were injured.

Sept. 24

Parete, Italy. An explosion in a fireworks factory killed 18 persons and injured 12 others.

Sept. 25

Kobe, Japan. A rubber shoe factory burned to the ground, killing 14 workers and injuring 7 others.

Oct. 31

Indianapolis, Indiana. The state fairgrounds coliseum, scene of an ice show performance, was ripped by a blast caused by leaking propane gas; 73 spectators were killed, and at least 350 others were injured.

Nov. 18

Atlantic City, New Jersey. Fire swept through the sixty-room, four-story Surfside Hotel, occupied mostly by elderly persons; 25 of the guests died as the fire spread to several nearby Boardwalk hotels, and 22 other persons, including firemen and policemen, were injured.

Nov. 23

Fitchville, Ohio. A rapidly spreading fire completely destroyed the Golden Age nursing home; flames trapped and killed 63 of the elderly patients.

Dec. 25

Charleston, South Carolina. An oil heater exploded and set fire to a frame house; flames took the lives of 12 children of the 18-member family.

Dec. 29

Jacksonville, Florida. Fire broke out in the first-floor ball-room of the thirteen-story Roosevelt Hotel; although the flames were held to the two lower floors, 22 persons perished (20 from smoke inhalation) and 72 others were hospitalized.

1964
Jan. 6
Tetelzingo, Mexico. An erratic skyrocket set off a fireworks explosion during a religious celebration, killing 10 persons and injuring 15 others.
Feb. 22
Cheraw, South Carolina. A fire swept through a three-room home, killing all 11 members of the family.
March 2
Santiago, Chile. The premature explosion of a dynamite charge in a nearby quarry killed 11 workers.
March 3
Itaocara, Brazil. An explosion of undetermined origin de-stroyed a dynamite plant; 12 persons were reported dead, and 70 others were injured.
May 8
Manila, Philippines. Two explosions set fire to a six-story office and apartment building; at least 30 persons perished.
May 26
Liège, Belgium. Fire consumed a state-managed vacation home and burned to death at least 19 elderly persons.
July 8
Aurangabad, India. An explosion at a fireworks factory killed 20 persons and injured 30 others.
July 15
Tokyo, Japan. Flames sweeping through the harbor district set off explosions in ten warehouses stocked with drums of oil, chemicals, and paint; 19 firemen perished, and about 50 other persons were injured.
July 23
Bóne, Algeria. A U.A.R. munitions ship *Star of Alexandria* exploded while being unloaded at dockside; at least 100 per-sons (many of them port area residents) were dead or missing, and another 160 were injured.
Aug. 24
Atlatlahuca, Mexico. Fireworks for a religious celebration exploded, igniting several gas tanks and blasting away the sides of a masonry house; of the 100 persons inside the house, 45 were killed, and at least 33 were injured.

Sept. 12
Kasota, Minnesota. A two-story home burned to the ground before firemen, summoned by a 14-year-old who escaped the flames, could save 10 other children sleeping inside.

Nov. 29
Lamia, Greece. A 15-year-old land mine exploded during commemorative ceremonies at the Gorgopotamus railroad bridge 60 miles northwest of Athens; the blast killed 13 persons and injured 40 of the 5,000 spectators gathered nearby.

Dec. 18
Fountaintown, Indiana. An overheated basement furnace set fire to a rural convalescent home during near-zero weather; 20 of the elderly, bedridden patients burned to death; 14 others and 3 nurses escaped.

1965

March 1
Montreal, Quebec, Canada. An explosion, followed by fire, leveled a large apartment building in the La Salle suburban area; 28 persons (including 15 children) were killed, and 29 others were injured.

March 4
Natchitoches, Louisiana. A large natural-gas pipeline exploded, set fire to the surrounding houses, and destroyed four; 17 persons (including 9 children) perished, and 6 others were injured.

May 16
Bien Hoa, Vietnam. A series of accidental explosions destroyed or severely damaged 40 U.S. military planes at the Bien Hoa airfield; 27 Americans were killed, and 99 others were injured.

Aug. 9
Searcy, Arkansas. An explosion and fire in a U.S. *Titan II* missile silo trapped and burned to death 53 civilian workmen.

Aug. 25
Louisville, Kentucky. A neoprene-manufacturing plant was completely wrecked by 26 successive explosions that killed 11 persons and injured 37 others.

Sept. 7
Trois-Rivières, Quebec, Canada. An explosion in a pressurized caisson under the St. Lawrence River, at a bridge construction site, killed 12 men and injured 12 others.

Oct. 21
Tila Bund, Pakistan. An explosion caused the collapse of a

canal bridge; at least 80 workmen were buried under the debris.

Oct. 30

Cartagena, Colombia. An explosion in a marketplace killed at least 48 persons and injured 200 others.

Nov. 24

Keokuk, Iowa. A National Guard armory, scene of a Thanksgiving Eve dance, was destroyed by an explosion that blasted through the floor and caused the deaths of 20 persons.

Dec. 20

Yonkers, New York. Fire swept through a Jewish community center trapping a group of students in a fourth-floor music room; 12 persons (3 adults, 9 children) perished in the flames.

1966

Jan. 18

Taipei, Taiwan. Fire destroyed one of the city's largest buildings, the Cosmopolitan dance hall, killing 28 persons, most of them hostesses in the hall.

Jan. 18

Seoul, North Korea. An overheated stove started a fire that burned down more than 100 shacks in a slum area; 23 persons, many of them children, perished; more than 2,000 others were left homeless.

Jan. 28

Boston, Massachusetts. An explosion and fire wrecked two hotels and killed at least 12 persons; about 60 others were injured.

Feb. 4

Buenos Aires, Argentina. A factory explosion killed 13 persons and injured 20 others.

Feb. 6

Miami, Florida. Fire swept through a crowded tenement building, killing 10 persons, 7 of them children.

Feb. 7

Iloilo, Philippines. A large section of the city was razed by a fire that caused damages estimated at $14 million; 18 persons died, and 12 others were missing.

March 11

Numata, Japan. Two ski resort hotels were destroyed in a predawn blaze that took the lives of 31 persons.

April 23

Lapinlahti, Finland. Fire broke out in a mental hospital and destroyed the building within two hours; 29 patients perished.

April 26

Amraoti, India. An explosion and fire in a cottonseed oil mill killed 32 mill workers; 26 others were seriously injured.

May 1

Vitoria, Brazil. Fire caused an explosion in a warehouse stored with dynamite and fireworks; 14 persons died, and 56 others were injured.

Aug. 13

Melbourne, Australia. A Salvation Army hotel went up in flames, trapping most of the guests; 29 persons perished.

Sept. 6–8

Near Sintra, Portugal. Forest fires in the Sintra Mountains killed 37 soldiers who were among the nearly 4,000 fire fighters.

Sept. 12

Anchorage, Alaska. A fire of unknown origin destroyed the Wooden Lane Hotel; 14 persons were burned to death.

Oct. 9

Bulacan Province, Philippines. A half-ton of firecrackers exploded in a fireworks factory; several houses were leveled, and 14 persons were killed.

Oct. 11

Tamaulipas, Mexico. A two-story building was destroyed by a fire in which 12 persons of the same family died.

Oct. 13

La Salle, Quebec, Canada. Explosions ripped through a chemical plant when a chemical reaction went out of control; 11 persons were killed, and 10 others were injured.

Oct. 17

New York, New York. A stubborn five-alarm fire in a commercial building in the Madison Square area took the lives of 12 firemen.

Oct. 31–Nov. 4

California. Brush fires in the hill country of Southern California took 16 lives: 4 U.S. Marines and 12 members of the "El Cariso Hot Shots," an elite fire-fighting unit.

Dec. 7

Near Erzurum, Turkey. A gas stove explosion ignited a fire that raged through the Dumlu barracks, killing at least 68 soldiers and injuring 24 others.

1967

Feb. 7

Montgomery, Alabama. A penthouse restaurant atop a ten-story apartment building became a blazing trap for 35 persons, 25 of whom were burned to death.

Feb. 7–9

Tasmania, Australia. Brush fires burning over the southern part of the island state destroyed twelve townships and threatened the capital city of Hobart; more than 60 persons perished.

Feb. 13

Itterbeek, Belgium. A rest home for the elderly was razed by an early morning fire that killed 21 of the 116 residents.

Feb. 17

Hawthorne, New Jersey. A chemical plant was ripped by several explosions that killed 11 persons and injured 17 others.

March 6

Taninges, France. An historic 700-year-old monastery in use as an orphanage was gutted by fire; 18 children died, 28 other children and 5 staff members were injured.

May 4

Samar Province, Philippines. A dynamite explosion in the fishing village of Mapanas killed 21 persons and injured 110 others.

May 22

Brussels, Belgium. The city's second largest department store was destroyed by a fire of unknown origin; the official death toll was placed at 322 persons.

July 16

Jay, Florida. Brawling convicts broke a gas line that set off a fire in the wooden barracks of a state prison road camp; 37 inmates died, and 6 others were injured.

Oct. 20

Near Dionisio, Brazil. A forest fire in a Minas Gerais state park trapped and burned to death 11 rural police fire fighters.

Nov. 8

Central Peru. A dynamite explosion at a hydroelectric project produced gas fumes that killed 15 workers.

Dec. 25

Moscow, U.S.S.R. An explosion, probably caused by a gas leak, wrecked a newly constructed six-story apartment house; at least 20 persons were believed dead.

1968

Jan. 9

Brooklyn, New York. A four-story tenement and factory building blazed for five hours in the sub-zero cold; 13 persons, including 9 children, perished in the flames.

Feb. 11

Franklin, Pennsylvania. Becoming confused in their blazing home as their mother attempted to lead the way to safety, 10 children burned to death.

Feb. 12

Kowloon, Hong Kong. A five-story building caught fire; 18 persons burned to death, and 8 others were injured.

Feb. 16

Moberly, Missouri. Fire in a downtown tavern trapped and killed 12 persons.

Feb. 26

Shrewsbury, England. Several floors of a 100-year-old mental hospital were consumed by flames that killed 22 elderly patients; 13 others were seriously injured.

April 6

Richmond, Indiana. An explosion in a sporting goods store rocked the city's business district, destroyed eight buildings, and killed 43 persons; 15 others were missing, and 91 were injured.

May 11

Vijayawada, India. A photographer's gasoline lamp ignited a fire in a wedding pavilion; in the ensuing panic at least 58 persons were burned or crushed to death, and more than 200 others were injured.

Aug. 16

Alicante, Spain. An explosion in a toy-pistol factory killed at least 21 workers.

Oct. 9

Zürich, Switzerland. A downtown hotel was swept by flames from a fire started by a disgruntled employee; 10 persons died and 20 others were injured.

Nov. 1

Near Algiers, Algeria. A forest fire in the Miliana Forest killed 22 persons.

Nov. 9

Iloilo, Philippines. Children ignited leaking gasoline, which caused the explosion of a nearby fuel storage tank; 14 persons burned to death, and 56 others were injured.

Nov. 18

Glasgow, Scotland. Fire in a window-barred furniture factory killed at least 24 trapped workers; 3 others escaped.

Nov. 25

Froissy, France. Flames swept through the dormitory floor of a home for the retarded; 14 adolescents died.

Dec. 29

Rio de Janeiro, Brazil. Loosened by nearby blasting, a slum hillside slid down into the valley below, carrying along twenty shacks with 40 to 70 occupants, all of whom were buried beneath tons of rock.

1969

Jan. 15

Victoria State, Australia. Week-long bush fires fanned by strong winds raged through thousands of acres of forest and range land; 17 persons were known dead, and 200 homes were destroyed.

Jan. 26

Dunville, Ontario, Canada. The fifty-room Victoria Hotel was gutted by a fire in which 13 persons died.

Feb. 6

Koriyama, Japan. Fire engulfed a resort hotel and spread through an amusement center, killing 30 persons.

Feb. 19

Bologna, Italy. A four-story apartment building was wrecked by an explosion resulting from a gas leak; 10 persons perished, and 17 others were injured.

Feb. 25

New York, New York. Ignited by tracing paper, a fire in the office of a Fifth Avenue architectural firm killed 11 persons and injured 5 others.

March 9

Manila, Philippines. A slum apartment building was destroyed by fire; 14 persons died.

April 5

Oakwood Bayou, Arkansas. Gasoline, used to light a wood-burning stove, set off an explosion and fire in a fourteen-room home; of 12 family members and friends gathered for an Easter reunion, 10 died.

April 6

Bridgeport, Connecticut. An early-morning fire swept through an old wooden tenement, trapping the sleeping occupants, of whom at least 11 perished.

July 10

Near Posen, Michigan. A two-story family farmhouse burned to the ground, killing 10 members in a family of 12.

Dec. 2
Notre-Dame-du-Lac, Quebec, Canada. A three-story wooden home for the aged and infirm was ravaged by a fire that killed 38 of the elderly pensioners; 29 persons survived.

Dec. 18
Brooklyn, New York. A flash fire, believed to have been started by defective Christmas lights, gutted the top stories of a small frame house as the 27 occupants were sleeping; 10 members of one family (9 children, 1 adult) perished.

Dec. 26
Saffron Walden, England. The sixteenth-century Rose and Crown Hotel was swept by a fire thought to have started in the television room; 11 persons died, and a number of others were injured.

1970

Jan. 4
St. Roche de l'Achigan, Quebec, Canada. A weekend family reunion turned to tragedy when the home in which it was held caught fire and burned so rapidly that none of the 13 family members could escape.

Jan. 9
Marietta, Ohio. Fire, presumably caused by a smoldering cigarette, blazed through a nursing home; 31 elderly patients were killed.

Jan. 24
Eilat, Israel. A munitions explosion ripped through a military dock as soldiers unloaded arms and ammunition from an army truck; 18 men were killed and 42 others were seriously injured.

April 8
Osaka, Japan. Explosions set off by leaking gas at a subway construction site erupted into a crowded street, tearing a hole 450 feet long and 30 feet wide; 27 buildings were destroyed, about 75 persons died, and more than 300 others were injured.

May 22
United Arab Republic. Brush fires, ignited by the 118° F temperature reached on the hottest day in sixty years, brought death to 41 persons and destroyed 660 homes.

Aug. 5
Minneapolis, Minnesota. An old three-story apartment building was swept by fire that started on a wooden back porch; 11 persons died, and 4 others were injured seriously.

Sept. 13

Los Angeles, California. Predawn flames gutted a four-story downtown hotel and caused the death of 12 persons; 22 others were injured.

Sept. 25–30

Southern California. Brush and timber fires of five days' duration ravaged more than 200,000 acres in Los Angeles, Ventura, and San Diego counties; 14 persons died, and 1,500 buildings were burned.

Nov. 1

Saint-Laurent-du-Pont, France. Flames caused by a discarded match raced through the plastic- and papier-mâché-decorated interior of an Alpine dance hall, driving the occupants toward unopened exits where 142 young revelers perished; 4 of the seriously burned died later, bringing the total fatalities to 146.

Nov. 5

Montreal, Quebec, Canada. A suburban home for the aged caught fire after an explosion in a basement furnace; 17 elderly persons died of asphyxiation; 17 other residents escaped.

Dec. 11

New York, New York. A three-story nineteenth-century building was ripped by a gas explosion and reduced to rubble by flames that killed 10 persons.

Dec. 20

Tucson, Arizona. Fire of unknown origin raced through the upper eight floors of the eleven-story Pioneer International Hotel and trapped many of the 112 guests, 28 of whom perished in the flames; 27 others were injured.

1971

Jan. 4

Auch, France. An explosion caused by accumulated gas shattered a concrete building and damaged a home; 14 persons died, and 12 others were injured.

Feb. 3

Rolde, The Netherlands. Fire sweeping through the wards of a home for the mentally retarded brought death to at least 13 patients.

Feb. 3

Brunswick, Georgia. A Camden County munitions manufacturing complex was rocked by a blast thought to have been caused by magnesium trip flares; 25 persons were killed, and more than 100 others were injured.

Feb. 16
Bangkok, Thailand. An explosion and fire wrecked one wing of the Imperial Hotel and caused the deaths of at least 25 persons.

April 25
Seattle, Washington. Careless smoking was the apparent cause of a fire that raged through a three-story apartment building; 14 persons perished, and 9 others were injured.

June 27
Czechowice, Poland. An explosion blew up a number of oil refinery tanks; 14 persons were killed, and 56 others were injured.

June 28
Near Mexico City, Mexico. A fireworks explosion wrecked a building, killing at least 13 persons and injuring 6 others.

Oct. 19
Honesdale, Pennsylvania. Leaking gas was believed to have caused a blaze that swept a nursing home; 15 of the elderly residents perished, mostly from smoke inhalation.

Oct. 21
Glasgow, Scotland. A busy shopping center was severely damaged by a gas explosion that blasted 15 newly built stores, killed 13 persons, and injured at least 100 others.

Dec. 2
Hammond, Ontario, Canada. A farmhouse was set afire when an oil furnace overheated in sub-zero temperature; 12 members of the family perished, and 2 others were severely burned.

Dec. 14
Mufulira, Zambia. Nine freight cars being loaded with explosives blew up and killed 29 persons.

Dec. 25
Seoul, South Korea. The worst hotel fire in history was believed to have started in a second-floor coffee shop of the plush 22-story Taeyonkak Hotel; the twelve-hour holocaust took the lives of at least 157 persons and injured more than 100 others.

1972

Jan. 16
Tyrone, Pennsylvania. Electrical overload in zero-degree weather caused a fire that leveled the Pennsylvania House Hotel and brought death to 12 persons; 33 others were injured.

Feb. 24

São Paulo, Brazil. Starting on the mezzanine floor of the Pirani Department Store, a fire quickly spread upward through the 29-story building, which also housed offices, forcing thousands of workers and shoppers to jump from windows; at least 16 persons died, and more than 400 others were injured.

March 6

Barcelona, Spain. An early dawn explosion, attributed to a gas leak, caused the collapse of a ten-story apartment building and killed 18 persons.

March 30

Rio de Janeiro, Brazil. A fire and explosions in Brazil's largest oil refinery claimed the lives of 21 persons, and 48 others were severely injured.

May 6

Springfield, Illinois. The Carver Convalescent Home, which was cited for numerous public health violations, was the scene of an early morning fire that brought death to 10 elderly patients.

May 13

Osaka, Japan. Patrons of the Play Town cabaret, atop a seven-story department store, were cut off from escape when a discarded cigarette started a fire on the third floor; 117 persons died of asphyxiation or injuries received in jumping or falling to the ground, and at least 37 others were hurt.

July 2

Seoul, South Korea. In refueling a lamp, a child mistakenly used gasoline in place of kerosene and set fire to a farm home in which 13 children died; 7 others were hospitalized.

Sept. 23

Rhodes, Greece. Started by an electrical short-circuit, a fire swept through the plastic decorations of the two-story Oscar Club, a tourist restaurant; 31 of the 80 persons trapped on the upper floor perished, and 16 other visitors were hurt.

Oct. 29

Barcelona, Spain. Reportedly caused by a gas leak, an explosion reduced a four-story apartment building to rubble and buried the occupants beneath tons of debris; at least 12 persons were dead or missing, and 21 others received injuries.

Nov. 21

Singapore. Robinson's Department Store, a landmark institution of colonial days, was destroyed by a fire that killed at least 12 persons trapped in two elevators.

Nov. 30
Rome, Italy. An explosion and fire in an illegal fireworks factory caused the deaths of 15 persons and injured 65 others.

Dec. 2
Seoul, South Korea. Fire raced through Citizens Hall, gutting the city's largest theater building; caused by faulty stage lights, it killed 51 persons and injured 76 others.

Dec. 15
Weirton, West Virginia. A natural-gas leak was believed to have touched off a series of violent explosions in a new coking plant at the Weirton Steel Company; falling girders and chunks of cement caused the death of some of the 19 workmen killed, and 10 others were injured in the blasts.

1973

Jan. 13
Kampala, Uganda. Flames burst from an overturned gasoline truck when a lighted cigarette was dropped into the leaking fuel; 10 persons were burned to death, and 70 others were hospitalized.

Feb. 2
Eagle Grove, Iowa. A café and several other downtown buildings were destroyed by fire following a gas explosion; 14 persons died.

Feb. 10
Staten Island, New York. An explosion in a huge 287-foot circular storage tank for liquefied gas caught members of a repair and cleaning crew in a hail of concrete and flaming debris, killing 40 workmen.

March 10
Neufmesnil, France. Flames swept through a home, killing 10 of 13 children in the family; the parents and 3 other children escaped with injuries.

Sept. 1
Copenhagen, Denmark. An early morning fire destroyed the 74-year-old Hafnia Hotel, a city landmark that fire officials had several times warned was a firetrap; fire, smoke, falling debris, and desperate leaps from windows and roof killed 35 foreign tourists.

Sept. 29
Hoboken, New Jersey. An early morning fire swept through four tenements in a predominantly Puerto Rican area of the city, killing 10 persons and injuring 6; some 50 others were rescued.

Nov. 29

Kumamoto, Japan. A fire swept through the seven-story Taiyo Department Store, blinding and choking thousands of shoppers as it raced from the third floor, up the stairwells, and toward the roof; 103 bodies were recovered.

Dec. 13

Tachov, Czechoslovakia. A faulty heating system caused a violent explosion that demolished a dormitory where teenage apprentice workers were sleeping; about 80 persons died.

Dec. 17

Near Quito, Ecuador. A can of gasoline, dropped on the floor of a crowded bus, exploded into flames when a passenger lit a match; 23 persons were burned to death.

1974

Jan. 23

Heusden, Belgium. A night fire, possibly started by illicit smoking and fueled by wooden partitions and bedding, swept through the Sacred Heart College dormitory; 23 teenage boys were asphyxiated or burned to death.

Feb. 1

São Paulo, Brazil. A fire, started by an electrical short circuit in an air conditioner, engulfed the upper fourteen stories of a newly constructed twenty-five-story bank building, trapping hundreds of workers as the flames fed on combustible interior-finish materials; due to inadequate escape facilities, at least 227 persons lost their lives.

March 11

Dublin, Ireland. In the worst private home fire in Dublin in almost thirty years, a news vendor, his pregnant wife, and 10 of their 13 children were burned to death.

June 1

Flixborough, England. A violent explosion completely destroyed the recently completed Nypro chemical plant about 180 miles north of London; 28 persons died, some victims of the raging fire, others of toxic fumes that required evacuation of neighboring areas.

June 17

Lahore, Pakistan. A building was completely gutted by a fire that took at least 40 lives; six entire families reportedly perished.

June 30

Port Chester, New York. Heavy smoke and flames from a

cellar fire next door poured into a crowded two-level disco-theque on the New York-Connecticut border, trapping scores of dancers who struggled blindly for the exits after the lights failed; of the 24 persons who died, some were apparent-ly trampled to death in the panic.

Aug. 1
Alcalá de Henares, Spain. A raging prison fire claimed the lives of the warden and 13 inmates.

Sept. 5
Southern Nigeria. Fire swept through a riverboat in southern Nigeria; 67 persons were killed, and more than 180 were in-jured.

Oct. 16
Sumatra, Indonesia. The Swedish tanker *Palma* caught fire and burned in a Sumatra harbor; the captain and 12 crewmen were missing and believed dead.

Oct. 17
Seoul, South Korea. Fire erupted on the fifth floor of the ten-story New Namsan Hotel in downtown Seoul; 15 persons died, and more than 20 others were injured.

Oct. 31
Near Allahabad, India. Two coaches of the Upper India Ex-press exploded and burned with the loss of 52 lives; about 60 others were injured.

Nov. 3
Seoul, South Korea. A seven-story hotel and entertainment center known as Daewang Corner was badly ravaged by a fire; of the 88 persons who lost their lives, 72 died in the Time Club discotheque.

Dec. 15
Nottingham, England. An early morning fire accompanied by heavy smoke swept through a city-owned nursing home; 18 of the 49 residents died, most from asphyxiation.

1975
Jan. 22
Marikina, Philippines. A fire that broke out in a five-story building trapped workers on the upper floors when flames engulfed the exits; about 50 persons died, most of them wom-en, and some 80 others were seriously injured.

Jan. 29
Taichung, Taiwan. An explosion in a firecracker factory set off a raging fire that engulfed more than a dozen buildings

and claimed the lives of some 20 persons; about 50 others were severely injured.

March 27

Santa Maria Maggiore, Italy. The Excelsior Hotel, a multistory resort lodging, was consumed by an early morning fire; 16 persons were killed, and about 40 others were injured.

March 28

Rijeka, Yugoslavia. Faulty electrical installation at the Dr. Zdravko Kucic Hospital was blamed for a fire that killed 25 babies in incubators.

Mid-April

Cologne, West Germany. The 270-ton Dutch excursion ship *Princess Irene* caught fire and sank while tied to its Rhine River moorings; most of the 19 persons presumed dead were elderly and infirm.

May 14

Buhut, Egypt. A fire, fanned by winds from a powerful sandstorm, destroyed a village of straw-roofed homes in the Nile delta; at least 12 persons lost their lives, and more than 200 were injured.

June 10

Keelathattapara, India. Explosives blew up in a southern India village, killing 12 persons and injuring 65.

July 23

Near Toulon, France. An explosion and fire aboard the ferryboat *Vénus des Iles II* claimed the lives of at least 12 persons; scores of terrified passengers leaped into the Mediterranean Sea and were rescued by nearby helicopters and surface vessels.

July 23

Near Comilla, Bangladesh. A mine discovered on a riverbank by children exploded when it was tossed into a fire by neighbors; 10 persons were killed, and 32 were injured.

Dec. 13

Mina, Saudi Arabia. A fire that began with the explosion of bottled gas swept through a tent city of Muslims who were among 2 million religious pilgrims gathered in or near Mecca for the annual feast of Id al-Adha; 138 persons lost their lives, and 151 others were injured.

Dec. 25

Sydney, Australia. A fire that started in an elevator shaft swept through the Savoy Hotel, located in the King's Cross area; 14 persons were killed and many others severely burned.

1976

Jan. 1

La Louvière, Belgium. A fast-spreading fire that set off a gas explosion in a small ground-floor café gutted a three-story building and trapped many of the young patrons inside; 15 persons were burned to death, and nearly 40 others were injured.

Jan. 9

Hamburg, West Germany. A boiler explosion aboard the 18,-500-ton *Anders Maersk*, under construction at the Bloehm und Voss shipyard, claimed 18 lives when the workmen were engulfed in searing steam; at least 20 other workers were seriously injured.

Jan. 10

Fremont, Nebraska. A gas leak in the basement of the six-story Pathfinder Hotel triggered an explosion and fire that killed 18 persons and injured about 60.

Jan. 30

Chicago, Illinois. A fire that apparently started in a clothes closet on the fourth floor of the Wincrest Nursing and Rest Home took the lives of 23 elderly persons, most of whom succumbed from heavy smoke that poured into the chapel during morning services.

Feb. 4

New York, New York. An intense early morning fire that started in a back apartment on the ground floor spread quick-ly upward through a six-story building; 7 of the 10 persons who died were young children.

Feb. 16

Tiaret, Algeria. A gas explosion that demolished two houses took the lives of 35 persons and injured 36 others.

April 13

Lapua, Finland. A brick unit of an ammunition factory was totally destroyed by an explosion of gunpowder; the casualty toll included more than 40 persons dead and about 70 in-jured.

Aug. 12

Chalmette, Louisiana. An explosion in the fractionating tow-er of a refinery operated by the Tenneco Oil Company killed 13 workers and seriously injured 6 others.

Aug. 29

Bangkok, Thailand. A chemical explosion and fire in a Bang-kok factory killed 14 persons, 12 of whom were teenage girls.

Dec. 24

Chicago, Illinois. A three-story brick building was set ablaze when a can of lighter fluid, used to ignite an indoor charcoal grill, burst into flames and the burning fluid sloshed onto the hall floors and staircase while someone was trying to carry it outdoors; among the 12 fatalities were 10 children attending a Christmas Eve birthday party on the upper floor.

Dec. 26
Numazu, Japan. A predawn explosion and fire, probably triggered by a gas leak in a bar, claimed the lives of at least 15 persons.

Dec. 26
Goulds, Newfoundland, Canada. Chafe's Rest Home, a two-story wooden structure, was totally destroyed by an early morning fire; 21 persons lost their lives.

1977

Jan. 28
Breckenridge, Minnesota. A predawn fire that swept a four-story brick hotel in blizzard-like conditions, with a prevailing wind chill factor of −85°F (−65°C), claimed the lives of 22 persons.

Feb. 25
Moscow, U.S.S.R. A major fire caused by a technical fault in an elevator motor shot upward through an elevator shaft from the 5th floor to the 12th floor of the Rossiya, the world's largest hotel; a Soviet medical source reported at least 45 fatalities.

May 9
Amsterdam, The Netherlands. After a fire gutted the Polen Hotel, 5 guests were still missing in the debris and 28 others were dead.

May 22
Brussels, Belgium. A raging fire broke out in the first floor snack bar at the Duc de Brabant Hotel, where 150 guests were registered; 40 persons were injured, 15 were killed, and another 12 were missing and presumed dead.

May 28
Southgate, Kentucky. A fast-burning fire poured heavy smoke throughout the Beverly Hills Supper Club, where some 3,500 persons awaited the arrival of singer John Davidson; a private investigating team linked a short circuit to the cause of the blaze that killed 164 persons.

June 9
Abidjan, Ivory Coast. A fire trapped patrons of a nightclub

when flames destroyed an electrical system operating an automatic exit; 41 persons perished in the blaze.

June 21

Saint John, New Brunswick, Canada. An intense fire that apparently started in padding ripped from the walls of a jail cell fused the locks on several cell doors; 20 prisoners died.

June 26

Columbia, Tennessee. A fire started by a prisoner in his cell at Maury County Jail burned vinyl-covered plastic foam padding, sending noxious cyanide and carbon monoxide fumes through the ventilation system; 34 inmates and 8 visitors died.

Nov. 11

Iri, South Korea. An explosion aboard a freight train loaded with 33 tons of dynamite leveled some 400 buildings, left a crater nearly 50 feet deep, injured more than 1,300 persons, and killed more than 50 others in the city of Iri.

Nov. 14

Manila, Philippines. An early morning blaze, aggravated by ferocious typhoon winds, swept through a hotel; at least 47 persons were killed, 9 others were injured.

Nov. 27

Rio de Janeiro, Brazil. A fire that broke out in a convention center adjoining a luxury hotel killed at least 11 persons.

Dec. 9–10

Cartagena, Colombia. A series of explosions at a petrochemical plant claimed the lives of at least 25 workers and seriously injured 30 others.

Dec. 16

Manila, Philippines. A fire in an overcrowded mental hospital destroyed the interior of a building that housed some 1,200 patients, although it was only designed for 400; rescue workers said the 32 persons who were killed would have been saved had they cooperated with the rescue team.

Dec. 22

Westwego, Louisiana. A chain-reaction explosion that apparently started in the weighing office of a 73-silo grain elevator completely leveled the structure of reinforced steel and concrete to a 120-foot pile of rubble; rescue workers reported that 36 persons were killed and 10 others were injured.

Dec. 27

Galveston, Texas. An explosion and fire destroyed a 230-foot dockside grain elevator at the Farmers Export Co. Terminal, killing 18 persons; among the dead were several federal grain inspectors.

1978

Jan. 3

Manila, Philippines. A fire that broke out in a Chinese Buddhist temple in Manila claimed the lives of 15 persons; it was the city's third major fire in two months.

Jan. 28

Kansas City, Missouri. A fire swept through the historic Coates House Hotel, where three U.S. presidents had once stayed after it opened in 1867; 16 persons were killed.

Feb. 27

Near Bangkok, Thailand. A boiler explosion at a sawmill and plywood factory claimed the lives of 21 persons.

March 14

Villa Devoto, Argentina. A fire started by rioting inmates at Villa Devoto Prison, 10 miles north of Buenos Aires, burned to death or asphyxiated at least 55 persons and injured 70 others, when rampantly spreading flames roared through the cellblock.

May 12

Ankara, Turkey. A fire that started in a leather-worker's shop in a six-story office and shopping complex reduced the center to a charred shell; 42 persons were killed, some of whom

A historic landmark is destroyed by fire on January 28 in Kansas City, Missouri. Firemen delayed the search for victims fearing that the century-old frame and stone hotel would collapse.

jumped to their deaths.

June 10

Borős, Sweden. A fire that swept through a five-story hotel claimed the lives of 20 teenagers celebrating their graduation from high school; 55 other persons were injured.

June 28

Bolivia, near the Argentine border. Gas from a ruptured pipeline exploded into flames when it came in contact with open fires in private homes; 10 persons were killed, and 6 others were seriously injured.

June 28

Damietta, Egypt. A five-year-old mortar shell exploded after it was picked up by a group of military students returning from a training course; at least 20 of them lost their lives, and 20 others were injured.

July 5

Near Taunton, England. A fire that started in the overnight sleeper of a passenger train traveling from Penzance to London killed 11 passengers who were sleeping when the fire broke out; more than 30 others were injured.

July 9

Manila, Philippines. A fast-burning fire swept through a crowded downtown theater; 16 persons were killed, and 70 others were injured.

Oct. 10

Caracas, Venezuela. A drunken national guardsman doused a downtown bar with gasoline and set a match to it after quarreling with two other patrons; 22 persons lost their lives because the emergency exit was blocked by boxes.

Oct. 12

Singapore. A powerful explosion aboard a Greek oil tanker docked for repairs at a Singapore shipyard stunned workers who had just reboarded following a lunch break; at least 57 persons were killed, and 86 others were seriously burned.

Nov. 2

Near Villahermosa, Mexico. A fiery explosion resulted when a natural gas pipeline ruptured; the blast, which sent a fireball flashing through several small restaurants and taco stands in the area, killed at least 52 persons.

Nov. 5

Honesdale, Pennsylvania. A 138-year-old hotel, denounced as a "fire trap" by the local county coroner, was destroyed by flames; 11 persons died in the blaze, and another 4 persons remained unaccounted for and were presumed dead.

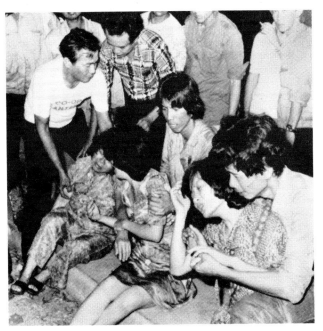

Relatives of victims grieve following the explosion of a Greek oil tanker on October 12 in a Singapore shipyard.

Nov. 5
Des Moines, Iowa. An early morning explosion, followed by a blazing fire, gutted a department store in a Des Moines shopping mall; at least 10 persons died in the fiery blast.

Nov. 26
Greece, New York. A roaring fire that started in a basement stairwell virtually destroyed a 15-year-old Holiday Inn hotel; 10 persons died after being trapped in rooms or hallways, and at least 34 others were injured.

Dec. 7
Newark, New Jersey. An early morning fire swept through a century-old, three-story frame tenement and reduced the building to rubble; 7 children and 4 adults were killed.

Dec. 9
Ellisville, Mississippi. An early morning dormitory fire at the Ellisville State School for the mentally retarded claimed the lives of 15 women patients and injured 16 others.

3.
Marine Catastrophes

Shipwreck is a danger mankind has faced ever since people first began to sail on the seas. The perils of the oceans can be every bit as terrifying today as they were in the time of Jonah or Ulysses. In fact, some of the worst marine disasters have occurred in more recent times.

The Queen Charlotte

On March 17, 1800, the enormous British frigate *Queen Charlotte* was sailing along the coast of Italy, off the port of Leghorn. As many as 700 British seamen were aboard. Suddenly, flames were discovered—a fire had broken out in some hay that was lying under an upper half deck. In an attempt to squelch the flames, an officer led several squads of men below decks to work the pumps.

The fire, however, quickly spread to the ship's sails and to the wooden gun deck, causing the heavy cannon to crash through to the next deck where the pumping crew was working. Once the ship foundered, it sank quickly. Most of the crewmen drowned. The handful who survived were plucked from the water by an unidentified ship of American registry.

The Medusa

In 1816 France was a defeated and demoralized country occupied by foreign troops. Napoleon Bonaparte's empire had ended the year before in the Battle of Waterloo, and the Bourbon king Louis XVIII had been installed on the throne by the victorious powers. In this atmosphere occurred one of the sorriest episodes in the history of the seas.

When King Louis returned from his exile in England, he brought with him a host of aristocratic followers who expected to be rewarded for their loyalty during his enforced residence abroad. One of these followers was Hugues Deroys, vicomte de Chaumareys. On the strength of his having been a naval officer twenty-five years earlier, de Chaumareys was given command of the forty-four-gun frigate *Medusa*. On June 17, 1816, the *Medusa* and three other ships left Rochefort, bound for the West African colony of Senegal. There were about four hundred persons aboard, including two hundred and fifty black troops and the colony's newly appointed governor, Julien Schmaltz.

From the first, Captain de Chaumareys showed little interest in the welfare of his ship. He was frequently drunk, and he spent a great deal of time with his mistress. The *Medusa* soon became separated from the rest of the squadron, and at one point it was discovered that the ship was a hundred miles off course. When the ship crossed the Tropic of Cancer on July 1, the captain celebrated the event in traditional style with dancing and general merriment, ignoring warnings from the other officers that they were dangerously close to the Argun Bank, an area of reefs just off the African coast. In the midst of the revelry the *Medusa* ran aground. All attempts to move her off the rocks failed, and that night she was badly damaged by a gale. On the morning of July 2, de Chaumareys decided to abandon ship.

There were only six lifeboats, not enough to accommodate everyone on board. Because the ship was only sixty miles from land, the boats probably could have made it to shore and back again for a second load of passengers. But nobody wanted to be left behind, and everyone distrusted de Chaumareys and feared that the ship might break up at any time. Governor Schmaltz suggested that they build a raft for the extra people and have the boats tow it. A raft approximately twenty by sixty feet in size was hastily put together, and 147 people who could not be taken in the boats were loaded onto it. At the last minute, seventeen men decided to take their chances and stay on the ship. The rest set off for the African coast, but before they had gone far the weight of the overloaded raft threatened to swamp the boats. The raft was cast adrift, and the people on it were left to fend for themselves.

Then began an ordeal that was to last for seventeen terrible days. The unfortunate people left on the raft were a motley collection of crew members—officers and men—soldiers, and civilian passengers. Some of the soldiers and seamen had been drunk when they left the *Medusa*. For provisions, they had only flour and casks of water and wine. Twenty people were swept into the sea during rough weather on the first night. Two of the passengers, Alexandre Correard and Dr. Jean Baptiste Savigny, and one of the midshipmen put up a mast and hung a sail from it, but the barely seaworthy raft continued to drift helplessly in the water.

Meanwhile, other officers rationed out the water and guarded the wine casks to prevent them from being seized by the sailors and soldiers, who were becoming mutinous. Despite their efforts, a group of sailors managed to get hold of one of the casks on the third day; a full-scale battle developed between the officers and passengers on the one side and the crazed mutineers on the other. When the fight was over, only sixty-seven persons were left alive. Too exhausted to continue the struggle, the two factions retired to opposite sides of the raft.

All of the kegs of flour had gone overboard, and in the absence of any other food the survivors began to eat the bodies of those who had been killed. Twelve more persons were lost in the sea that night, and more fighting over the next couple of days reduced the number of survivors to twenty-seven. Twelve of the remaining survivors were clearly not going to live; asking God's forgiveness, the others abandoned the dying to the sea, hoping thereby to increase their own chances. Correard and Savigny, assuming leadership of the fifteen who were left, persuaded all to throw their weapons away and to make peace.

In the days that followed, the survivors succumbed to delirium from hunger and exposure, no longer aware of what was happening to them, until at last they were picked up by the brig *Argus* and taken to Senegal on July 19. Six more persons died after they had been rescued. Although the life-

In an idealized painting French artist Théodore Géricault depicts the struggle for survival aboard "The Raft of the Medusa."

boats had reached the African coast within a few days, by the time anyone got around to sending help to the men who had been left on the *Medusa*, all but three of them were dead. Altogether, 152 lives were lost in the *Medusa* tragedy, most of them needlessly.

When Correard and Savigny returned to France, they published an account of their experiences, which led to the recall of Schmaltz and de Chaumareys. The French artist Théodore Géricault commemorated the shipwreck in a rather idealized romantic painting, "The Raft of the Medusa," which hangs in the Louvre.

The Birkenhead

Among the many sea sagas in which men faced inevitable death with courage, the men who went down with the troopship *Birkenhead*, an iron-hulled paddle frigate employed in transporting British regiments to South Africa, set a particularly high standard of disciplined heroism. The troop ship with 680 persons on board, 56 of whom were women and children—sailed from Queenstown, England, headed for Algoa Bay, South Africa, on January 17, 1852. Stopping at the Simonstown naval base, it took on provisions and disembarked several women, children, and some of the soldiers too sick to travel. Dozens of officers' horses also were loaded aboard.

Rounding the Cape of Good Hope on February 26, the *Birkenhead* pounded into an uncharted rock that jutted from the end of the appropriately named Danger Point, fifty miles from Cape Town, South Africa. Torrents of seawater poured into the troop compartments below decks, drowning dozens of soldiers as they slept. When the *Birkenhead* backed off the reef, it began to take on water even more quickly.

Major Alexander Sexton of the 74th Highlanders, the troops' able thirty-seven-old commander, ordered all surviving troops on deck, where they formed ranks and stood at attention, as the women and children aboard were lowered safely into lifeboats. The ship listed badly, but still the troops stood silently at attention. Even the horses aboard had been driven into the water to give them a chance for survival, before Major Sexton ordered his men to break ranks and to save themselves by jumping overboard and swimming to some small lifeboats that had been lowered for them as the *Birkenhead* began breaking in half. The order was a useless one; hundreds of the men couldn't swim. Many simply held their formation and went down with the ship. Of the valiant troopers, 458 died at their posts.

The Atlantic

One of the more deplorable marine tragedies occurred on April 1, 1873, when the British White Star Line's luxury liner *Atlantic* wrecked itself on the rocks off Meagher Island, near the entrance to Halifax Harbor, Nova Scotia, Canada. The incident was curious namely in that, though it happened in sight of land and though more than 400 persons survived, not one woman made it alive to shore and only one child was among those saved. In all, about 560 passengers and crewmen perished.

The *Atlantic* left England and sailed for New York, New York, in late March. It was the period when ships were in transition from sail to steam, and the *Atlantic*—though powered by four 150-horsepower engines—also had four 150-foot ship-rigged masts. Its skipper, Captain John A. Williams, tended to rely more on the sails than on the engines; and he evidenced a woeful indifference when it came to relying on charts illustrating dangerous landfalls.

Waters were turbulent and the ship had rough going, using up great quantities of fuel. The *Atlantic* was still 1,100 miles out of New York when the captain was informed that only slightly more than 400 tons of coal remained to power the engines. He deemed it a sufficient amount, feeling that he could always rely on his sails if need be. By March 31, however, the *Atlantic*'s coal supply was down to 100 tons, and the liner was still 460 miles out to sea. Reluctantly, the captain decided to make for Halifax, Nova Scotia, to resupply his fuel.

Despite the fact that the Halifax harbor had a reputation of being a dangerous harbor to enter, Captain Williams chose not to consult his charts or maps. Even worse, he mistakenly concluded that a red light spotted in the distance was Sambro Light, which was near the harbor entrance. It was, in fact, Peggy's Point Light, which warned of dangerous reefs. Putting his third officer in charge and telling him to "keep to course until six bells" (3 A.M.), Captain Williams took to his berth.

At 3 A.M. came the lookout's cry: "Breakers ahead!" Before the awakened captain could make it to his bridge, the *Atlantic* had plowed onto some huge rocks, ripping open its hull in the process, and drowning more than 300 sleeping passengers.

Passengers attempt to escape the sinking Atlantic *on April 1, 1873, after the ship struck some huge rocks off the coast of Nova Scotia. About 560 victims perished in the shipwreck, and although more than 400 men were rescued not one woman survived.*

Panic ensued. Passengers in upper deck cabins fled onto the decks. Many were washed overboard; men deserted wives and children as they climbed riggings and masts to escape the encroaching waves.

Captain Williams, to his credit, had a rope taken from the ship to the shore; he and his crew spent hours passing survivors along this fragile escape route. Hysterical, spray-frozen victims kept dropping from the decks and masts of the striken ship. The few women who had managed to make their way into the rigging were found dead, frozen grotesquely in place by the icy spray. The one child who survived, a twelve-year-old boy, was pulled by his hair through a porthole by a crew member.

Later, before a Canadian Board of Inquiry that would strip him of his sailing certificate for two years, Captain Williams, a broken man, exlaimed: "It's horrible. To think that while hundreds of men were saved, every woman should have perished. It's too terrible, it's too terrible!"

H.M.S. Victoria

The story of the British ship *Victoria* must surely be one of the most bizarre in the annals of sea disasters. Launched in 1887, she was a steam-powered ironclad, one of the largest, fastest, and most heavily armed warships of her day—the pride of the British Navy.

In 1893 the *Victoria* was the flagship of the Mediterranean fleet, commanded by Vice Adm. Sir George Tryon. Tryon was as much admired by the British public as his flagship. Known as a brilliant and daring tactician, he was also an iconoclast, impatient with tradition and anxious to reform and modernize the British Navy. He believed that after decades of peace it had become too set in its ways and needed waking up to enable it to respond to new challenges. A hard taskmaster, Tryon demanded a lot from his subordinates; he was especially fond of having the fleet perform elaborate and unconventional maneuvers requiring considerable skill and initiative. It was his custom never to explain these exercises ahead of time, and the captains of the other ships in the fleet frequently held their breaths while they waited to see how he would bring the maneuvers off. Tryon liked to keep his men on their toes.

On May 27, 1893, the Mediterranean squadron, consisting of eleven ironclads and two light cruisers, left its base at Malta for summer maneuvers. On the afternoon and evening of the twenty-eighth the fleet performed evolutions and practiced firing at sea and then lay off the coast of Libya for a few days before proceeding to Acre and Haifa on the Palestinian coast. Leaving Haifa on June 16, they went through more exercises at sea and then spent several days at Beirut, where the men had shore leave.

When Lord Tryon's fleet sailed from Beirut on the morning of June 22 it was in a characteristically unconventional fashion. At anchor, the ships had been in two parallel divisions, the one closest to shore headed by the *Victoria*, the one on the seaward side headed by the *Camperdown*, which was the flagship of Tryon's second-in-command, Rear Adm. Albert Hastings Markham. Normally the two columns would have left port in that order, but as they got under way, Tryon signaled Markham to pass his division between the ships of the first division and then pursue a diagonal course until the whole fleet was in one line abreast.

The next port of call was Tripoli, a short distance north along the coast, where the fleet expected to arrive that afternoon. At two o'clock Admiral Tryon sent for the *Victoria*'s captain, Maurice Bourke, the staff commander, Thomas

Hawkins-Smith, and Lord Gillford, his flag lieutenant. Tryon told them that they were to begin their entry into the anchorage at Tripoli by forming two divisions, six cables (twelve hundred yards) apart; the divisions were then to reverse course, the left division by turning right, and the right division by turning left. It occurred to the others that if this were done, the ships of the two divisions would collide, because each needed more than three cables to make a full turn. When Hawkins-Smith suggested that the columns should be farther apart, the Admiral at first seemed to agree, but when he was giving instructions to Gillford, who was responsible for transmitting orders to the rest of the fleet, he again said the distance should be six cables. The officers were puzzled, but when Bourke and Gillford asked about the order a second time a few minutes later, Tryon reconfirmed the original order. They could only suppose that, as had happened in the past, the Admiral had some trick up his sleeve that would make the maneuver come out all right.

At 2:20, as ordered, the squadron formed two divisions behind the *Victoria* and the *Camperdown* respectively. Shortly after three o'clock the town of Tripoli was visible in the distance as they entered the bay where they were to drop anchor. At 3:25 the flagship signaled the first division to alter course, ship by ship, sixteen points to starboard, and the second division to do the same, sixteen points to port. On the bridge of the *Victoria*, Bourke and Gillford looked anxiously at one another and at Tryon, but the Admiral gave no indication of being aware that anything was amiss. All of the other vessels were required to acknowledge receipt of the signal before the evolution could begin. Minutes went by and the *Camperdown* failed to respond. At 3:31 Tryon signaled impatiently to Markham: "What are you waiting for?" Markham then acknowledged that he understood, and the two lead ships began to turn toward one another. As the *Camperdown* got closer, Bourke repeatedly tried to draw Tryon's attention to the danger of a collision, but the Admiral ignored him, his eyes fixed on the *Nile*, the second ship in the other division. Finally, when the *Victoria* and the *Camperdown* were less than 400 yards apart, Tryon turned around and for the first time seemed to grasp what was happening. He quickly ordered Bourke to go astern, but it was too late. A minute or so later, the *Camperdown's* bow, equipped with a steel ram designed for use against enemy ships in combat, tore into the starboard side of the *Victoria* at a speed of six knots, forcing the flagship sixty feet to port.

Still reeling from the shock, Tryon found himself facing Markham on the bridge of the *Camperdown*, less than fifty yards away. "Go astern! Go astern with both engines!" he shouted. "Why didn't you . . .?" Tryon could not make himself heard in all the confusion, but it did not matter. The damage had been done, and *Camperdown*'s engines, like the *Victoria*'s, had been reversed at the time of the collision anyway. The *Camperdown* pulled away, leaving the stricken ship to her fate.

At first Tryon did not realize how badly the *Victoria* had been hurt. Some of the nearby ships were lowering their boats in case they might be needed, but the Admiral signaled that no help would be required. Because land was only a short distance away, he told Hawkins-Smith to steer for shore and beach her, but the ship could not make any headway. Within a few minutes the bows were under water, and the *Victoria* was listing badly. By 3:44 Tryon realized that they were not going to make it, and he gave the order to abandon ship. There was no time to launch the boats; the *Victoria* was turning over, capsizing. Everyone who could jumped over the side, but those below decks did not have a chance. Eleven minutes after the collision, H.M.S. *Victoria* sank to the bottom of Tripoli Bay. Sir George Tryon made no attempt to leave the ship and went down with her. Some of the seamen who had escaped into the water were pulled down by the force of the sinking vessel, and many more were killed by the debris that came shooting up to the surface like projectiles from a gun after she had sunk.

Officers and men watching from the decks of the other ships could hardly believe their eyes. In the midst of routine maneuvers and within sight of land, their commander in chief and his flagship had been suddenly destroyed by an accident so absurd as to defy reason.

The explanation for the tragedy was sought by a court-martial held at Malta the following month. Captain Bourke, who survived the disaster, was cleared of all blame for the loss of the *Victoria* and the 358 men who perished with her. Rear Admiral Markham was criticized for having done nothing to prevent the collision. He admitted that, because the evolution had seemed impossible to him, he had delayed acknowledging the signal—he could not believe that he had understood it correctly. He had gone ahead when pressed to do so by Tryon, thinking that perhaps the first division was going to turn in a wider arc than the second and pass around it on the outside. Others have suggested that Tryon may have intended the second division to circle around the first. Since Tryon was not there to tell the court what he had intended, it had no choice but to fix the responsibility for the tragedy on him.

There were those who maintained that the *Victoria* was unstable, that she should not have capsized, and certainly should not have sunk so quickly. The Admiralty denied that there had been anything wrong with her design; nevertheless, her sister ship, the *Sans Pareil*, was modified after the accident, and many considered her unsafe until she was eventually scrapped in 1907.

The General Slocum

The 250-foot-long excursion steamer *General Slocum* was one of the largest of its class working out of the New York, New York, harbor. Aboard, that sunny morning, June 15, 1904—when it pulled away from its Third Street Pier at 9 A.M.—were almost 1,500 persons, mostly women and children members of the German immigrant congregation of St. Mark's church school in the Bronx. It was to be a full day's outing, and a holiday mood prevailed. Hundreds of young children raced about the decks, playing. Yet, little more than an hour later, the ship had become a blazing funeral pyre; and by noon, more than 1,000 of those excursionists had perished.

The *Slocum* was making its way up the East River and by 10 A.M. was at a point approximately opposite 130th Street—when, suddenly, a woman shouted "Fire!" Flames were shooting from a paint locker in the forward part of the ship. A fresh coat of white paint, covering the *Slocum*'s brittle, cracking wooden frame, made the ship highly combustible, and the flames spread with maddening ferocity. Screaming, hysterical women and children rushed frantically for the stern—a tragic mistake, for there most of them would die.

The *Slocum*'s captain, William Van Schaick—a man already notorious for earlier navigational blunders—inexplicably ordered his pilot to steer the vessel to North Brother Island, rather than toward the Manhattan shore, only three hundred yards away. There, the ship could have been beached in a matter of minutes, and hundreds of lives might have been saved. Instead, as the ship plied the longer route to the island, a stiff northeast wind fanned the flames, driving

General Slocum *(above)* caught fire and burned to its waterline on June 15, 1904, during an excursion on New York City's East River. More than 1,000 bodies were later recovered *(below)*.

them from the bow backward to the stern, where most of the panic-stricken passengers had taken refuge. Mothers fought each other to get life preservers for their children only to have the rotting devices fall apart in their hands. Fire hoses, too, were rotten—never, apparently, having been inspected—and, when the crew tried using them, water came through in useless trickles.

When the *Slocum* finally rammed itself onto the rocky shoals of North Brother Island, it proved a most inaccessible spot both for the nearby tugs and the one fireboat that tried to render assistance and for the hopeless passengers trapped on the stern. The water, at the point where the stern jutted out into the river, was close to thirty feet deep. While hundreds of victims—most of whom could not swim and many of whom spoke no English, thus adding to the confusion—were either dying in the flames or falling or jumping into the river, where they drowned in countless numbers, Captain Van Schaick and his two pilots, who were on the *Slocum*'s bow when it grounded, jumped safely onto the deck of a tugboat moored nearby. Their uniforms were only slightly singed. Crewmen, too, for the most part, made little effort to save the passengers and thought mostly of saving their own lives.

The *Slocum* burned to her waterline. The jam of floating bodies in the water became so thickly crowded together that it formed almost a carpet on which the final surviving passengers could walk safely ashore. Although 407 persons survived, the final death count reached 1,021, almost all of whom were women and children.

Arrested and charged with manslaughter, Captain Van Schaick was accused likewise of gross negligence for having failed to train his crew in life saving techniques and for having inadequate and faulty equipment aboard his vessel. (Two New York City safety inspectors were dismissed immediately from their jobs.) Eventually, Van Schaick was convicted of the charges against him and sentenced to ten years in prison. The burning of the *General Slocum* was the worst harbor disaster in U.S. history since the steamboat *Seawanhaka* burned and sank off Ward's Island in the East River, on June 28, 1880, killing 60 passengers.

The Eastland

In Chicago, Illinois, on July 24, 1915, another excursion ship disaster took a similarly terrible toll in lost lives. Still at dockside, and crammed with more than 3,500 passengers and

On July 24, 1915, the packet boat S.S. Eastland *capsized in the Chicago River; 852 passengers were drowned.*

crewmen, the packet boat S.S. *Eastland* was readying itself to cast off for Michigan City, Indiana, where the excursionists— most of whom were employees of the Western Electric Company—were to spend the day picnicking on the sand dunes.

Unknown and unnoticed, perhaps, by most of the fun-seeking, festive-minded passengers, the vessel, in service only five years, had certain "built-in" structural deficiencies that caused it to tilt precariously. That morning, when it was noticed that a photographer was taking pictures off the port side, hundreds of persons rushed to the port railing, and the *Eastland*, already at a dangerous list, tilted even further toward the water. It never stopped until, capsizing completely, it lay flat on its side on the bottom of the Chicago River. Only about eight feet of its starboard side remained above water and, on it, hundreds of bewildered passengers scrambled to await rescue. Hundreds of others were capsized into the water or were trapped below decks. In all, 852 persons drowned.

The Titanic

At 10:30 P.M. on Sunday, April 14, 1912, the Leyland steamer *Californian*, en route from London, England, to Boston, Massachusetts, ran into an ice field off the Grand Banks. Captain Stanley Lord, deciding that it was unsafe to proceed, brought his vessel to a halt. A little after eleven o'clock the lights of another ship could be seen a few miles to the north, headed in a westerly direction through the clear starlit night. It was the British White Star liner *Titanic*, the largest oceangoing vessel in the world, on the fifth day of her maiden voyage from Southampton, England, to New York, New York. She was carrying a full complement of wealthy and socially prominent passengers, who kept her radio operator busy sending personal messages to their friends and relatives in the United States. When the *Californian*'s radio operator tried to warn the *Titanic* about the icebergs, he was told not to interrupt their transmission of messages to Newfoundland.

The great ship found out about the icebergs soon enough on her own. Her lookout spotted one directly ahead at 11:40 and notified the bridge at once. Less than a minute after the lookout's warning, the ship was almost on top of it. First Officer William M. Murdoch ordered the helm to starboard and breathed a sigh of relief as the ship seemed to be passing close by the side of the towering iceberg. Then he heard a grinding noise from below the waterline. A submerged portion of the floating mass of ice had ripped a gash in the hull of the *Titanic*. Capt. Edward J. Smith came rushing up onto the bridge from his cabin as Murdoch brought the ship to a stop and ordered the watertight doors closed. On the *Californian* Third Officer Charles Groves saw the lights of the *Titanic* suddenly disappear; not realizing that she had changed direction, he thought the lights had merely been put out for the night.

Some of the passengers on the White Star liner had seen the iceberg, but it was gone now. Others had heard the grinding noise or felt the impact, but most did not notice anything until the ship stopped. A section of the starboard weather deck was littered with chunks of ice, which some of the steerage passengers picked up and threw at one another playfully. On the A and B decks, first-class passengers came out of their cabins to see what was going on. Even those who knew that the vessel had struck something were not worried. The *Titanic*, a floating palace equipped with every modern convenience, was considered unsinkable.

J. Bruce Ismay, managing director of the White Star Line, thought that she was. He had come along on the maiden voyage and now made his way to the bridge to learn the extent of the damage. He found Captain Smith in consultation with Thomas Andrews, the builder of the ship. The infor-

On its maiden voyage from Southhampton, England, to New York City the "unsinkable" Titanic (above) collided with an iceberg (below) that ripped a 300-foot gash in her hull. More than 1,500 people died in the sinking ship or were drowned in the icy cold waters of the North Atlantic.

mation they were receiving about the *Titanic*'s condition came as a grim surprise. The gash torn by the iceberg in the ship's side was 300 feet long, cutting across the first five watertight compartments. Those who had pronounced her unsinkable did so on the assumption that in no circumstances would more than two or three of the compartments be flooded. But now the inconceivable had happened: water was pouring into five compartments, and the *Titanic* seemed doomed.

Shortly after midnight the captain ordered the crew to ready the lifeboats for launching and told the radio operator to send a call for assistance. There was no general alarm. Stewards went around to the first- and second-class cabins, informing everyone that there had been an accident and that they were to go up on deck wearing their life jackets. The passengers obediently filed out into the biting cold, each class keeping to its own area, and waited to be told what to do.

There were eight wooden lifeboats on each side of the ship, and four "Englehardts"—collapsible canvas boats—that were designed to be fitted into the davits after the wooden boats were lowered. The total capacity of these boats was 1,178 persons. In other words, there was room for only slightly more than half of the 2,207 people on board. The Board of Trade regulations did not require passenger ships to carry enough boats to accommodate everyone, and it had not seemed necessary. Modern shipbuilding, it was thought, had made the *Titanic* invulnerable to the hazards of sea travel. Few passengers had any idea that they were in imminent danger. At the worst, they thought that they might have to be transferred to other ships. Charles M. Hays, president of the Grand Trunk Railroad, assured his fellow passengers that the *Titanic* was good for another eight hours. Andrews and Captain Smith knew that it was more likely to be two hours.

People were reluctant to get into the boats. Women and children were given priority, but many women refused to go without their husbands. Sometimes the men were allowed to go along, sometimes not. At 12:45 A.M. the first boat was lowered, but it was only half filled. When it became clear that the ship was going to be abandoned, some of the passengers went below again to collect valuables that they had left behind. Many found their cabins already flooded. One woman, a lady's maid who had been sent by her employer to fetch some jewelry, heard the key turning in the lock of the stateroom door while she was inside. The stewards were locking the doors to prevent looting. Her cries brought them back to let her out; she ran up to the deck again, forgetting the jewelry.

Little thought was given to the more than 700 third-class passengers. They were assembled several levels below the boat deck, and a steward had taken the initiative of guiding small groups of women and children up so they would not lose their way. But this was slow work, and others who tried to reach the boat deck on their own were turned back by crew members when they blundered into first- and second-class areas.

In the radio shack, wireless operator John Philips was receiving some answers to his call for help. The Cunard liner *Carpathia*, fifty-eight miles away, signaled that she was coming as fast as she could. The *Californian*, barely ten miles away and within sight of the *Titanic* on that clear night, did not receive the distress call. Her radio set had been closed down for the night at 11:30.

Quartermaster George Thomas Rowe had been standing watch on the stern of the *Titanic* when she struck the iceberg. More than an hour later he was still at his post, unaware of what was happening. He probably would have remained there, forgotten, if he had not noticed one of the lifeboats in the water and telephoned the bridge to ask about it. He was told to come forward at once and to bring some signal rockets with him to signal the *Californian*. Rowe brought twelve rockets, and they were fired at five-minute intervals. The signals were seen by officers on the *Californian*, who reported them to Captain Lord, below in his cabin. He suggested that they try to contact the *Titanic* by signal lamp to see if anything was wrong, and he then went back to bed.

Meanwhile, one by one the remainder of the wooden boats and two of the collapsibles were lowered, most of them not filled to capacity. By the time the last one, collapsible D, was launched at 2:20 A.M., it was obvious that the ship would not last much longer. The whole forward area was submerged, and the stern had risen high into the air, ready for the final plunge. Still ablaze with lights, the *Titanic* presented an awesome spectacle to those who looked back from the boats. Some who had been left behind dived into the water, but most stayed where they were—including millionaires John Jacob Astor, Benjamin Guggenheim, and Mr. and Mrs. Isador Straus, as well as Captain Smith and Thomas Andrews. The ship's band, which had been playing ragtime music,

switched to a hymn. At 2:20 the *Titanic* became almost per-
pendicular to the surface, then settled back a little, and slid
smoothly down into the calm sea.

After the ship went down, the water was filled with people
crying for help. A few were picked up by the boats that had
been launched earlier. A few more saved themselves by
climbing onto collapsibles A and B, which had floated free of
the wreck. But no one survived for long in the icy water, and
more than fifteen hundred persons were lost. The exact number was never determined. The lifeboats rowed around in the
dark for the next couple of hours, sending up flares to attract
the attention of any vessels that might be in the vicinity. The

Survivors from the ill-fated Titanic *are rescued from one of
the crowded lifeboats by crewmen of the* Carpathia.

collapsibles barely remained afloat; several men awaited rescue standing on top of collapsible B, which was upside down.

At the first light of dawn, the *Carpathia* arrived on the scene and began to pick up the survivors, who were scattered over a four-mile area dotted with icebergs. Finally alerted, the *Californian* appeared shortly thereafter. By mid-morning, the 705 people in the boats had been taken on board, and the *Carpathia* headed for New York City leaving the *Californian* to search for any more survivors. None were found.

A number of reforms were instituted as a result of the *Titanic* disaster. The International Ice Patrol was established, and Atlantic shipping lanes were moved farther south in the winter. All ship radios were ordered to be in operation on a twenty-four-hour basis, and, perhaps most important, new regulations required lifeboats for everyone on board.

The Morro Castle

Other marine tragedies have led to other reforms. In 1934, for example, when the passenger liner *Morro Castle* caught fire and burned six miles off the coastline of New Jersey, 133 persons—mostly passengers—were killed.

Subsequently, an inquiry board ruled that a laxity in fire regulations and improperly implemented safety precautions had contributed to a needlessly high death toll. As a result, strong new marine laws governing fire hazards were enacted, and more modern fireproofing systems were made mandatory.

The San Francisco and the Daphne

Tragically enough, the *Titanic* is not alone in being the only ship never to complete a maiden voyage. Others share in this dubious distinction; among these, the 3,000-ton paddle steamship *San Francisco*, completed in late 1853 and put into immediate service without so much as a trial run.

Because the transcontinental railroad had not yet been completed, the ship was sorely needed as a means of transporting a United States artillery regiment from New York to their new duty station in California. Accordingly, on December 21, 1853, the huge ship set sail with about 750 persons—including eight companies of troops (about 500 men), 200 dependents, and 50 crewmen.

Two days out, the *San Francisco* encountered heavy seas. The ship's paddle wheels, being too deeply immersed in the water, made the vessel sluggish and unmaneuverable. Then

In 1934 the Morro Castle *burned six miles off the coast of New Jersey, killing 133 persons.*

the engines gave out. Buffeted by stormy seas and high winds, the ship's mast splintered and its decks were soon a pile of shattered timbers and fallen sails. About 150 soldiers and sailors were attempting to clear away the debris, when one gigantic wave—estimated to be more than thirty feet high—broke over the ship, carrying with it virtually everybody and everything above deck. It also swept the decks clean of lifeboats and rafts.

For days the ship wallowed helplessly, waves crashing across decks and into cabins, carrying additional victims into the sea. Crewmen and soldiers labored at the pumps and

The San Francisco, *a paddle steamship carrying a military regiment, flounders in stormy seas on its first and last voyage.*

manned bucket lines to no great appreciable effect. Morale flagged, and as it became increasingly obvious that the *San Francisco* was a mortally wounded ship, discipline crumbled. Men broke into the food and spirits lockers, gorging themselves into severe attacks of cramps and diarrhea. Cholera broke out, and the death toll rose even higher.

Finally, two relief vessels were able to reach the stricken ship and begin to take off the survivors. Even after rescue, another 60 of the food "debauchees" succumbed. Altogether, an estimated 300 persons died; and, finally, on January 14, 1854, the ill-fated ship broke into fragments and sank beneath the waves.

Even more incredible was the sinking—immediately upon launching—of the 460-ton packet steamer *Daphne*, in the River Clyde at Glasgow, Scotland, on July 3, 1883. The ship, it was discovered, had little or no ballast—except for 195 workmen who were aboard. Thus, when it hit the water, with virtually no stability, it rolled over forty-five degrees, took in huge amounts of water through a large deck opening, and sank. The 195 workmen died within seconds.

The Andrea Doria

On the night of July 25, 1956, the Italian luxury liner *Andrea Doria*, nine days out of Genoa with 1,134 passengers aboard, was off the coast of New England bound for New York City. As she approached the Nantucket Lightship, fifty miles from Nantucket Island, a dense fog settled over the area. Captain Piero Calamai took the usual precautions in conditions of restricted visibility: he closed the *Doria*'s twelve watertight doors, sounded the fog signal at regular intervals, kept a radar watch, and posted a lookout on the bow to give warning of any obstacle in the ship's path. According to the Rules of the Road at Sea, vessels navigating in foggy weather were supposed to keep to a "moderate speed," but the *Doria* went ahead at nearly twenty-two knots, only a little less than its normal cruising speed. Because failing to make port on schedule involved expense for the owners, most captains were reluctant to slow down unless absolutely necessary, and the *Doria*'s master was no exception. In any case, it was thought that radar would give sufficient warning of any vessels approaching through the fog.

Proceeding toward the Nantucket Lightship from the opposite direction was the Swedish liner *Stockholm*, which had left New York City that morning for Copenhagen, Denmark, and Göteborg, Sweden. Around ten o'clock Capt. H. Gunnar Nordenson went down to his cabin, leaving Third Officer Ernst Carstens-Johannsen in charge on the bridge. Visibility was excellent; there was no trace of fog to be seen. At 10:30 a dot indicating another ship appeared on the radar screen. The ship seemed to be about twelve miles away and heading in the direction of the *Stockholm*'s course. Carstens calculated that she would pass within a mile of them, and as the distance between the two ships decreased, he scanned the horizon for some sign of her. He wanted to be able to alter his course if necessary, in order to give the other vessel as wide a berth as possible. Captain Nordenson's standing orders were that the *Stockholm* should always stay at least a mile away from any other ship at sea. Half an hour passed and Carstens grew more and more puzzled; although the radar showed the other ship to be less than four miles away, he was still unable to see any lights over the water.

A dot representing an approaching ship showed up on the *Andrea Doria*'s radarscope at 10:45. Like Carstens, Captain Calamai and his watch officers thought that there would be a considerable distance between the two vessels as they passed each other. The *Doria* was still enshrouded in fog, and the *Stockholm* was sailing through a clear moonlit night. Shortly after eleven o'clock, the ships sighted each other as the *Stockholm* reached the western limit of the fog shelf.

With the visibility so poor, each misjudged the other's position. The *Stockholm* made a right turn so as to pass the *Doria* port to port; minutes later the *Doria* turned sharply to the left, heading across the bows of the oncoming *Stockholm*. When he realized what was happening, Carstens frantically gave the signal for full speed astern, but the ship could not be stopped in time. At 11:10 the bow of the *Stockholm* hit the

The Italian luxury liner Andrea Doria *lists to the starboard following a collision with the Swedish liner* Stockholm. *Although the ship remained afloat long enough for rescue vessels to save 1,662 persons, 52 others died.*

starboard side of the *Doria*, penetrating the Italian liner to a depth of thirty feet. For a few seconds the two ships were locked together, the *Doria* dragging the smaller vessel along with her. The *Stockholm* then wrenched free and disappeared into the night.

The sea poured into the huge hole in the *Doria*'s side, and she began to list heavily to starboard. Captain Calamai was astounded to discover that his ship, supposedly designed never to list more than fifteen degrees, was already at an eighteen-degree angle. When the list increased to twenty degrees, he knew that she was in danger of sinking. Calamai ordered the boats to be launched and directed his engineers to keep the pumps going as long as they could. The degree of the starboard list, however, made it impossible to get the portside boats into the water. Because there would only be room in the remaining boats for half the people on the ship, Calamai notified the radio operator to send out a call for immediate assistance. The passengers had been told to don life jackets and proceed immediately to their lifeboat stations. After the failure to launch the portside boats, organization seemed to break down, and the passengers were left without any further instructions. As for the starboard boats, they were hanging so far out over the water that people could not reach them from the deck.

Everything on the *Doria* was arranged to work on the assumption that she would never list more than fifteen degrees. When that assumption proved incorrect, nothing could proceed according to plan. The starboard boats were lowered into the water, but in order to reach them, the people on deck had either to jump into the sea or lower themselves on ropes. Most of the boats left the side of the ship before they were filled, and some of them contained mostly crew members—porters, waiters, and kitchen help—none of whom were supposed to leave the ship before the passengers.

About a mile away on the *Stockholm*, Captain Nordenson assessed the damage done to his ship. The bow was completely crushed, but the watertight doors had been closed in time; although the forward section was riding low in the water, she seemed to be in no immediate danger. The only problem was that the ship could not be moved. The anchor chains had unwound during the collision and had become tangled with something underneath the water, holding the ship fast. Nordenson picked up those who came over in the *Doria*'s boats but refused to lower the *Stockholm*'s boats to help the Italian ship, feeling that there was still a chance that the boats might be needed for his own passengers.

The *Doria*'s SOS was received by several vessels in the area around Nantucket, but the only one with enough boats to help was the 44,000-ton liner *Ile de France*, en route from New York City to Le Havre, France. She changed course and headed toward the scene of the collision. Two other ships, the *Cape Ann*, a United Fruit Company cargo ship, and the *Private William H. Thomas*, a U.S. Navy transport, arrived first. After the appearance of the *Cape Ann* at 12:45, the *Stockholm* began sending lifeboats to the *Doria*, which by that time had a thirty-degree list. Those watching from the other ships were amazed that she was still afloat and felt sure that she would not last much longer. But the *Doria* held on, and with the arrival of the *Ile de France* just before two o'clock the panic died down, and rescue work began to go more smoothly.

By four o'clock all of the passengers had been taken off, and Captain Calamai ordered most of the remaining crew members to abandon ship. He and his senior officers remained on board a while longer, hoping that U.S. Coast Guard tugboats might still get there in time to take their ship in tow and save her. At 5:30 the officers transferred to lifeboats and continued to wait. By the time the cutter *Hornbeam* arrived with towing equipment at nine in the morning, the *Doria*, lying completely over on her side, was beyond saving. At 10:09, eleven hours after the collision, she disappeared beneath the waves.

The casualties in this dramatic marine disaster were much lighter than might have been expected, chiefly because the *Doria* remained afloat as long as she did. Fifty-two persons were lost, forty-six of them from the *Doria*. The great majority died in the collision. One of the survivors, fourteen-year-old Linda Morgan, was swept out of her bed on the *Doria* and was later found alive on the bow of the *Stockholm*. Her sister, who had been sleeping beside her, was killed. The 1,662 persons who were saved from the wreck were taken to New York City on the *Ile de France*, the *Cape Ann*, the *Thomas*, and on the *Stockholm*, which was able to navigate satisfactorily once its anchor chain had been cut loose.

The Italian Line and the Swedish-American Line brought suits against one another for the losses suffered because of the accident, and a pretrial discovery proceeding was held in New York City the following September. The question of who was responsible for the collision could not really be settled; the logbooks of the *Andrea Doria* had been lost with the ship, and without them it was impossible to determine what her exact course and position had been as the two vessels approached each other. But the Swedish Line claimed that, no matter who was responsible, the collision should not have caused the *Doria* to sink. She went down, they said, because she was not properly ballasted.

On the *Doria's* bottom deck, where she had been hit by the *Stockholm*, there was a fuel storage compartment containing ten oil tanks. As the oil in these tanks was used up during the voyage, they were supposed to have been refilled with water. On the night of July 25 they had been empty. If the *Stockholm* had struck any of the other lower deck compartments, seawater would have flooded them all the way across, and the *Doria* would have stayed on an even keel. As it was, the *Stockholm* tore open the five starboard tanks, filling them with seawater and causing the ship to list to starboard and, ultimately, to capsize. If the portside tanks had been properly ballasted, the imbalance would not have occurred, and the *Doria* would not have gone down. When evidence of this came to light, the Italian Line dropped its suit and made an out-of-court settlement.

Other Marine Catastrophes, 1959–78

1959
Jan. 30
Off Cape Farewell, Greenland. A Danish passenger-cargo ship on her maiden voyage struck an iceberg and sank; 95 persons were lost.
Feb. 9
Northeast of Newfoundland, Canada. Two trawlers capsized; all 47 men aboard the vessels were believed lost.
Feb. 17
Off southwest Iceland. A lighthouse tender sank in a gale; all 12 crew members were lost.
April 14
New Delhi, India. A small boat capsized on the Sarda River, drowning 35 persons.
May 8
Cairo, Egypt. An estimated 200 persons drowned when a pleasure steamer turned over in the Nile.
May 14
Santiago, Chile. A boat capsized on the Talten River, drown-

ing 14 persons.

Aug. 22

Palawan, Philippines. A Philippine interisland ship sank in a typhoon, with a loss of 90 persons.

Sept. 22

Munising, Michigan. A mother and her 10 children drowned when their small boat sank.

Oct. 4

Lake Pielinen, Finland. Two motorboats collided in a rainstorm, drowning 15 persons.

Dec. 7

Oporto, Portugal. A tugboat sank in a heavy storm, drowning 17 men aboard.

Dec. 7

North Sea. In a gale, 13 fishermen perished.

Dec. 9

North Sea. A Norwegian freighter capsized, drowning 20 crewmen.

1960

Feb. 24

Near Chittagong, Pakistan. A riverboat carrying Hindus to a religious festival capsized, drowning 20 of 60 persons aboard.

March 21

Red Sea. A boat sank; 50 persons drowned.

March 22

Near Taipei, Taiwan. A ferry carrying schoolchildren capsized, drowning 18 of them.

April 6

Persian Gulf. A motor launch capsized in a storm, drowning 57 persons.

May 12

Andhra State, India. A boat overloaded with pilgrims capsized in the Krishna River; about 60 persons drowned.

June 13

Warsaw, Poland. An excursion boat capsized in the Dunajec Mountain River; 18 schoolchildren, a teacher, and 2 boatmen drowned.

July 11

Belém, Brazil. A passenger launch on the Amazon River overturned and sank with 32 persons aboard.

July 19

Off Newport Beach, California. Two U.S. Navy destroyers collided in a fog, killing 11 crew members.

July 30

Andhra State, India. A motor launch capsized in the Gadavari River, drowning 29 persons.

Aug. 18

Lourenço Marques, Mozambique. A boat carrying 46 passengers capsized in Delagoa Bay, drowning all aboard.

Oct. 21

Persian Gulf, near Qatar. The Norwegian tanker *Polyana* was set afire after a series of explosions; 14 crewmen were missing and presumed dead, and 29 were rescued.

Oct. 22

Near Buras, Louisiana. The U.S. passenger freighter *Alcoa Corsair* and the Italian freighter *Lorenzo Marcello* collided in the Mississippi River; 10 persons were killed, and at least 25 were injured.

Dec. 2

North Atlantic Ocean. The Liberian freighter *Iri* was reported missing; all 23 persons aboard were presumed drowned.

Dec. 14

Istanbul, Turkey. The Yugoslav tanker *Peter Zoranic* and the Greek tanker *World Harmony* collided in the Bosporus, after which the *Peter Zoranic*, out of control, drifted across the strait and rammed the drydocked Turkish passenger ship *Tarsus*, which burned and sank; 50 persons were missing and presumed dead, and 40 others were injured.

Dec. 21

Persian Gulf. A motor launch caught fire and sank; 50 of the 53 persons aboard drowned.

1961

Jan. 7

Persian Gulf. A motor launch en route from Iran to Kuwait caught fire and sank; 88 persons perished.

Jan. 11

Off Albucemas Bay, Morocco. The motor launch *Price* sank in a storm; 43 Moroccan Jews, on their way to an Israel-bound ship in Gibraltar, drowned.

Jan. 15

Atlantic Ocean, off the New Jersey coast. A "Texas Tower," a U.S. Air Force radar installation, collapsed and sank following a heavy storm; all 28 men aboard drowned.

Feb. 16

East Pakistan. Two launches collided on the Meghna River, 70 miles from Dacca; about 100 persons drowned.

April 8

Off the Trucial and Bahrein coasts. The British liner *Dara* caught fire in a raging storm and sank in the Persian Gulf; 212 persons were missing and presumed dead.

June 11

Off the Tenasserim coast, Burma. The 995-ton motor launch *Aungteza* sank; 94 persons drowned.

July 8

Near Quelimane, Mozambique. The Portuguese ship *Save* ran aground during a storm, exploded, and burned; 259 of the 549 persons aboard were killed or missing and presumed dead.

Sept. 3

Off Buenaventura, Colombia. The tourist boat *Vencedor* capsized and sank; 54 persons drowned, and 20 others were missing.

Sept. 11

Gujarat state, India. The boat *Salamat*, loaded with 130 evacuees from the flooded village of Gopali, sank in the Narbada River; 95 persons drowned.

Nov. 6

Mediterranean Sea, off Tunis. The 7,129-ton British freighter *Clan Keith*, battling a storm, exploded and sank; 61 persons aboard died, and 7 were rescued.

Dec. 19

Off the southern coast of Korea. A ferryboat capsized and sank near Wan Island; 34 persons drowned.

1962

Jan. 1

Mhapal, India. A crowded passenger boat sank in the Savithri River; at least 70 persons drowned.

Jan. 1

Off eastern coast of South Korea. A fishing fleet of ten small boats was caught in a gale; 94 fishermen were lost and presumed dead.

Jan. 8

English Channel. The Yugoslav freighter *Sabac* and the British freighter *Dirington Court* collided three miles east of the Goodwin lightship; 17 Yugoslav seamen drowned, and 11 others were missing and presumed dead.

April 28

Near Hong Kong. A junk loaded with escapees from Communist China overturned in heavy seas; of 23 persons aboard, 22 were presumed drowned.

May 27

Kyushu Island, Japan. A small Japanese fishing boat broke up in rough seas 150 miles offshore; 15 crewmen were missing and presumed drowned.

June 10

Taipei, Taiwan. The fishing trawler *Chieh Shin*, loaded with students watching a boat race, capsized in the Yun River; at least 22 children drowned.

July 11

Portuguese Guinea. A small Portuguese motorboat capsized in a canal; of the 35 persons aboard, 30 drowned.

Aug. 18

Quincy, Florida. During a Sunday school picnic a small boat sank in Lake Talquin; 17 children and their teacher drowned.

Sept. 7

Near Seoul, Korea. A ferryboat overturned in the rain-swollen Han River; of the 55 passengers, 24 drowned.

Oct. 20

Lutcher, Louisiana. The 13,500-ton Norwegian tanker *Boheme* collided with a string of oil barges in a fog on the Mississippi River; the cargo of explosives caught fire, and 19 crewmen were killed.

Oct. 21

Off Vikna Islands, Norway. A Norwegian coastal liner, *Sanct Svithun*, ran aground on a reef and sank; 48 persons were rescued, and 33 others perished.

Nov. 15

Atlantic Ocean. The Greek freighter *Captain George* caught fire and was abandoned in the storm-tossed sea 500 miles northeast of Bermuda; 7 crewmen were rescued, and 18 others were lost and presumed dead.

Nov. 18

Tokyo Bay, Japan. A Japanese tanker and a Norwegian tanker collided and burst into flames; 13 crewmen from the Japanese vessel were killed, and 26 others were missing.

Nov. 18

New Bedford, Massachusetts. The fishing scalloper *Midnight Sun* was lost off the Georges bank, east of Nantucket; 11 crewmen were presumed drowned.

Nov. 19

Lake Nyasa, Southern Rhodesia. A lifeboat overturned while taking passengers ashore from a cargo ship; at least 15 persons drowned.

Dec. 6

South Korea. A fleet of eight fishing boats was missing off the east coast after a severe snowstorm; 127 men were presumed drowned.

Dec. 16

Off The Netherlands coast. The 3,218-ton German freighter *Nautilus* sank in mountainous seas; 23 crewmen were lost.

Dec. 18

Hong Kong. A junk loaded with refugees from Communist China capsized near an offshore island; 22 persons were lost and presumed dead.

1963

Jan. 14

North Sumatra. A Toba Lake tourist ferry sank in flames after a fuel tank was touched off by a fire in the engine room; at least 105 persons burned to death or drowned.

Jan. 18

Mokpo, Korea. A coastal ferry sank in a storm off the south coast; all of the estimated 80–100 persons aboard drowned.

Feb. 3

Off southeastern Atlantic coast. The U.S. tanker *Marine Sulphur Queen* vanished and was believed to have gone down in a heavy storm; all 39 crewmen aboard were presumed dead.

Feb. 25

Kobe harbor, Japan. The Japanese freighter *Richmond Maru* and the ferryboat *Tokiwa* collided in the dark; 47 persons drowned.

March 21

Atlantic Ocean, off North Africa. The 3,884-ton Norwegian freighter *Hoegh Aronde*, buffeted by high winds, sank in the heavy seas; 19 crewmen perished.

April 10

Atlantic Ocean, off Massachusetts. The U.S. Navy nuclear submarine *Thresher* failed to surface after making deep-diving tests in an 8,400-foot depth area; all 129 persons aboard perished.

May 4

Maghagha, Egypt. A ferryboat loaded with more than 220 Muslim pilgrims capsized in the Nile River; at least 200 persons drowned.

May 21

Off Luzon Island, Philippines. A boat returning to Jomalig Island from a fiesta on Luzon capsized in shark-infested waters; 22 persons were believed to have perished.

June 25
Off western coast of Greenland. The motor trawler *München* sank after striking a reef; 27 crewmen drowned.

July 2
Moulmein, Burma. A Burmese schooner sank about a mile from port; of the 213 persons aboard, 113 were missing and presumed drowned.

July 9
Kingston, Jamaica. Search was abandoned for the missing Jamaican fishing boat *Sno' Boy*, which disappeared after setting out July 1 for the Pedro banks; all 40 persons aboard were presumed drowned.

July 11
La Plata, Argentina. The ferryboat *Ciudad Asunción*, operating in a dense fog, struck a sunken ship, caught fire, and sank in the Rio de la Plata; 53 persons drowned, and 12 others were missing.

July 20
Near Quebec, Quebec, Canada. A British ore carrier, the 13,000-ton *Tritonica*, collided with the 6,000-ton British freighter *Roonagh Head* and sank in the fog-shrouded Saint Lawrence River; 33 *Tritonica* crewmen died.

Aug. 17
Off Naha, Okinawa. The Japanese ferryboat *Midori Maru*, reportedly sabotaged, sank about 18 miles out in the East China Sea; 112 persons died, and at least 150 others were rescued.

Sept. 24
Piraeus, Greece. A Greek ship with 26 persons aboard, missing for thirty days, was officially declared lost in the Gulf of Aden.

Oct. 23
Near Hoju, Korea. A small ferry returning schoolchildren from a picnic capsized in the Han River as the children rushed to disembark; 49 persons (37 of them children) drowned.

Oct. 23
Off Land's End, England. The 682-ton Spanish freighter *Juan Ferrer*, lashed by heavy seas, foundered on the rocks; 11 of the 15 crewmen were lost.

Dec. 23
Atlantic Ocean, north of Madeira Island. Fire broke out on the 20,314-ton Greek luxury cruise liner *Lakonia* and forced

1,041 passengers and crewmen to seek safety over the side; 155 persons died or were lost in the chilly water.

Dec. 30

North of Anholt Island, Denmark. The 4,261-ton French ship *Capitaine Louis Malbert* and the 12,410-ton Danish tanker *Rosborg* collided in a dense fog; the French ship sank with 13 of her crew aboard, and 5 crewmen of the *Rosborg* were lost in a rescue attempt.

1964

Jan. 10

Onitsha, Nigeria. The collision of a canoe and motor launch on the Niger River resulted in the drowning of at least 30 persons.

Jan. 15

Tehran, Iran. Three launches sank during a storm in the Persian Gulf; 19 persons drowned.

Jan. 26

Near North Cape, Norway. An East German tanker sliced through a wooden fishing vessel obscured by an Arctic blizzard; 14 fishermen were lost and presumed drowned.

Feb. 10

Ulladulla, New South Wales, Australia. The Australian Navy destroyer *Voyager* sank in Jervis Bay shortly after colliding with the aircraft carrier *Melbourne*; 82 men of the *Voyager* (including the captain) were missing and presumed drowned.

Feb. 19

Atlantic Ocean. The 10,000-ton British freighter *Ambassador*, disabled the day before by raging storms 660 miles southeast of Halifax, sank later during a salvage attempt by the Dutch ocean tug *Elbe*; 14 crewmen were lost and presumed dead, and the captain's body was pulled from the sea.

March 23

Grand Cayman Island. An open boat reached shore after drifting for eighteen days in the Caribbean Sea in an attempted flight from Cuba; 17 of the 18 persons aboard had died.

March 29

Near Suva, Fiji. The Fiji schooner *Kadavulevu,* which was sailing on a pleasure trip to nearby Nairai Island, caught fire and capsized; more than 70 persons were lost and presumed dead.

April 10

Persian Gulf. An Iranian launch, reportedly loaded with Italian workers being smuggled into Kuwait, caught fire and sank; an estimated 113 persons perished.

May 1

Trapani, Sicily. A motorboat capsized offshore, drowning 16 boys and a priest.

June 30

Off Morgan City, Louisiana. The U.S. oil-drilling ship *C. T. Baker*, working 78 miles out in the Gulf of Mexico, exploded, burst into flames, and sank within fifteen minutes; 20 of the 43 men on board were lost and presumed dead.

July 3

Off Cape Finisterre, Spain. Thick fog was blamed for the collision of two tankers, the 12,942-ton Spanish *Bonifaz* and the 32,125-ton French *Fabiola*; fire on the latter ship was brought under control, but the *Bonifaz* sank in flames; 21 crewmen were lost and presumed dead.

Sept. 29

Off Coromandel coast, India. A fleet of seventy-five fishing boats was reported missing after a cyclonic gale on the high seas; about 450 fishermen were lost and presumed drowned.

Oct. 25

Off Lugus Island, Philippines. A motor launch on its way from Jolo to Siasi Island capsized in high waves; 58 passengers were lost and presumed dead.

Nov. 19

Lakhnoor, India. A motor launch plying the Chenab River capsized with 150 persons aboard, of whom at least 125 drowned.

Nov. 26

Off New Jersey coast. The Norwegian tanker *Stolt Dagali* was sliced in two when she crossed the bow of the Israeli luxury liner *Shalom* as the ships collided in darkness and heavy fog; 19 of the tanker crewmen lost their lives as the 140-foot stern section of the *Stolt Dagali* foundered and sank; the *Shalom* returned to port with a 40-foot gash in her bow.

Dec. 8

Rauma Harbor, Finland. A tugboat working in icy rain rammed into a military motorboat transporting a group of 28 teenage girls to an artillery ball; 16 of the girls and 3 soldiers drowned.

1965

Jan. 9

Lake Victoria, Kenya. A passenger boat capsized in a severe storm on the lake; at least 26 persons drowned.

Jan. 10

Norway. The *Nysa*, a 486-ton Polish motor vessel, broke up in a heavy storm off the southwest coast; all 18 men aboard were missing and presumed dead.

Jan. 10–12

South Korea. Heavy snowstorms off the coast were blamed for the loss of about sixty fishing boats; 27 men were known dead; 252 others were missing and presumed dead.

Jan. 23

Casablanca, Morocco. A Moroccan fishing boat sank ten miles offshore; 19 men were believed drowned.

Feb. 11

Bering Sea. U.S.S.R. planes and ships abandoned a two-week search for four oceangoing fishing trawlers lost in icy gales; at least 100 fishermen were presumed dead.

March 18

Gobindsagar Lake, India. A boat loaded with pilgrims on their way to a shrine capsized in a sudden squall; at least 100 persons drowned.

April 15

Vijayavada, India. A procession of eight joined boats taking pilgrims to a temple across the Krishna River capsized as passengers panicked when one boat sprang a leak; 40 persons drowned.

May 7

Straits of Mackinac. Caught in a dense fog, the U.S. Great Lakes freighter *Cedarville* collided with the Norwegian motor launch *Topsdalsfjord* and sank; 10 of the *Cedarville* crewmen drowned.

May 23

Zomba, Malawi. A ferryboat loaded with passengers, many in trucks, buses, and cars, capsized when a guide cable snapped; of the more than 200 persons flung into the crocodile-infested Shire River, at least 150 were believed dead.

June 5

Bandar Mashur, Iran. The 20,747-ton Italian tanker *Luisa* caught fire and exploded in the port; at least 32 crew members were killed.

June 27

Dryden, Ontario, Canada. A Lake Wabigoon houseboat, struck by a sudden 75-mph windstorm, overturned and sank; 12 of 14 family members aboard drowned.

July 14–15

Southern coast of China. Typhoon Freda struck the Chinese mainland after sinking forty fishing boats off Macao and drowning 200 fishermen.

Aug. 4

Off Esposende, Portugal. The Portuguese trawler *Padre Cruz*, rammed in a dense fog by the 1,337-ton German freighter *Apollo*, split in two and sank; 28 of the 39 fishermen aboard perished.

Aug. 15

Off San Vincente, Chile. The Chilean Navy cutter *Janequeo*, driven shoreward by a winter gale, broke apart on the rocky coast; 45 of the 72 crewmen perished.

Aug. 24

Off Samar Island, Philippines. An overloaded motor launch capsized and threw about 150 passengers into the water; 45 persons drowned or were missing and presumed dead.

Sept. 23

Off Izmit, Turkey. An explosion and fire ripped through the 9,403-ton Turkish tanker *Barbaros*; 15 men were killed, and 6 others were injured.

Nov. 1

São Luis Bay, Brazil. A motor launch struck a reef and sank; at least 57 persons drowned.

Nov. 2

Off Yucatán Peninsula, Mexico. A fishing boat loaded with Cuban refugees struck offshore reefs and sank; 39 of the 45 persons aboard were believed drowned.

Nov. 13

Bahamas. The Panama-registered cruise ship *Yarmouth Castle*, bound from Miami, Florida, to Nassau with 550 passengers aboard and making her way through the New Providence Channel, was suddenly enveloped in flames and quickly sank; 89 persons perished, and many others were severely burned.

1966

Jan. 5

Off the Faeroe Islands. A Soviet fishing trawler sank; 14 of the 24 men aboard were reported missing.

Jan. 10

North Atlantic Ocean. A Spanish freighter, the 10,500-ton *Monte Palomares*, sank in storm-tossed waters about 840 miles northeast of Bermuda; 32 of the 38 crewmen died.

Jan. 25

Belawan, Indonesia. An Indonesian state-owned oil company ship *Permina* sank near the North Sumatra port of Belawan; 89 of the 200 passengers drowned.

Jan. 31

Off Kuril Islands. Two Japanese fishing boats were reported lost in a North Pacific storm; 30 crewmen were presumed dead.

Feb. 16

Nagoya, Japan. A Japanese tanker, the new 33,800-ton *Bridgetown Maru*, was gutted by fire as it lay in the harbor; at least 16 workmen were killed.

Feb. 19

Off La Coruña, Spain. Two fishing boats foundered in a violent Atlantic storm; 17 seamen drowned.

March 24

Escondido River, Nicaragua. An overloaded river launch capsized and sank, drowning 19 persons.

April 3

Off Donna Nook, England. The British 300-ton pleasure ship *Anzio* was caught in a sudden North Sea storm and smashed to pieces near the mouth of the Humber River; 10 persons perished.

April 5

Pacific Ocean. The U.S. tanker *Comet Commander* was split in two during a violent storm 600 miles northwest of Midway Island; 11 of the 42 crewmen were missing and presumed dead.

April 9

Off Iloilo Province, Philippines. An overloaded sailboat capsized, drowning 16 passengers.

May 16

Malispascua Island, Philippines. Typhoon Irma, with 80-mph winds, grounded and overturned the 740-ton interisland passenger ship *Pioneer Cebu*; at least 132 of the 262 persons aboard perished.

May 23

Pandora Banks, New Zealand. The 2,500-ton British collier *Kaitawa* ran aground in a gale and broke up off the northernmost tip of New Zealand; all 29 crewmen were missing and presumed dead.

June 16

New York Harbor. An empty U.S. tanker, *Texaco Massachusetts*, collided with the naphtha-laden British tanker *Alva*

British and U.S. tankers burst into flame after the two ships collided in New York Harbor off Bayonne, New Jersey, on June 16. The British ship was carrying highly combustible naphtha.

Cape as the two ships maneuvered through Kill Van Kull, a narrow neck in the harbor; spilling naphtha caused a fire that killed 33 seamen.

June 18

Near Shelburne, Nova Scotia, Canada. A collision between the 5,771-ton Liberian freighter *Bordapian* and the 118-foot Nova Scotian trawler *Reliance*, during a thick coastal fog, resulted in the deaths of 12 fishermen.

July 22

Penmaenpool, Wales. The small Welsh excursion steamer *Prince of Wales*, caught in a crosscurrent as it neared dockside, struck a bridge support and overturned; 11 passengers drowned.

July 31

Off the Cornish Coast, England. A British pleasure launch, the 46-foot *Darlwin*, chartered for a 40-mile cruise along the coast, disappeared in a sudden windstorm; all 31 persons aboard were presumed dead.

Sept. 14

North Sea. A West German Navy training submarine, *Hai*, vanished in a storm while en route to a goodwill visit to Scotland; 19 crewmen drowned.

Sept. 19

Paraná River, Paraguay. An Argentinian cargo ship, *El Inca*, struck a hidden rock and sank; 14 passengers drowned.

Sept. 30

Quebec, Quebec, Canada. The Canadian barge *Manseau 101*, under tow by a tug, capsized and sank; 11 of the 23 crewmen aboard were lost.

Oct. 22

Manila Bay, Philippines. A collision of the 7,598-ton U.S. freighter *Golden State* with the Philippine passenger ship *Pioneer Leyte* resulted in the death of 71 persons.

Oct. 23

Near Patna, India. A riverboat, loaded with passengers going to a country fair, sank in the Kosi River; more than 100 persons were believed drowned.

Oct. 26

Gulf of Tonkin, Vietnam. Touched off by a flare that ignited in a locker, flames swept the forward decks of the U.S. Navy aircraft carrier *Oriskany*; 43 men perished, and 16 others were injured.

Nov. 2

Off Lobos Island, Mexico. A Mexican oil drilling barge, the *Mercury*, sank in heavy seas; 22 crewmen were missing and presumed dead, and 23 others were rescued.

Nov. 29

Lake Huron. A U.S. ore carrier, the 13,500-ton *Daniel J. Morrell*, broke in two under 60-mph winds and sank about 26 miles off Harbor Beach, Michigan; 28 crewmen perished, and one was rescued.

Dec. 8

Aegean Sea. A Greek ferryship, the 8,922-ton *Heraklion*, was torn apart when heavy seas caused a 16-ton trailer to wrench loose from its ropes and smash about uncontrolled; sinking within fifteen minutes, the ship took the lives of at least 264 persons; about 47 others survived.

Dec. 25

Off Newfoundland. The British trawler *St. Finbarr* was swept by flames; 12 seamen perished, and 13 others were rescued.

1967

Jan. 14

Off the south coast of Korea. *Hanil-Ho*, a 140-ton Korean ferryboat, collided with the Navy destroyer-escort *Chung-nan-Ho* and sank near Kadok-Do Island; at least 72 ferryboat passengers drowned or were missing.

Jan. 25

Off Sardinia. *Hashlosha*, a 1,338-ton Israeli freighter, sank; all 20 officers and seamen aboard were lost.

Feb. 21

Halifax Harbor, Nova Scotia, Canada. The Canadian trawler *Cape Bonnie* grounded and broke up when a gale drove her onto a rocky ledge near Woody Island; 15 men drowned.

Feb. 26

Buenos Aires, Argentina. An overloaded Argentine excursion boat hit a submerged log in the Paraná River and sank; at least 16 persons died.

Feb. 28

Near Hanstholm, Denmark. *Tukan*, a 2,433-ton Soviet fish-processing boat, sank in gale-swept waters off the Jutland coast; 57 of the 79-member crew perished.

May 4

Off Chandpur, East Pakistan. A Pakistani motor launch capsized during a cyclonic storm and dumped about 150 persons into the Meghna River; at least 90 passengers died.

May 23

South of Toulon, France. *Circe*, a 11,157-ton Greek oil tanker, exploded and sank in the Mediterranean Sea with 39 persons aboard, only one of whom survived.

July 27

Bombay, India. A passenger boat capsized in the flooded Malaprabha River, drowning about 30 of the 80 persons aboard.

July 29

Off North Vietnam. The 75,900-ton U.S. Navy aircraft carrier U.S.S. *Forrestal* broke into flames following an explosion on the flight deck; 134 aircraft and ship personnel died, and at least 100 others were injured.

Aug. 6

Lake Tel, Romania. A lake steamer crowded with picnickers sank suddenly, drowning between 100 and 300 persons.

Aug. 12

Off southern Chile. The Chilean iron-ore ship *Santa Fe*, apparently caught in heavy seas between Chonos Archipelago and the Gulf of Peñas, was reported missing with her 39-man crew.

Oct. 9

North Pacific. *Panoceanic Faith*, a U.S. freighter, went down in a storm-tossed area about 870 miles southwest of Kodiak Island; 13 crewmen died, 23 others were missing, and 5 were rescued.

1968

Jan. 25

Eastern Mediterranean Sea. An Israeli submarine, the 1,280-ton *Dakar*, was reported missing and presumed lost with 69 men aboard.

Jan. 27

Mediterranean Sea. The 850-ton French submarine *Minerve*, on maneuvers southeast of Toulon, suddenly disappeared and was presumed lost with its crew of 52 men.

March 8

Persian Gulf. An Arab dhow, which was overloaded with 400 Pakistanis en route home from a pilgrimage to Mecca, Saudi Arabia, struck a sandbar in Dubai Harbor and sank; 200 passengers were missing, and at least 90 others were known dead.

March 28

Near Chapra, India. Strong winds upset a boat crossing the Gogra River; all 60 persons aboard drowned.

April 4

Persian Gulf. A motor launch carrying Pakistani pilgrims capsized off Dibal, Trucial Oman; at least 75 persons drowned.

April 10

Wellington Harbor, New Zealand. The 8,994-ton interisland ferryboat *Wahine*, laboring in a 123-mph gale, was ripped open on Barrett's Reef, went aground, and capsized; of the 727 persons on board, an estimated 52 perished.

April 11

North Pacific. A Soviet diesel-powered Golf II-class submarine exploded and sank in waters three miles deep, 750 miles northwest of Hawaii; its entire 70-man crew perished.

May 21

Near the Azores. The 3,075-ton U.S. nuclear submarine *Scorpion*, making a submerged crossing of the Atlantic to its home base in Norfolk, Virginia, failed to report; all 99 officers and crewmen were presumed dead.

Survivors from the wreck of the interisland ferryboat
Wahine *are pulled ashore in Wellington, New Zealand, on*
April 10.

June 14
Indian Ocean. The Liberian-registered *World Glory*, a 28,323-ton storm-tossed vessel, broke in two and caught fire about 90 miles northeast of Durban, South Africa; 21 men were missing and presumed drowned; 10 others were rescued.

Oct. 11
Off Mindanao Island, Philippines. A Philippine ferryboat, *Dumaguete*, heavily loaded with passengers on their way to participate in a religious festival in Zamboanga, foundered after springing a leak and went down in a shark-infested strait of the Sulu Sea; between 300 and 500 persons perished.

Oct. 19
Rourkela, India. A local riverboat capsized as it crossed the Koel River; 40 persons were missing and presumed drowned.

Oct. 31
North Atlantic Ocean. Fire and explosions aboard the Norwegian tanker *Etnefjell* caused it to be abandoned by its 25-man crew who, after a nineteen-day search by the U.S. Coast Guard, were presumed dead; the captain and two officers who remained aboard the *Etnefjell* were rescued by a salvage vessel.

Nov. 18
Cebu, Philippines. The Philippine interisland boat *Iruna* col-

lided with the 5,338-ton British freighter *Eastern Moon*, split in two, and sank; 40 passengers were rescued, and 200 others were missing and presumed dead.

Dec. 7

Off White Castle, Louisiana. The U.S. Coast Guard buoy tender *White Alder* was sheared in half by the 400-foot Taiwan freighter *Helena* when the vessels collided in midstream; 17 of the 20-man Coast Guard crew drowned.

Dec. 21

Grenadine Islands, West Indies. The British interisland schooner *Federal Queen* capsized for an unknown reason; 41 persons drowned, but 37 others were rescued.

1969

Jan. 14

Pearl Harbor, Hawaii. The U.S. nuclear aircraft carrier *Enterprise* was swept by fire and explosions centered on the flight and hangar decks; 27 men died, and 82 others were injured.

Jan. 24

Dacca, East Pakistan. Two boats collided on the Buriganga River, dumping the passengers into the water; 50 persons drowned.

Feb. 22

Assiut, Egypt. A small sailboat in the Nile, overloaded by 62 persons going home from a funeral, overturned and drowned 40 of the passengers.

March 13

Oregon Inlet, North Carolina. A 125-foot Soviet fishing trawler sank after colliding with the 36,000-ton Panamanian tanker *Esso Honduras*; as many as 25 Soviet sailors were presumed dead.

April 6

New Orleans, Louisiana. The Taiwan freighter *Union Faith*, passing under the Greater New Orleans Mississippi River Bridge, collided with the lead barge of a string of oil barges; explosions and fire sank the *Union Faith*; 25 men were missing and presumed dead.

April 13

Off Kuwait. A small boat loaded with Iranians attempting illegal entry into Kuwait capsized and sank five miles offshore; 30 persons drowned, and 5 others were missing.

June 2

South China Sea. The U.S. Navy destroyer *Frank E. Evans*, on SEATO maneuvers with about forty other warships. misinterpreted an order and was sliced in two by the Australian aircraft carrier *Melbourne*; when the sheared-off forward portion of the *Evans* sank, 74 officers and enlisted men went down with it and were presumed dead; 200 others were rescued.

June 21

Beira, Mozambique. A barge transporting 150 Portuguese troops and their vehicles, en route to reinforce a garrison beleaguered by guerrillas, sank and drowned 108 of the men.

Aug. 9

Near Shikotan Island, Japan. A Soviet patrol boat collided with a Japanese fishing boat, the *Fukuju Maru*; 11 fishermen of the 12-man crew were killed.

Aug. 15

Cairo, Egypt. A river launch sank in the Nile River and drowned 24 persons; 16 others were saved.

Aug. 18

Évian-Les-Bains, France. The pleasure boat *Fraidieu*, loaded with vacationing French teenage girls, plunged beneath the waters of Lake Geneva and carried 19 persons to their death; 34 others were rescued.

Aug. 25

North Sydney, Australia. The 1,465-ton Australian freighter *Noongah*, battling high seas and strong winds, turned over and sank; 24 missing crewmen were presumed dead, and 2 others were rescued.

Oct. 8

Near Cape Shiono, Japan. A South Korean freighter, the 1,051-ton *Dragon*, sank about 20 miles offshore; 12 seamen drowned, and 8 others were saved by a passing British ship.

Nov. 5

Off the New Jersey coast. A transatlantic oil tanker, the 629-foot Liberian *Keo*, broke up in heavy seas 120 miles southeast of Nantucket; after a fruitless three-day search by the U.S. Coast Guard, the 36 lost crewmen were presumed dead.

Dec. 24

Barrancabermeja, Colombia. A ferryboat, overcrowded by families homeward bound for Christmas, collided with four oil barges and sank in the Magdalena River; between 25 and 40 persons drowned.

Dec. 26

Northeast of Midway Island. The U.S. munitions ship *Badger State* began to break up in heavy seas and was abandoned by the crew; one body was recovered from the rough waters, 25 crewmen were lost and presumed dead, and 14 were rescued.

1970

Jan. 18

Off southern Hokkaido, Japan. The sinking of a 2,302-ton collier brought death to 18 seamen.

Feb. 6

Off Middlesbrough, England. A Scottish coastal ship, the 522-ton *Lairdsfield*, capsized and sank in the Tees River estuary; all 10 crewmen were lost and presumed dead.

Feb. 27

Jaffna, Ceylon. A pilgrimage vessel sailing from Jaffna to Palaitivu capsized with 82 persons on board, 61 of whom drowned.

March 4

Cape Camaret, France. A French submarine, the 850-ton *Eurydice*, disappeared during diving maneuvers, possibly as a result of an inboard explosion; all 57 crewmen were lost.

April 9

Off Genoa, Italy. The storm-lashed 24,700-ton British ore carrier *London Valour* was crushed against a rocky breakwater, killing 13 of the 57 crewmen on board.

June 12

China Sea. The Philippine fishing boat *Baby Princess* capsized in a violent storm 300 miles southwest of Manila; 22 persons were rescued; 22 others were devoured by sharks.

July 3

Dong Ha, South Vietnam. A South Vietnamese riverboat making a scheduled run on the Cua Viet River struck a floating mine and exploded, killing 46 of the 50 civilian passengers.

July 5

English Channel. The West German freighter *Hagen* collided with the Greek ship *Bougaria*, which sank; 17 *Bougaria* officers and crewmen were lost, and 12 were rescued by the *Hagen*.

July 5

Near Masulipatnam, India. A large cargo launch, in use as a ferry between two Krishna River towns, capsized and sank; about 150 persons were presumed drowned.

Aug. 1

Off Basseterre, St. Kitts Island. Overcrowded with more than 200 passengers, the Caribbean ferryboat *Christena*, on a ten-mile trip from Basseterre to Charlestown on Nevis Island, capsized and plunged the passengers into shark-infested waters; about 125 persons were believed to have perished.

Sept. 3

Tangadad, India. The flooded Krishna River claimed a boat-load of festival-goers on their way to a feast on a neighboring island; at least 68 persons (many of them children) drowned.

Oct. 23

English Channel. The 42,000-ton Liberian-registered oil tanker *Pacific Glory* collided with the Liberian tanker *Allegro* off the Isle of Wight; 30 Chinese crewmen were rescued from the burning *Pacific Glory*; 13 others were dead or missing.

Nov. 5

Kristiansand, Norway. Working on the sprinkler system aboard the dry-docked 19,180-ton Norwegian tanker *Pollo*, more than 60 workmen were overcome by leaking carbon dioxide gas; 12 men died, and the others were hospitalized.

Dec. 15

Korea Strait. A South Korean ferryboat, the 362-ton *Nam-yung-Ho*, capsized because of an unbalanced cargo and flung its 278 crewmen and passengers into the icy waters; at least 261 persons perished.

Dec. 23

Off Jakarta, Indonesia. Two U.S. oil company ships, the *Northern Dancer*, a 9-ton passenger vessel, and the 900-ton supply carrier *Aquadud*, collided in the Java Sea; *Northern Dancer* sank, and 24 of its 42 passengers drowned.

Dec. 23

Northwest of Pescara, Italy. The 500-ton Italian fishing boat *Rodi* was shipwrecked during a storm in the Adriatic; all 22 crewmen perished.

1971

Jan. 5

South Korea. Stormy weather in the eastern and southern coastal waters claimed sixteen fishing boats; 28 sailors were missing and presumed dead.

Jan. 12

English Channel. A West German freighter. the 2,695-ton *Brandenburg*, hit the submerged bow of an oil freighter, the 20,545-ton *Texaco Caribbean* (which had sunk two days before), and sank within two minutes, taking 21 persons to their death.

Jan. 22

Off Cagliari, Sardinia. Explosions and fire struck the empty

U.S.-owned oil tanker *Universe Patriot*, killing 16 crewmen.

March 6

Off Folkestone, England. The 2,000-ton Greek freighter *Niki* foundered after striking wreckage in the English Channel and sank with an estimated 23 persons aboard.

March 27

Off Cape Hatteras, North Carolina. The 661-foot *Texaco Oklahoma*, on a run from Port Arthur, Texas, to Boston, Massachusetts, with a cargo of 220,000 barrels of heavy sulfur fuel oil, encountered heavy seas and broke in two; 28 of the 44-man crew were missing and presumed dead.

May 22

Off Vancouver, British Columbia, Canada. The Norwegian cruise ship *Meteor* was severely damaged by an explosion and fire in the Strait of Georgia; all passengers were successfully evacuated, but 32 seamen were lost.

June 12

Manila Bay, Philippines. An excursion boat carrying factory workers on a trip around Corregidor Island capsized in stormy weather; 54 of the 120 excursionists drowned or were missing and presumed dead.

July 27

Near Palashipara, India. A Kharia river-crossing boat sank in midstream and at least 40 West Bengalis drowned.

Aug. 6

Persian Gulf. An Iranian boat that was transporting Iranian laborers headed for illegal entry into Kuwait struck a submerged rocky shelf and sank; an estimated 300 passengers drowned.

Aug. 28

Off Brindisi, Italy. An overcrowded Greek ferryboat, the 11,-674-ton *Heleanna*, caught fire during an overnight trip from Pátrai, Greece, to Ancona, Italy; 25 of the 1,127 persons aboard perished.

Nov. 9

Atlantic Ocean. Encountering a severe storm about 600 miles off the French coast, the 9,400-ton French freighter *Maori* broke up and sank; most of the 39 crewmen were presumed lost.

Nov. 21

Central Philippines. A 30-ton wooden cargo vessel ferrying passengers between Leyte Island and Cebu ran into turbulent waters and sank; about 100 of the 200 persons aboard drowned or were missing and presumed dead.

1972

Jan. 1

Off Qais Island. The Qatari ship *Al-Rayyan* foundered in a heavy storm and sank in the Persian Gulf; at least 40 persons drowned; 2 others were rescued.

Jan. 1

Off Lower California. The Dutch freighter *Dordrecht* with 35 crewmen aboard was flooded in rough seas; 20 crewmen were rescued by the Liberian-registered freighter *Golar Arrow*, and 15 others were presumed dead.

Jan. 3

Persian Gulf. A launch bearing 160 falcons and a cargo of hunting equipment belonging to the ruler of Qatar sank and drowned 80 persons; 2 others survived.

Jan. 9

West of Vancouver Island, British Columbia, Canada. The *Dona Anita*, a 7,840-ton freighter of Somali Republic registry, fighting hurricane-force winds, went down when water flooded the engine room; all 42 crewmen aboard were lost and presumed dead.

Feb. 1

Gulf of Mexico. The 572-foot U.S. tanker *V. A. Fogg*, on a trip from Freeport to Houston, Texas, disappeared in 90-foot deep water about 32 miles south of Freeport; all 39 men aboard were presumed drowned.

May 4

Canea, Crete. A small fishing boat carrying a group of high-school girls on an outing overturned in a sudden squall; 21 girls drowned; 6 others and the boat's captain were rescued.

May 11

Montevideo, Uruguay. The collision at the channel entrance of the Rio de la Plata between the British cargo ship *Royston Grange* and the *Tien Chee*, a Liberian-registered tanker, caused the dumping of the broken tanker's 20,000 tons of crude oil, which ignited and burned both vessels as they foundered in the fog-enshrouded waters; all 74 persons aboard the *Royston Grange* and 10 others from the *Tien Chee* perished; 32 men were saved.

June 28

Bombay, India. An explosion aboard a Greek-owned tanker, the 17,103-ton *Tarsos*, undergoing repairs at dockside, killed at least 22 persons and injured 30 others.

Aug. 21

Off Cape Agulhas, South Africa. The collision of the 43,339-

ton tanker *Texanita* with the 48,320-ton tanker *Oswego Guardian*, both of Liberian registry, caused explosions that brought death to 47 of the 50-man crew of the *Texanita*.

Nov. 8

Brunswick, Georgia. A seabound freighter, the 11,000-ton *African Neptune*, smashed into the mile-long Sidney Lanier drawbridge and sent cars and people tumbling from the crumpling structure into the Brunswick River; divers recovered the bodies of 10 persons.

Dec. 25

Gulf of Alaska. Ships and planes searched stormy seas for traces of the 13,000-ton Liberian-registered freighter *Pacrover* in response to a signal of distress; the colliery ship en route from Vancouver, British Columbia, to Japan was presumed to have gone down with the loss of its 30-man Korean crew.

1973

Jan. 6

Off Sabang, Sumatra. A Cyprus oil tanker, the 20,000-ton *Anson*, quickly sank after colliding with the 15,000-ton Liberian tanker *Atlantic Faith* about 120 miles offshore; 10 crewmen from the *Anson* were lost and presumed dead.

Jan. 8

Posadas, Argentina. An explosion and fire on board a ferryboat crossing the Paraná River with 61 passengers returning from a gambling casino on the Paraguay side brought death to 16 persons; another 23 were missing and presumed dead.

Jan. 25

Off South Korea. A 76-ton Korean ferryboat ran aground and sank; many among the 100 passengers were believed drowned.

Feb. 7

Southeast of Tasmania. A Japanese tuna boat, the *Nissan Maru No. 8*, was wrecked as it ran aground about 25 miles south of Brunia; 21 fishermen were lost and presumed dead; one survivor clung to a rock and was rescued.

Feb. 21

Rangoon, Burma. A crowded ferryboat collided with the Japanese freighter *Bombay Maru* in the Rangoon River; an estimated 200 persons died when the ferry sank.

March 22

Southeast of Cape May, New Jersey. A Norwegian freighter, the 541-foot *Norse Variant*, foundering in stormy Atlantic seas with two flooded cargo holds, sank moments after the crew abandoned ship; of the 30 seamen aboard 29 perished, and one was rescued from a life raft.

May 5

Southeast of Dacca, Bangladesh. Carrying about 300 passengers, the riverboat *Ghazi* was rammed astern by another launch, the *Dirghirpir Express*, and sank almost immediately; at least 250 persons aboard the *Ghazi* were believed dead.

May 17

Near Magwe, Burma. A Burmese government-owned vessel, the *Tawpan*, sank in the Irrawaddy River, drowning more than 100 persons.

May 19

Off Port Judith, Rhode Island. The U.S. party boat *Comet*, on a day-long fishing trip, tipped over in choppy seas and broke in two; 12 persons died in the chilly waters, 5 were missing and presumed dead, and 11 survived.

June 2

Off Staten Island, New York. A steering-gear failure on the U.S. *Sea Witch* apparently caused the big container ship to ram into the Belgian oil tanker *Esso Brussels* as it rode at anchor in the Narrows of New York Harbor; fires were set off in both ships, bringing death to 16 persons.

June 16

Bay of Bengal. A motor launch carrying 150 members of a wedding party was caught in a gale and capsized and sank in the bay off Chittagong, Bangladesh; 31 persons drowned.

June 25

Off Cape Guardafui, Somalia. An Indian cargo and passenger vessel, the 5,973-ton *Saudi*, foundered in heavy seas and was abandoned; 105 persons died or were missing and presumed dead in the shark-infested waters off East Africa's horn.

June 27

South of Cebu, Philippines. A Philippine interisland ship with 400 passengers aboard struck a coral reef and sank; at least 20 persons perished.

July 16

Southeast of Manila. The *Mactan*, carrying about 700 passengers from the southern Philippines to Manila, sank near a small island during a typhoon; two bodies were recovered, and most of the 35 missing were believed drowned.

Oct. 28

Río de la Plata estuary, Argentina. The *Ushuaia*, an Argentine Navy transport, collided with an Argentine cargo vessel about 90 miles from Buenos Aires shortly after midnight; of the 89 persons aboard the *Ushuaia*, 24 were missing and presumed drowned.

Dec. 19

Northwest of Vancouver Island, British Columbia, Canada. The 10,000-ton Liberian freighter *Oriental Monarch* lost power and sank in heavy seas during a Pacific storm while carrying grain from Japan to Portland, Oregon; rescue ships that first spotted only empty lifeboats, rafts, and floating life jackets later recovered 27 bodies; 13 other crew members were presumed dead.

Dec. 24

Gulf of Guayaquil, Ecuador. The heavily overloaded ferryboat *Jambeli*, making its way from Puerto Bolivar to Guayaquil, capsized in converging currents near Puná Island; at least 191 persons drowned, 142 were rescued, and an undetermined number were unaccounted for.

1974

Jan. 5

Central Philippines. The ferryboat *Tagbilaran* sank in high seas and strong winds shortly after midnight; 37 bodies were recovered, but another 45 of the 217 persons aboard were reported missing.

Jan. 17

English Channel near Guernsey. The 2,000-ton Cypriot timber freighter *Prosperity* was wrecked on a reef by a 100-mph gale; 16 bodies were recovered, and 2 other crewmen were presumed drowned.

Jan. 18

Near Pilottown, Louisiana. The U.S. tanker *Key Trader* collided with the Norwegian ore freighter *Baune* in the mouth of the Mississippi River; exploding oil and gasoline caused the death of 16 persons; 8 others were reported injured.

Feb. 8

Arctic Ocean. The ultramodern 1,106-ton British trawler *Gaul* apparently foundered and sank in stormy seas and freezing temperatures north of Norway; after an extensive but futile eight-day air and sea search all 36 crew members were presumed dead.

Feb. 22

Off Chungmu, South Korea. A South Korean Navy tug, returning from a training cruise with 311 recruits and a crew of 5, sank in Chungmu Harbor; 15 persons were known to have died, but 144 others were missing.

Late March

Mato Grosso, Brazil. Two navy ships collided while rescuing flood victims in Mato Grosso, a state in the west region of Brazil; 13 persons died in the accident.

April 3

Piauí, Brazil. A barge carrying 80 persons was reported to have gone down in the Paranaíba River; at least 30 persons lost their lives.

April 12

Off Cape Hino, Japan. The 999-ton South Korean freighter *Kaiei Ho* collided with the 21,467-ton American container ship *President Pierce*; 18 of the 26 Korean seamen were missing after their ship split in two.

April 12

Off Cape Shinono, Japan. The 284-ton fishing boat *Shohei Maru* collided with the 11,144-ton freighter *Ocean Sovereign*; 14 of the 17 Japanese tuna fishermen were missing and presumed drowned.

April 23

Southeast of Rangoon, Burma. A fishing schooner was reported sunk some 155 miles from Rangoon with a loss of about 100 lives.

May 1

Bay of Bengal. A motor launch capsized in waters off Bangladesh, killing 250 persons.

Late August

Off the southwestern coast of South Korea. Six fishing boats, battered by severe gales and heavy rains, were presumed to have capsized with the loss of 71 lives.

Mid-September

Black Sea. A Kashin-class Soviet destroyer armed with guided missiles exploded and sank with the loss of its entire crew, according to unofficial sources; the death toll was conservatively estimated at 225—and may have exceeded 300—making it one of the worst peacetime naval disasters in modern history.

September

Bay of Bengal. A ferryboat capsized in the Bay of Bengal, drowning about 160 persons.

Sept. 28

Hong Kong. The Panamanian freighter *Sun Shang* sank after being caught in a typhoon 400 miles east of Hong Kong, killing 31 of 34 crewmen aboard.

Late October

Near Fiji. A burned-out Korean fishing boat, without life-boats and crew, was discovered on Nov. 1; the 22-man crew was presumed drowned.

Nov. 9

Tokyo Bay, Japan. The Liberian freighter *Pacific Ares* collided with the 43,700-ton Japanese tanker *Yuyo Maru*, which was carrying butane, propane, and naphtha; 21 persons died and 12 others were missing as a result of violent explosions and raging fires that destroyed both vessels.

Nov. 20

Near Sundarbans, Bangladesh. A ferryboat capsized about 90 miles from Dacca with the loss of at least 85 lives.

Nov. 28

Bay of Bengal. A cyclone that struck Bangladesh was believed to have claimed the lives of 79 fishermen who were still missing after a sea and air search.

1975

Jan. 10

Hanstholm, Denmark. Trapped between their capsized Polish trawler and a pier, 10 seamen were crushed to death just beyond the reach of a rescue party; 17 others were saved by an air force helicopter.

Jan. 25

Off the southwestern coast of England. The 1,093-ton British cargo ship *Lovat* was sunk by strong gales while on its way from Wales to France with a load of coal dust; only 2 of the 13 crewmen were rescued.

Jan. 25

Near Dacca, Bangladesh. A ferryboat that collided with a steamer on the Buriganga River sank about seven miles from Dacca; about half of the estimated 200 persons aboard were presumed drowned.

Aug. 3

Near Canton, China. Two triple-deck excursion ferries, plying the Hsi River during heavy rains in the early hours of the morning, collided and sank; as many as 500 persons were believed to have drowned.

Aug. 25

João Pessoa, Brazil. During a festival for dependents of military personnel, a group of small army boats capsized on a lake; 29 persons died, most of them children.

Mid-September

Northern Thailand. Thousands of Meo tribesmen, many of

them women and children, fled their sanctuary in northern Thailand when Pathet Lao troops began firing on their village; several hundred of the refugees drowned while attempting to escape in boats across a mountain river.

Sept. 18

Northern India. A crowded ferryboat carrying about 200 flood victims to a relief center capsized on the Rapti River; about half the refugees perished.

Oct. 24

Pyamalaw River, Burma. A two-deck ferryboat carrying about 230 passengers capsized and sank on a branch of the Irrawaddy River; at least 150 of those aboard were believed drowned.

Oct. 25

Near Rangoon, Burma. A ferryboat capsized and sank in the Twante Canal; 18 persons were known to have died, and 49 others were missing.

Nov. 10

Near Cooper Mine Point, Ontario, Canada. The 729-foot ore carrier *Edmund Fitzgerald*, battered by 20-foot-high waves and 65-mph winds, sank in Lake Superior; although sea and air rescue parties discovered three self-inflatable lifeboats, none of the 29 crewmen survived.

Dec. 19

Gulf of Mexico. The 7,000-ton Mexican freighter *Tlaxcala* capsized when its cargo of aluminite shifted during a storm; 23 persons were missing, including the captain, his wife, and their two-year-old daughter.

1976

Jan. 3

Rangoon River, Burma. A double-deck ferryboat burned and sank after an explosion was set off by careless smoking near a leaking drum of gasoline; 12 persons were known to have died, 27 were severely burned, and some 150 were missing.

Jan. 9

Off Surat Thani Province, Thailand. Two ferryboats collided off the southern coast of Thailand; although many passengers were rescued after one of the boats sank, 15 lost their lives and 50 others were reported missing.

Jan. 18

Off the eastern coast of Mindanao, Philippines. Two crewmen from the 224,000-ton Norwegian supertanker *Berge Istra* were rescued by a Japanese fishing boat after being adrift on a life raft for twenty days; they reported that three explosions on Dec. 30, 1975, had ripped apart the hull of the *Berge Istra*, which sank with the loss of 30 lives.

Jan. 19

Southern Bangladesh. A sea wave that swept into the Ganges Delta from the Bay of Bengal took the lives of an estimated 800 fishermen in the vicinity of Barisal.

Jan. 20

Ichamati River, India. A launch carrying about 150 persons capsized in the Ganges Delta; early reports indicated that probably more than 40 persons drowned. ·

Late January

Off southern Burma. About 160 of an estimated 200 passengers aboard a ferryboat reportedly lost their lives after a collision with a fishing trawler in the Andaman Sea.

March 25

Southern coastal waters, Haiti. About 100 persons died when fire broke out aboard the ferryboat *St. Sauveur* as it was making its way from Dame Marie to Port-au-Prince.

Aug. 7

Gulf of Thailand. An overloaded three-deck ferryboat, operated by an unlicensed skipper, capsized several hundred miles south of Bangkok; nearly 30 persons were known to have died, and dozens of others were presumed drowned.

Aug. 16

Gulf of Saint Lawrence, Canada. A 14-foot motor launch capsized in stormy weather after setting out from Percé, Quebec; all of the 9 French tourists and 3 of the 4 Canadian crewmen were presumed drowned, inasmuch as only the empty boat and one body were recovered from the water.

Aug. 29

Mindanao Province, Philippines. Huge waves capsized a boat at the mouth of the Davao River; 19 of the 25 persons aboard were missing and presumed drowned.

Oct. 15

West of Bermuda. The 590-foot vessel *Sylvia L. Ossa*, en route from Brazil to Pennsylvania with a cargo of iron ore, broke up in heavy seas and sank about 140 miles due west of Bermuda; rescue teams spotted pieces of wreckage but found no evidence that any of the 37 crewmen had survived.

Oct. 20

Near Luling, Louisiana. The Norwegian tanker *Frosta* and the automobile ferry *George Prince* collided on the Mississippi River; rescue divers recovered 71 bodies and more than 30 vehicles from the river, but an estimated 27 other persons were missing and presumed drowned; 18 persons survived.

Mid-October

English Channel. Two small German ships, the tanker *Böhlen* and the freighter *Antje Oltmann*, were lashed by gales in the English Channel; a total of 32 seamen were presumed to have lost their lives in the turbulent waters.

Oct. 19

Off Newfoundland, Canada. The small Dutch freighter *Gabriella* was abandoned in heavy seas about 60 miles off the coast of Newfoundland; 13 of the 15 persons aboard died.

Nov. 11

Northeast of Honolulu, Hawaii. The 486-foot Japanese lumber ship *Carnelian 1* flooded and sank in stormy seas about 1,400 miles from Honolulu; 14 crewmen were rescued, but 19 others were missing and presumed dead.

Dec. 25

Red Sea. An Egyptian passenger ship, the *Patria*, caught fire and sank about 50 miles from Jidda, Saudi Arabia; most of the passengers were Muslim pilgrims returning to Egypt after visiting sacred shrines in Mecca and Medina; the death toll was put at about 150 persons.

1977

Jan. 17

Barcelona Harbor, Spain. A 56-foot U.S. Navy launch, rounding a pier in early morning darkness, collided with the 380-ton *Urela*, a Spanish coastal freighter; of the more than 100 sailors and marines being ferried back to the helicopter carrier *Guam* and the landing ship *Trenton*, at least 46 persons were killed, and 18 others were seriously injured.

Jan. 19

Gulf of Mexico. The Panamanian freighter *Ukola* snapped in two and sank about 200 miles off the coast of Florida, after being buffeted by a gale and 20-foot-high waves; of the 23 crew members aboard, only 3 survived.

March 20

Southeast of Wilmington, North Carolina. The *Claude Conway*, a 43,000-ton Panamanian oil tanker carrying 536,000 gallons of oil, exploded and split in two when sparks from a welding torch ignited gas fumes deep within the tanker's hold; the captain and 9 crewmen lost their lives.

June 11

North of Sabah, Malaysia. A boat carrying Vietnamese refugees en route to the Philippines capsized when it struck a cluster of rocks off the northern coast of Borneo; only 4 of the more than 30 persons aboard were rescued.

Aug. 17

South Pacific. A South Korean fishing vessel sank in the South Pacific; rescue teams were unable to locate the 17 crewmen reported to be afloat on a life raft.

Oct. 31

Bay of Biscay. The Greek freighter *Tina* sank in the Bay of Biscay north of Spain; 10 of the 21 crew members aboard the vessel were killed, and 6 others were believed drowned.

1978

Jan. 21

Off the southwestern coast of Japan. A Singapore-registered freighter sank off the southwestern coast of Japan; three Japanese navy vessels rescued 12 crewmen but reported 10 deaths and listed 3 other sailors as missing.

Feb. 17

Off the eastern coast of Korea. A freighter and two fishing boats sank off the eastern coast of Korea, and seven other fishing boats overturned or went aground when snowstorms created stormy seas; a total of 54 persons were drowned.

March 22

Zambezi River, Mozambique. A boat capsized on the flooded river; 20 persons drowned.

April 4

Bay of Bengal. A fleet of about 100 cargo boats sank during a violent Bangladesh storm; authorities believed that as many as 1,000 persons may have drowned.

April 8

Bay of Bengal. A boat capsized about 300 miles northwest of Rangoon, Burma; at least half of the 200 passengers were missing and presumed dead.

April 21

Northeast of Dacca, Bangladesh. An overloaded launch capsized in the Ghorautra River, about 200 miles northeast of Dacca; at least 100 of the persons aboard drowned.

May 24

Jamuna River, Bangladesh. A passenger launch capsized during a storm; 30 of the nearly 200 persons aboard drowned.

June 11

Lake Timiskaming, Ontario, Canada. A canoe excursion was bombarded by violent thunderstorms accompanied by high winds and four-foot waves; 13 of the 31 persons on the trip, including 12 students and a teacher of St. John's School, drowned when their canoes capsized.

June 18

Lake Pomona, Kansas. The two-tiered paddlewheel steamboat *Whippoorwill* was returning to shore when a tornado struck, flipped over the showboat, and hurled most of the 46 passengers and 13 crew members overboard; 15 passengers were killed, and 14 others were injured, 2 seriously.

Mid-July

Atlantic Ocean. A boat carrying 28 Haitian refugees from the Bahamas to Florida capsized during a storm; at least 10 persons drowned, and 3 others were missing.

July 20

Near Taejon, Korea. A small motorboat capsized while carrying 17 children to school; 3 boys and the skipper of the vessel swam to safety, but 14 others were feared drowned.

Oct. 4

Mediterranean Sea. The *Colo*, a 1,598-ton Algerian ship, sank after colliding with the 8,390-ton Italian *Expresso Marilyn*, 60 miles east of the Cape of Palos; 26 of the 30 crewmen aboard the *Colo* were missing and presumed drowned.

Mid-October

Northern India. A leaky boat capsized in the Hindon River, in the Swai Madhopur district, when its passengers panicked after realizing the craft was taking on water; 26 persons drowned, including 13 women and 6 children.

Oct. 20

Chesapeake Bay. The 125-foot U.S. Coast Guard cutter *Cuyahoga* sank in 70 feet of water minutes after it collided with the *Santa Cruz II*, a 521-foot Argentine coal freighter; the Coast Guard was unable to rescue 11 of the *Cuyahoga's* 29-member crew.

Nov. 22

Off the coast of Malaysia. A boat packed with Vietnam refugees sank in the Kuala Terengganu estuary, after it was forced back to sea by Malaysian police and villagers; 200 persons reportedly drowned.

Dec. 2

South China Sea. A boat filled with Vietnam refugees sank off the coast of Malaysia after being denied permission to land in that country; at least 143 persons were believed dead.

Dec. 12

Atlantic Ocean. The 37,000-ton West German freighter

Following a collision with the Argentine freighter Santa Cruz II *on October 20, the U.S. Coast Guard cutter* Cuyahoga *is dragged from the floor of Chesapeake Bay.*

München, with 28 persons aboard, disappeared—after sending distress signals—during a storm, from a point about 400 miles north of the Azores; nine days later, there was still no sign of any survivors, though several empty life rafts and other wreckage had been sighted.

Dec. 21

Off Fuerteventura, Canary Islands. A ferry with 32 persons aboard sank in heavy seas after breaking apart on the rocks; 12 persons drowned or were missing and presumed dead.

Dec. 24

Manila, Philippines. A boat loaded with holiday travelers capsized, killing 15 persons.

Dec. 28

Off the coast of Portugal. The 315-foot Greek freighter *Tenorga* sank in a violent storm near the entrance to the port of Leixoes; 21 of the 24-man crew perished.

Dec. 31

Off the coast of northwestern Spain. When the Greek supertanker *Andros Patria* cracked in heavy seas and gale force winds, 29 of the 32 persons aboard took to the lifeboats and drowned in rough waters; three men who remained on board were rescued by a helicopter.

4.
Mining Calamities

As shown by injury and fatality rates, the working environment of a miner, especially a coal miner, is decidedly more hostile than that in most other occupations. Stringent safety standards, periodic mine inspections, and vigorous safety training programs for workers have been established by legislation and through efforts by mine management, labor unions, and other groups. These factors coupled with improved mining techniques have substantially reduced the number of work injuries in the past few decades. The majority of underground fatalities result from falls of the roof or ground, haulage activities, gas or dust explosions, and the operation or movement of machinery.

Falling roof or ground has generally been the most prevalent cause of deaths in mining accidents. Surface coal mines, such as strip or open-cast and auger operations, present a much lower degree of hazard to workmen than does underground mining. Consequently, the death rates for surface mines are much lower.

Accidents caused by the falls of mine roofs and sides usually involve only one or two men, although on occasion single incidents do result in many deaths. This is particularly the case in mines liable to rock bursts. In certain circumstances the rock itself can disintegrate violently when the elastic strain energy in stressed strata, or layers, of rock is released suddenly. Such a rock burst on a large scale can be accompanied by air-pressure waves of sufficient violence to disrupt a mine's ventilation circuit. Although much has been learned about this phenomenon, and safety measures have been introduced, rock bursts still constitute a major hazard in many coalfields, particularly in North America.

Relatively small falls of rock, however, occurring as they do with terrible regularity, account for most deaths. Prevention of this type of accident depends on adequate support of the roof and sides of the mine. Normal support systems may be supplemented by protective pillars of coal that are left unmined. In the United States a technique known as roof bolting is widely employed. This involves drilling holes in the strata and inserting steel rods, which are subsequently anchored in position. These rods, several feet in length, either secure the immediate sidewall to a stronger stratum or secure several individually weak roof layers to form in effect one thick compound beam. In Europe hydraulically powered supports are used.

Mine haulage systems are often very extensive, and it is not unusual for a coal mine to require large numbers of haulage workers. Haulage accidents, like falls of the ground, tend to be limited in their individual effects, but they occur frequently. Apart from the obvious dangers associated with the large-scale movement of men and material, mine haulage is made more dangerous by lack of working space and poor lighting.

Provision of adequate ventilation is one of the most essential safety features of underground coal mining. The average weight of air passing daily through a coal mine is much greater than the weight of coal produced during the same period; many mines require the circulation of more than half a million cubic feet of air a minute. Most of the air is necessary in order to dilute the harmful gases or "damps" (from the German word *dampf*, meaning "vapor") produced during mining operations.

The gas that occurs naturally in coal mines is nearly always methane, a highly inflammable gas that is explosive when present in the air in a proportion of from 5 to 14 percent. Several gas explosions are recorded each year in the United States. In Great Britain methane is frequently called "marsh gas" or "firedamp," although more correctly the latter term means an inflammable mixture of methane and air. Methane, which is absorbed in coal under the earth, is liberated when the coal is disturbed. It is usually given off gradually, but in the course of mining some seams yield up to five thousand cubic feet of methane for each ton of coal. In order to render this gas harmless, it is necessary to circulate large volumes of air to reduce the percentage of methane below a prescribed figure. The legal maximum methane contact varies from country to country, but it normally does not exceed 2 percent.

Methane is also given off in the form of outbursts—sudden, violent discharges of short duration that are usually accompanied by the displacement of large quantities of broken strata and dust. Although very destructive outbursts are comparatively rare, firedamp, however formed, is a major hazard, and despite improvements in detection and ventilation techniques, dangerous accumulations still occur.

To reduce the danger from inflammable gas underground,

long boreholes may be drilled through the earth to the area where the coal is being extracted and the methane drawn out and piped to the surface. This technique, known as methane extraction, is common in Europe. Although many instruments have been designed specifically to detect the presence of firedamp underground, the principles of the flame safety lamp devised by the English chemist Sir Humphry Davy in 1815 still form the basis of many detectors. Methane air mixtures can be ignited by a naked flame, but Davy discovered that a flame burning within a metal gauze would not ignite firedamp. Moreover, such a flame would burn with a clear yellow flame in good air but with a blue-capped flame in explosive air. In addition to ignition by naked flame, firedamp can also be set off by frictional sparking, which has accounted for many serious underground explosions. It has also been found that firedamp can be ignited by electrical energy, and to avoid this danger only specially designed electrical equipment may be used in mines where methane constitutes a possible hazard.

The mixture of gases found in a mine after an explosion or fire is known as "afterdamp." Its actual composition varies with the nature and amount of the materials consumed by the fire or with the extent to which firedamp or coal was involved in the explosion. Afterdamp is deficient in oxygen, and among other dangerous characteristics it has a high carbon monoxide content. By far the greater proportion of deaths in coal mine explosions and fires is due to the toxic effects of afterdamp.

The menace of gas explosions in coal mines was widely recognized as long ago as the early years of the nineteenth century. The danger of coal dust in mines, however, was not appreciated until comparatively recently. Few people heeded the English physicist Michael Faraday's thesis in 1845 that the ignition and explosion of firedamp would raise and then kindle coal dust. Eventually it was realized that coal dust presents a far greater danger than methane, in that coal dust explosions are far more violent and widespread than simple firedamp explosions. The latter are usually fairly localized in their effect; their principal danger lies in the fact that a firedamp explosion may initiate a far more serious coal dust explosion.

Fires are also a danger in coal mines. Apart from the fact that a naked flame may cause an explosion, there is the added complication that the coal itself provides a virtually inex-

Members of a rescue party, overcome by gas fumes, are carried from the Midlothian coal mine in Coalfield, Virginia, after an explosion on February 3, 1882, killed 32 persons—just 28 years after a similar accident at the same mine killed 55. The danger of gas explosions had been recognized since the early part of that century.

haustible source of fuel. A modern development in the field of underground fire fighting is the "foam plug" technique. Air-water foam—tens of thousands of cubic feet per minute —is generated on the upwind side of the fire. The foam completely fills the mine's roadway and is pushed by the normal airstream into the fire zone where it blankets the fire.

Sunderland, England, 1880. The great Seaham coal mine near Sunderland in northern England had been in operation for forty years without any major accidents, normally being worked by sixteen hundred men in three shifts around the clock. On August 17, 1880, however, the midnight-to-morning shift was under strength, consisting of only 246 men. At 2:30 in the morning there was a terrific explosion in the main shaft of the colliery, which had been filled with dangerous amounts of coal dust and combustible gases. The walls and ceiling of the main tunnel fell in. The blast was probably caused by an open flame in one of the miner's lamps coming

The first dead body is hoisted from the mine after a terrible explosion occurred in the main shaft of the Seaham coal mine near Sunderland, England, on August 17, 1880. In all, 161 miners died.

into contact with firedamp. Many of those who were not killed in the explosion found themselves trapped by falling debris in small side tunnels.

The experience of a group of nineteen trapped miners was described by Ralph Marley, one of their number. After recovering from the initial shock, the men burrowed through the fallen rock that had blocked off their section of the mine. Once on the other side, they made their way along a passageway littered with dead bodies, keeping as close to the floor as possible in order to avoid breathing the gas that filled the upper part of the chamber. When they reached the elevator that normally carried them down into the mine and back to the surface again, they found that it had been put out of commission by the explosion. The air was clearer around the shaft leading to the surface, and there was nothing for them to do but sit down and wait to be rescued. The greatest danger at that point was that there might be a second explosion, but although the adjacent passages were filling up with gas, nothing more happened. Rescuers finally dug their way through at about five in the morning. The eighteen with Marley and sixty-six others got out alive. It took several days to find all the 161 bodies of the dead.

Pocahontas, Virginia, 1884. The Laurel Mine in Pocahontas was operated with little concern for the safety of the miners. It was poorly ventilated and contained dangerous amounts of dust and firedamp. The quantities of black blasting powder used to loosen the coal increased the hazard. At one o'clock on the morning of March 13, 1884, when about 150 men were working in the mine, it was rocked by an explosion that was heard for miles around. Machinery and equipment came flying out of the mine shaft, killing a number of men who were working around the entrance, decapitating several of them. The explosion destroyed nearby houses and trees and deposited half an inch of coal dust on the mountainside opposite the entrance.

The interior of the mine was an inferno; the distraught people of Pocahontas stood helplessly outside, not knowing what to do. Some tried to get in, wrapping themselves in wet blankets for protection, but the heat was too great, and they only succeeded in getting badly burned. The fires were still raging several hours later, when Col. George Dodds, a representative of the company, arrived with a party of mining engineers. Disregarding the possibility that some of the miners inside might still be alive, Dodds decided to put out the fires by flooding the mine with water. All the entrances were closed off, and the water was pumped in through hoses.

It was another two weeks before anyone was able to get down the shaft again. When investigators did make the descent, they discovered 112 bodies. Evidence showed that some of the victims had died by drowning, the result of Dobbs's decision to flood the mine. Great outrage was expressed when the incident was publicized, but conditions like those at the Laurel Mine continued to be commonplace.

Krebs, Oklahoma, 1892. In the Osage Company mines at Krebs the "shot-firers" who set the explosive charges used to loosen the coal deposits usually worked at night, when there was nobody else around. On the afternoon of January 7, 1892, however, a crew of six shot-firers arrived early at Mine Number Eleven. They were already in their work area when the miners quit for the day and lined up to be taken to the surface in iron cages. One of the cages had just reached the top of the main shaft when the shot-firers detonated an enormous blast, the force of which blew the cage through the roof of the shaft, fifty feet into the air.

In the mine the carnage was terrible. Miners who escaped serious injury climbed up the shaft by themselves to escape the deadly gases forming in the wake of the explosion. Others, too badly hurt to move, were carried up in baskets. Men from nearby mines came to lend a hand with the rescue work; making their way to the bottom of the shaft of Number Eleven, they began to sift through the fallen rock for the bodies of the dead. "Here a head, there a hand or leg protruding from the mass. . . ." ran one account. "A number of burned lamps, caps and dinner buckets completed the desolation of the scene. The bodies were removed with all possible care, but this did not prevent an arm or leg, almost severed from the body, from being completely torn off when taken from under the wreckage." The number of dead was estimated at 100.

An ugly racial incident developed in the midst of the rescue efforts. Some of the volunteers were blacks who had been excluded from work in the mines. White miners accused them of gloating over the disaster, and a fight started. A posse was called in "to drive the colored men from the place with Winchesters."

Hanna, Wyoming, 1903 and 1908. The town of Hanna and nearly everything in it was owned by the Union Pacific Railroad. It had a large population of Finnish migrants who would work for a while in the Wyoming coalfields, return to Finland, and then come back again. They were always welcome at Hanna, where the company valued their habits of sobriety and hard work. More than 200 miners—mostly Finns, along with some Poles, blacks, and Chinese—were working in the Hanna mine on the morning of June 30, 1903, when two disastrous explosions occurred. As in so many other instances, they were probably caused by blasting with inadequate safety procedures. Ignited gases and dust spread flames through every part of the mine.

The hero of the day was a black miner, William Christian, who risked his life repeatedly, descending several times through the only entrance not blocked by fire, and rescuing twenty men. Twenty-six more were saved within the next twenty-four hours, but 169 men never came out again. As usual there was a loud outcry from the press about unsafe working conditions in the coal mines; the Hanna mine was closed for a few months but was soon operating again under the same conditions as before.

In March 1908 gas fires broke out again on the lower levels. Despite the obvious danger, men were kept working on the levels closer to the surface. On March 28 there was another explosion, in which fifty-nine miners were killed. This time the mine was closed down for good.

Monongah, West Virginia, 1907. A tragic accident occurred in the Monongah coal works, a large complex run by the Fairmont Coal Company, on December 6, 1907. In Mine Number Six several cars of a railroad train carrying coal out to be processed broke loose on an upgrade and went rolling back down through the tunnel. They jumped the track and crashed into a wall, cutting some electric cables; sparks from the cables ignited the coal dust that filled the tunnel, causing an explosion that ripped through Mine Number Six and Mine Number Eight, which connected with it. A total of 362 were killed; some were burned to death, and others were crushed or suffocated when the roof and walls of the mine collapsed. It took weeks to locate all of the bodies. Ironically, one of the victims was not an employee of the Fairmont Company at all; he had been in the mines giving away cigars to the workmen, trying to sell them life insurance.

This was only one of the many disasters that plagued the United States in 1907, a year in which more than 3,000 lost their lives in the coalfields. Major accidents also occurred in Yolande, Alabama, Primero, Colorado, Fayette City and Jacob's Creek, Pennsylvania, and Stuart and Thomas, West Virginia.

Marianna, Pennsylvania, 1908. The rash of accidents caused by unsafe conditions continued in the following year. One of the worst took place at Marianna, south of Pittsburgh, on the morning of November 28, 1908. An exposed flame set off two successive explosions in Shaft Number Three of the Rachel and Agnes Mine. The ventilation system was put out of order by the blasts; by the time it was repaired hours later, 154 men trapped in the mine had died, either in the initial explosion or of asphyxiation caused by the afterdamp. One man who was blown clear was the only survivor.

The Rachel and Agnes Mine had a water system that was supposed to settle the dust raised by the mining operations, but it did not work properly. Despite this, safety inspectors had given the mine a clean bill of health. An inquiry into the causes of the calamity exonerated the coal company, blaming instead the immigrant miners' inability to understand instructions given in English.

Cherry, Illinois, 1909. In the following year there was a disaster at the St. Paul Company mine in the town of Cherry, near Peru in north-central Illinois. Shortly after noon on November 13, 1909, a fire started in some bales of hay just inside the mine entrance. Realizing the danger, two workmen threw the burning hay into a coal car to get it out into the open; before they could do so, however, the fire spread to the beams supporting the roof of the tunnel. In another few minutes there was an explosion. It sent the fire racing into the interior of the mine, where more than 400 men were at work.

Mine superintendent John Bundy and five others were standing outside when the explosion occurred. They decided to go down the main shaft in the elevator to see if they could help. By the time they reached the bottom of the shaft, Bundy and his companions were overcome by methane fumes. Alexander Nerberg, the only one who was still conscious, signaled frantically for the elevator to be raised again. It came slowly back up to the surface, and when it was opened, everyone inside was dead. The next group of volunteers to go down took the precaution of wearing gas masks, but in the short time that had elapsed the heat from the fire had grown so intense that they could not go to the bottom.

Meanwhile the wives and children of the miners kept an anguished vigil at the entrances to the mine, waiting until something could be done; as the hours went by, many of the women became hysterical. Some distance away, a farmer heard vague noises like gunshots coming from underneath the ground where the mine tunnels were; he though it must have been survivors of the blast trying to let people know they were still alive. In reality, what he had heard was one miner shooting several others to put them out of their misery.

When the fire at last died out on the morning of November 14, rescuers renewed their attempts to reach anyone who might still be alive. The relief operations continued for thirty-six hours; a good number of miners were saved, but several of the rescuers lost their lives in the process. One young man had gone down with his uncle to help out. After they had

Relatives and friends anxiously wait for news of miners who were trapped after a fire triggered an explosion in the St. Paul Company mine in Cherry, Illinois, on November 13, 1909. A total of 259 miners and rescue workers lost their lives in the disaster.

loaded a score of unconscious men into the elevator cage, he begged the older man to come up with him out of the gas-filled shaft. His uncle told him to go on alone. "I'll come up on the next trip," he said, and went back into the tunnel. That was the last time anyone saw him alive.

Some of the miners found their own way out. John Phillips and Edward Surrock managed to get to the cage by themselves, Phillips holding a tobacco pouch over his mouth to protect himself from the fumes. William Vicker and a friend helped each other through one of the shafts. Vicker later described what it was like:

> *At one point, we passed about sixty-five miners sitting by the roadside, almost in a stupor. I tried to rouse them and encourage them to go on, but they seemed to have given up all hope, and did not stir. The sight of my doomed comrades is something that will haunt me until my dying day. . . . I escaped death by just three minutes. When I arrived at the bottom of the shaft, the last cage was about to ascend. I shouted as the signal bell was ringing. Two men broke their way to me and dragged me to the cage. I then lost consciousness. When*

*I came to, I was safely on top. My buddy had followed
me closely all the way and . . . was carried with me
to safety.*

A total of 259 men were killed in the St. Paul Company
mine disaster, the worst in the history of the Illinois coalfields.

Littleton, Alabama, 1911. Littleton's Banner Mine, owned
and operated by the Pratt Consolidated Coal Company, was
worked mostly by convicts, many of them blacks. At 6:20 on
the morning of April 8, 1911, the mine foreman and a chain
gang boss were having coffee outside the mine when they
heard an explosion. Smoke poured out of the entrance, and
a few minutes later some of the prisoners staggered into the
open, gasping for breath. In all, 42 made their way to safety,
but 128 others were crushed or suffocated before they could
get out.

The explosion was probably caused by an open-flame lamp
coming into contact with the dynamite used for blasting. O.
W. Spradling, a convict overseer, was among those who perished. He was killed by a blow on the head, but the fact that
his body was found in a part of the mine where there had been
no cave-in caused some to suspect that his death might not
have been an accident.

Dawson, New Mexico, 1913. The Stag Canyon Fuel Company mines seemed safer than most. The level of methane in
the miners' work areas was generally low, and all explosive
materials were detonated by electricity to forestall the kinds
of accidents that so often resulted from the use of matches.
The weak spot of the Dawson mines, as in many other mines,
was the sprinkler system that was supposed to keep the air
free of coal dust. It covered only limited areas, leaving large
sections of the mine dry and dusty.

A dynamite blast, though electrically set off from outside,
accidentally ignited the dry coal dust on October 22, 1913,
causing an explosion that blocked off the main entrance of
Mine Number Two. There were 284 miners inside at the time.
The members of the first rescue party that tried to get
through to them were overcome by afterdamp and had to be
rescued themselves. Eventually twenty-one of the miners
were saved; the rest were killed.

Hastings, Colorado, 1917. After an explosion that caused
several fatalities in 1913, the Victor-American coal mine in
Hastings had acquired a bad reputation, but it continued to
be a thriving enterprise. In 1917 it was yielding about 1,000

tons of coal a day and was worked continuously by shifts of more than 100 men. After the 1913 accident, fire bosses were supposed to make daily checks to see that methane and coal dust did not accumulate above a safe level, but their inspections were not usually very thorough.

The mine was certified as clear of gas before the first shift went to work on April 17, 1917. The miners went down into the main shaft on the little railroad that was used to transport them. No sooner had they entered the mine than someone lit a match, and the entire mine blew up with a deafening roar, killing 129 miners almost instantly.

Benwood, West Virginia, 1924. At 7:35 on the morning of April 28, 1924, there was a mine explosion at Benwood, a few miles from Wheeling, West Virginia. Just before, 119 men had gone to work on the morning shift. In one tunnel, relatives and friends of the trapped miners who had been summoned to the scene dug through the fallen rock to try to reach them, but they were driven back by the deadly afterdamp on the other side of the debris.

When no one succeeded in getting to the miners by midafternoon, company inspector A. E. Lafferty decided there was no hope left for any of them. He advised the waiting townspeople to return home, but they remained at the gates to the mine area until all of the bodies were brought out hours later.

Parnassus, Pennsylvania, 1929. Parnassus (now New Kensington), just east of Pittsburgh, was the site of the Kinlock Mine, where a tragic accident occurred on March 21, 1929. A 300-foot conveyor belt used to transport coal to the surface broke and flew back down the shaft, raising a great quantity of coal dust. The dust was then ignited by an electrical spark from the mine machinery. A mine inspector described the resulting explosion as "violent, traveling up the slope where it destroyed the conveyor structure . . . and . . . into the mine [where it] destroyed doors, stoppings, overcasts and all equipment." Although 46 men were killed, 212 were saved by prompt and effective rescue measures. Emergency teams moved into the mine quickly with supplies of oxgyen to counteract the afterdamp; they put out the fires and got the survivors out by way of abandoned shafts that adjoined the Kinlock Mine.

West Frankfort, Illinois, 1951. The New Orient Mine Number Two at West Frankfort, Illinois, owned by the Wilmington and Franklin Coal Company, was inspected by federal authorities in July 1951. They recommended that the

A grieving woman waits for word of one of her relatives after 281 miners were trapped in the New Orient Mine Number Two at West Frankfort, Illinois, on December 21, 1951; though many were rescued, 119 lost their lives.

older parts of the mine be closed off to prevent methane gas from contaminating the areas still being worked. But the company was not being required by law to follow the recommendation and simply ignored it.

On the evening of December 21, 1951, Mine Number Two was wracked by an explosion that "knocked cars weighing several tons off the tracks and brought down overhead timbers." Of the 281 men working in the mine 119 were killed. The disaster caused great public indignation. Illinois governor Adlai Stevenson blamed the state's antiquated mine safety laws. He had earlier tried to get the legislature to enact a modern mining code, but the union, the operators, and politicians from southern Illinois successfully opposed the bill.

Marcinelle, Belgium, 1956. The Bois du Cazier Mine in Marcinelle, outside Charleroi, Belgium, was worked mostly

Relatives and friends keep a constant vigil outside the gates of the Bois du Cazier Mine in Marcinelle, Belgium, after the August 8, 1956, mining accident. All 270 men trapped in the mine were found dead when rescue workers finally reached them two days later.

by Italian migrant laborers. There were 276 men in the mine on the morning of August 8, 1956, when a coal car was derailed and ran into ventilating equipment. The collision cut electric cables, causing a short circuit that spread fires through the various mine shafts.

Six of the miners were able to get to an elevator and reach the surface before the elevator cables were burned through. The rest were stranded. No one was able to get through to the work areas for forty-eight hours, and by that time all 270 of the men in the mine were dead.

Dharbad, India, and Fukuoka, Japan, 1965. One of the worst mine disasters on record took place in Jharia coalfield, northwest of Calcutta, India, on May 28, 1965. Coal dust that had been allowed to accumulate in the shafts of the East Indian Mine was ignited by an electrical spark, causing an explosion that devastated an area of four square miles. Buildings in the vicinity of the mine were obliterated, and 100 people on the surface were killed. Later, 275 bodies were dug out of the ruins of the mine.

Only a few days later, on June 1, there was an accident at the Yamano coal mine, near Fukuoka on the Japanese island of Kyushu. The mine was torn apart by an explosion set off by escaping gas. Rock falls blocked many of the tunnels, but 279 miners were able to get out. The families of the remaining 236 waited outside for two days hoping that some of them might still be saved. After a dispiriting search of the wreckage, however, no one was found alive. Trade minister Yoshio Sakurauchi, whose department was held responsible for the lax safety measures, resigned in the wake of the disaster.

Other Mining Calamities, 1959–78

1959

Feb. 16
Near Quetta, West Pakistan. At least 13 persons were killed in a coal mine explosion.

May 29
Merlebach, France. A coal mine explosion killed 18 miners and injured 35.

Aug. 30
Utrillas, Spain. A mine explosion killed 12 miners and injured 6 others.

Sept. 18
Kirkintilloch, Scotland. Fire and gas trapped and killed 47 persons in a coal pit.

Nov. 25
Szuesci, Hungary. An explosion in a coal mine killed 31 men.

Dec. 24
Welkom, South Africa. An explosion in a gold mine killed 25 miners.

1960

Jan. 21
Coalbrook, South Africa. A mine cave-in killed 417 men.

Feb. 1
Hokkaido Island, Japan. A mine blast killed 32 miners.

Feb. 22
Zwickau, East Germany. A fiery explosion ripped through a coal mine, killing 49 men and leaving 75 trapped.

March 8

Logan, West Virginia. A coal mine fire killed 18 persons.

May 22

Ostrava, Czechoslovakia. A coal mine blast killed 54 miners.

June 28

Six Bells, Wales. A coal mine explosion and cave-in claimed 45 lives.

July 19

Salzgitter, West Germany. An iron mine fire killed at least 33 miners.

Aug. 17

Johannesburg, South Africa. A rockfall trapped and killed 15 men in a gold mine under the streets.

Sept. 20

Kyushu, Japan. A reported 67 miners drowned in a coal mine flooded as the result of a gas explosion.

Oct. 30

Shiranuka, Japan. A gas explosion in a coal mine caused the death of 17 miners.

1961

Feb. 17

Near Johannesburg, South Africa. An explosion of dynamite in a gold mine killed 30 miners and injured 40 others.

March 2

Terre Haute, Indiana. An explosion in a coal mine killed 23 miners.

March 9

Fukuoka, Japan. A fire in a coal mine raged out of control, killing 71 miners.

March 16

Yahata, Japan. A fire in a coal mine took the lives of 32 persons.

July 7

Dolna Suce, Czechoslovakia. A gas explosion in a coal mine took the lives of 108 men.

1962

Jan. 11

Carterville, Illinois. A methane gas explosion in the Blue Blaze coal mine killed 11 miners.

Feb. 7

Near Saarbrücken, West Germany. A methane gas explosion in the Luisenthal mine at Voelklingen killed 298 miners.

Feb. 27

Banovici, Yugoslavia. A double explosion ripped the main shaft of a large lignite mine; 54 miners died, and 11 others were injured.

March 9

Heessen, West Germany. A firedamp explosion 3,000 feet underground in the Sachen coal mine brought death to 31 miners; 6 others were injured.

March 22

Burnley, England. An underground gas explosion in the Hapton Valley coal mine killed 16 miners and injured 20 others.

May 2

Odendaalsrust, South Africa. A rockfall in a gold mine killed 15 miners.

Oct. 15

Gorgan, Iran. An explosion in a coal mine killed 13 workers.

Nov. 6

Spitsbergen Island. Two explosions ripped through a 650-foot deep shaft of an Arctic coal mine, killing 21 miners.

Dec. 6

Carmichaels, Pennsylvania. A violent explosion in a U.S. Steel mine killed 37 miners who were working 680 feet underground.

Dec. 12

Johannesburg, South Africa. A crushing plant at the West Driefontein gold mine collapsed, killing 29 African miners.

1963

Feb. 11

Patchefstroom, South Africa. A mine elevator stuck in a poorly ventilated shaft at the 7,000-foot level; 21 miners died of heat and suffocation.

April 25

Dola, West Virginia. An explosion of methane gas and coal dust at a Compass mine brought death to 22 miners.

Aug. 28

Moab, Utah. An explosion in the main shaft of a potash mine trapped 25 miners at the 2,700-foot level; 18 of the men died, and 7 were rescued.

Oct. 24

Broistedt, West Germany. A burst dam flooded the nearby Mathilde iron mine and trapped 129 miners; 29 men died, 86 men escaped within a short time, 3 men were rescued from an air pocket after eight days of drilling, and 11 others were

dramatically rescued after two weeks of entombment.
Nov. 9
Omuta, Japan. A coal dust explosion about 2,400 feet from the opening of the Mitsui Miiki mine killed 452 miners and injured at least 450 others.
Dec. 4
Tatabanya, Hungary. An explosion in one of Hungary's largest coal mines killed 26 miners.

1964
Jan. 27
Taipei, Taiwan. A coal mine explosion killed 12 men and injured 9 others; 15 were listed as missing.
Feb. 9
Keelung, Taiwan. An explosion in a 3,000-foot shaft of a nearby coal mine killed 17 miners.
May 25
Prestea, Ghana. A fire in a gold mine brought death to 12 workers.
June 12
Karkar, Afghanistan. An explosion in a coal mine killed 74 miners and injured 6 others.
Oct. 9
Wanli, Taiwan. A landslide engulfed a sulfur mine and killed 25 miners.
Nov. 16
Sasolburg, South Africa. A fire at the 450-foot level of a coal mine trapped 54 miners; 23 were unable to escape and died.

1965
Jan. 10
Near Kaljevo, Yugoslavia. The explosion of an air compressor 4,500 feet down in the Jarando coal mine killed 14 men.
Feb. 2
Lens, France. A gas explosion in a 2,345-foot deep coal pit killed 21 miners.
Feb. 10
Near Quetta, West Pakistan. The collapse of a protective wall 2,000 feet beneath the surface released poison gas that killed 17 trapped miners.
Feb. 22
Yubari, Japan. A gas explosion at the Hokkaido Colliery and Steamship Company mine caused a cave-in that killed 61 men and injured 17 others.

Feb. 23

Uricani, Romania. A gas explosion in a coal mine killed 41 miners and injured 16 others.

March 19

Amasya, Turkey. Gas explosions and fire in a nearby lignite mine trapped 126 miners 1,000 feet below the surface, killing 68 of the men.

April 9

Nagasaki, Japan. A gas explosion and cave-in at the Nitetsu Mining Company coal mine on a small nearby island took the lives of 30 miners and injured 15 others.

May 8

Real del Monte, Mexico. Broken cables plunged an elevator cage into the water-filled bottom of a shaft at the Purisma silver and gold mines; 27 of the 30 trapped miners drowned.

May 17

Tonypandy, Wales. A gas explosion in a narrow gallery of the Cambrian colliery 850 feet beneath the Rhondda Valley killed 31 men and injured 12 others.

June 7

Kakanj, Yugoslavia. An explosion of methane gas in the Orasi shaft of the Kakanj coal mine brought death to 125 workers and injured 21 others.

Nov. 24

Albi, France. A coal dust explosion 750 feet beneath the surface claimed the lives of 12 miners.

Dec. 15

Welkom, South Africa. A rock fall in the Virginia gold mine killed 12 workers.

1966

Feb. 16

Moers, West Germany. An explosion in a nearby coal mine brought death to 16 men; 3 others were missing.

Feb. 16

Near St. Gotthard Pass, Switzerland. Gas swept through an uncompleted tunnel, part of a hydroelectric project, and killed 17 workers.

July 8

Monomura, Japan. A cave-in blocked a section of an irrigation tunnel under construction and trapped 65 workers, 25 of whom died in a gas-filled pocket.

Oct. 24

Samacá, Colombia. A network of coal mines was ripped by

two explosions; 8 men were killed, and 11 others were buried by slides and were presumed dead.

1967
Jan. 19
Greymouth, New Zealand. An underground explosion blocked off a section of the Strongman coal mine and caused the deaths of 19 miners.
March 22
Barazana, India. A blast from an explosion in an iron mine killed 11 workers and injured 3 others.
April 3
Natal, British Columbia, Canada. Explosions and cave-ins occurring in the Boomer coal mine left 15 men dead and 17 injured.
June 28
Baguio, Philippines. Heavy rains caused cave-ins 4,000 feet down in a gold and copper mine; 21 miners died.
July 25
Carletonville, South Africa. Panic in a passageway of the Western Deep Level gold mine brought death to 50 workers.
Sept. 5
Antofagasta, Chile. Chuquicamata, a huge open-pit copper mine, was the scene of an explosion that killed at least 21 men and injured 50 others.
Sept. 9
East Wemyss, Scotland. Fire and explosions in the Michael colliery, 1,800 feet beneath the Firth of Forth, killed 10 men.
Oct. 13
Carletonville, South Africa. Fire, explosions, and a pressure cave-in at the Western Deep Level gold mine brought death to at least 14 miners; 9 others were missing.

1968
Jan. 26
Lengede, West Germany. An explosion in a 300-foot-deep shaft in an iron mine killed 12 miners.
March 6
Belle Isle, Louisiana. A fire in the 1,200-foot shaft of the Belle Isle salt mine destroyed the entrance and suffocated all 21 men trapped at the bottom of the shaft.
May 6
Hominy Falls, West Virginia. Water pouring into a coal mine cut off the crew about a mile from the entrance; 28 died.

Oct. 4

Luenen, West Germany. A Ruhr Valley coal mine caved in, causing the death of 17 miners.

Nov. 20

Mannington, West Virginia. A series of explosions set off fires that raged through a mine and trapped 78 men; recovery of the entombed bodies was deemed impossible, and the mine was sealed.

1969

Jan. 23

Welkom, South Africa. An explosion of methane gas at the President Steyn gold mine killed 15 miners and injured 13 others; 2 persons were missing.

March 31

Barroteran, Mexico. Deadly gases prevented rescuers from reaching miners trapped 800 feet underground when explosions ripped through two shafts of a coal mine belonging to Altos Hornos de Mexico; at least 180 miners were given up for dead.

July 7

Jui Feng, Taiwan. Floating coal dust set off an explosion that killed 24 miners; 53 others were injured.

Sept. 22

Izuwa, Japan. A cave-in following a coal mine explosion killed 14 miners.

Nov. 7

Buffelsfontein, South Africa. A dynamite explosion in a gold mine buried a shaft blasting team 1.5 miles beneath the surface, killing 60 members of the crew and injuring 14 others.

Nov. 14

Salisbury, Rhodesia. An elevator cage broke loose from its cables and plunged 3,500 feet down a mine shaft, killing 20 men.

1970

April 4

Near Ostrava, Czechoslovakia. A gas explosion ripped through the Paskov colliery and killed 26 miners; 3 others were missing.

June 6

Sharig, Pakistan. An explosion set off in a dynamite storeroom blasted a government-owned coal mine, killing 30 miners and officials; 20 others were injured.

Sept. 7

Sorrange, Pakistan. A cave-in caused by a gas explosion blocked the pit entrance to a coal mine and trapped the miners 150 feet below the surface; 24 workers died, and 10 others were missing.

Sept. 25

Lusaka, Zambia. Millions of tons of sand collapsed at the Mufulira copper mine, one of the world's largest, trapping 89 mine workers in seas of mud and water; all perished.

Dec. 15

Sapporo, Japan. A gas explosion blasted through a coal mine; 19 miners were dead or missing, and 11 others were injured.

Dec. 30

Wooton, Kentucky. Set off by a charge of explosives, a coal dust explosion blasted through a coal mine trapping 38 miners; all died.

1971

May 16

Near Quetta, West Pakistan. An explosion killed 32 workmen in a coal mine at Sinjabi.

June 24

Near Los Angeles, California. Natural gas exploded and triggered a 14-hour fire in a 5.5-mile water tunnel being drilled beneath the suburb of Sylmar; 17 workmen lost their lives.

Oct. 30

Hunedoara, Romania. The collapse of a settling tank caused a landslide that trapped a crew of miners working underground; 51 persons died, and 88 others were injured.

Dec. 1

Near Keelung, Taiwan. An explosion 7,260 feet underground in the Seven Star mine killed 41 miners; 7 others were missing, and 4 were seriously injured.

Dec. 11

Port Huron, Michigan. Deadly methane gas exploded and ripped through a six-mile water tunnel being drilled 250 feet under the surface of Lake Huron; 22 of the approximately 40 workers inside the tunnel died, and 9 others were injured.

1972

Jan. 31

South Africa. A fire in the West Driefontein gold mine, the world's richest, brought death to at least 13 African miners.

May 2

Kellogg, Idaho. A flash fire of unknown origin raced through the Sunshine silver mine, spewing flames, smoke, and carbon monoxide fumes throughout miles of corridors between the 3,100- and 3,700-foot levels and blocking hoist exits used by the miners working below the 4,600-foot level; 108 miners quickly escaped from the upper levels, but 91 others perished.

June 6

Wankie, Rhodesia. A violent explosion in a shaft of the Wankie colliery tore down walls of rock and coal and blew twisted machinery and a cable car up the shaft and into the open air; of the 426 men in the mine, 422 were trapped and killed, and 5 others were killed on the surface.

July 31

Ipswich, Queensland, Australia. To prevent further explosions at a nearby explosion-ridden and fire-ravaged colliery, bulldozers sealed the mine entrance, entombing 17 miners and rescue workers who had perished in the fires.

Nov. 6

Ishikari, Japan. A methane gas explosion in the Ishikari coal mine killed 31 miners.

1973

Feb. 8

Johannesburg, South Africa. It was reported that an underground fire in the nearby West Driefontein gold mine had killed at least 26 miners.

March 18

Dhanbad, India. A series of gas explosions in a coal mine brought death to at least 50 miners.

May 5

Changsong, South Korea. Six mine cars transporting miners into the coal pits went out of control and tipped over, killing 18 workers and injuring 18 others.

June 28

Near Johannesburg, South Africa. A surfacing mine cage rammed into steel girders of the hoisting machinery and killed 16 men.

1974

March 10

Near Soko Banja, Yugoslavia. Methane gas exploded in a coal pit in eastern Yugoslavia, taking the lives of 12 miners; 3 other workers were missing and presumed dead.

Mid-May

Near Erzurum, Turkey. A coal mine explosion in eastern Turkey took the lives of at least 10 miners.

Dec. 27

Liévin, France. An explosion and fire of uncertain origin took the lives of 42 miners working 2,300 feet below the surface in the state-owned Liévin coalfields.

1975

Sept. 20

Near Rockhampton, Australia. An explosion and fire at the Kianga coal mine in central Queensland took the lives of 13 miners who were trapped 650 feet underground.

Nov. 3

Figols, Spain. A gas explosion in a coal mine located about 50 miles from Barcelona killed 27 workers and seriously injured at least 2 others.

Nov. 7

Beek, The Netherlands. An explosion caused by leaking gas at one of the State Mine Company's three naphtha cracking units ignited storage tanks containing gasoline and liquid chemicals; 12 persons were killed and 2 were missing.

Nov. 27

Mikasa, Japan. A gas explosion deep inside a coal mine killed 10 workers and injured 7 others.

Dec. 27

Near Dhanbad, India. Two explosions at the Chas Nala colliery caused millions of gallons of water from old shafts to pour into underground areas where hundreds of coal miners were working; despite frantic rescue efforts, the death toll was reportedly as high as 431.

1976

March 1–11

Near Whitesburg, Kentucky. An explosion of methane gas in a mine operated by the Scotia Coal Company claimed the lives of 15 workers; a second explosion 36 hours later killed 11 others, including 3 federal safety inspectors.

Aug. 5

Breza, Yugoslavia. An explosion killed 17 miners who were working 600 feet underground; of the 100 workers who escaped, only a few were injured by the blast.

Sept. 7

Walbrzych, Poland. An explosion that shattered a coal mine shaft killed at least 17 workers and injured more than 30 others; some 70 other miners escaped unhurt.

Mid-September

Near Tete, Mozambique. A gas explosion inside a coal mine claimed the lives of more than 100 workers.

Oct. 4

Near Dhanbad, India. An explosion in a Sudamdih coal mine killed 39 workers and injured about 30 others.

Dec. 31

Chlebovice, Czechoslovakia. A gas explosion at the Staric coal mine trapped and killed 43 workers.

1977

May 11

Hokkaido, Japan. A gas explosion at the colliery of Mitsui Mining Co. on the northern island of Hokkaido killed 25 miners and injured 8 others.

July 15

Amaga, Colombia. A gas explosion at a mine in the northwestern department of Antioquia in Colombia was reportedly the worst in the country's history; 135 persons were killed in the blast.

Aug. 2

Moatize, Mozambique. An explosion that ripped through a coal mine in northern Mozambique trapped 150 miners and killed 70; rioting followed the explosion and claimed the lives of 9 additional persons.

Sept. 3

South Africa. An earth tremor caused cave-ins at Blyvooruitzicht and Hartebeestfontein gold mines, trapping miners beneath tons of rock and earth; at least 21 miners were killed, and 16 others were missing and believed dead.

1978

Feb. 16

Tatabanya, Hungary. A coal explosion in Tatabanya, a region of vast lignite deposits and the country's main mining center, killed 26 miners and injured 19 others.

April 3

Near Aleksinac, Yugoslavia. A gas explosion in a coal mine killed 12 persons and injured 26 others.

Nov. 10

Near Changsong, South Korea. A pit cage carrying coal miners experienced a mechanical failure and plummeted to the bottom of a mine shaft; 10 miners died.

5.
Train Wrecks

In the United States, no form of transportation has more romantic and legendary associations than railroads. There seems to be something about railroad trains, especially the steam-powered variety, that has an irresistible appeal for the American mind. It is an attraction that has remained strong, perhaps even grown, since the decline of American railroads in the 1960s and 1970s.

The American railroad tradition grew up rather quickly, considering the fact that the steam locomotive was unknown before the second quarter of the nineteenth century. Along with this tradition, however, especially in the early days, there was widespread antirailroad sentiment in the United States. Early critics of the railroads condemned them as unsafe, warning that it was dangerous to travel at speeds of thirty-five and forty miles an hour. The record of the first few decades of railroad operation showed that these charges were not entirely without foundation.

On April 23, 1853, a Michigan Central express collided with a Michigan Southern train near Jackson, Michigan, killing 21 persons.

After a modest beginning in the 1830s and 1840s, the railroad accident rate rose sharply. One of the worst years was 1853. There were a number of minor mishaps in January and February. Then seven people died in March when a mail train hit the rear of passenger cars in Mount Union, Pennsylvania, and twenty-one were killed in April when a Michigan Southern train collided with a Michigan Central express. The series of accidents reached a climax on May 6 with a calamity at South Norwalk, Connecticut.

Edward Tucker, the engineer of the New York and New Haven express bound for Boston, Massachusetts, on May 6, had been with the railroad since 1849. Two years earlier, he had been badly injured in a head-on collision with another train; after his recovery, he went back on the New York to Boston run. At eight o'clock that morning, Tucker pulled out of Manhattan's Canal Street Station with a trainload of passengers, including a number of well-known physicians returning home from a meeting of the American Medical Association. After passing the South Norwalk station, the express approached a bridge that spanned the Norwalk River. The central section of the bridge turned on a pivot to allow the passage of river traffic; when it was open in this way, a red ball that hung from a tower at the entrance to the bridge was lowered as a signal to trains that they should halt and wait. When the bridge closed, the ball was raised again, and rail traffic was free to proceed.

Shortly before 10:30 the bridge had been opened, and several witnesses on the scene later testified that the signal had been lowered as required by regulations. Despite the fact that the tower was visible from a distance of a thousand yards down the track, Engineer Tucker approached the bridge at an estimated speed of between thirty and fifty miles an hour. He didn't realize that the drawbridge was open until it was only a few hundred feet away. He signaled the brakemen on the passenger cars to stop the train, but when they saw what was ahead they jumped off, leaving the passengers to their fate. The fireman and conductor did the same, followed by Tucker himself. The engine shot out into the air, striking the abutment on the other side, and plunged into the river, taking the tender, two baggage cars, and two passenger cars along with it. A third passenger car was broken in half. "The scene which ensued," a reporter wrote, "was one of incredible horror."

In all, forty-six persons were killed and twenty-five were injured. The engineer had to be rescued from a lynch

The New Haven Railroad express approached an open drawbridge at full speed and plunged into the river (above) on May 6, 1853, at Norwalk, Connecticut. The bodies of the 46 victims were brought into the Norwalk depot (below) later that day.

mob. A coroner's jury found him and the other crewmen guilty of criminal negligence but put most of the blame on the directors of the New York and New Haven Railroad. The railroad officials ruled that from then on all trains were to come to a full stop before any drawbridge, and the state of Connecticut established a board of railroad commissioners to enforce safety regulations. Nevertheless, the accident rate continued to rise.

Most railroads had no more than a single track in the 1850s, and for a long time they failed to make use of the telegraph to communicate traffic and schedule information. Thus, when a train was running off schedule, as frequently happened, there was no way to alert other trains that might be using the same track. Head-on collisions were often the result.

Sometimes accidents were caused by one engineer trying to second-guess another one. On July 17, 1856, for example, a special excursion train was scheduled to leave Philadelphia, Pennsylvania, at 5:00 A.M. to take some schoolchildren to a picnic at Fort Washington, Pennsylvania. The train left the station late and was soon fifteen minutes behind schedule. If late, the engineer's instructions were to pull onto a siding to allow the first regular morning local to pass on its way into the city. But the engineer also knew that the local train was instructed to wait fifteen minutes before proceeding when an expected train had failed to show up on time. Assuming that the local would wait, the engineer of the excursion train did not. The engineer on the local, assuming that the excursion train would wait, also proceeded on his way. The two trains collided at Camp Hill, Pennsylvania, killing sixty people, many of them young children.

As this tragic example shows, one of the worst problems was that even the confusing and inadequate safety rules that did exist were not taken seriously enough. Railroad employees thought nothing of taking a chance that might endanger the lives of their passengers.

Poor brakes and coupling devices and the use of different track gauges by different rail companies also posed hazards to safety. All three factors were involved in the famous "Angola Horror" wreck of 1867. On December 18 an express train of the Lake Shore and Michigan Southern Railroad was traveling toward Buffalo, New York, along the eastern shore of Lake Erie. The last car on the train belonged to the Cleveland and Toledo line, which used a narrower gauge than the Lake

Shore, but the car was equipped with wheels whose treads were wide enough to run on tracks of either gauge.

The problem with these "compromise cars" was that they were easily derailed. At Angola, New York, a few miles from Buffalo, the train had to cross a bridge over Big Sisters Creek. Just before reaching the bridge, the wheels of the car went off the tracks; the brakes failed to stop the train quickly enough. As it proceeded across the bridge, the last car was so violently shaken as it ran along over the wooden railroad ties that its coupling came loose, and it fell over the side to the frozen creek fifty feet below. Forty-two persons lost their lives. The publicity given to this accident led to the elimination of compromise cars and the standardization of gauges on all U.S. railroads.

Improved brakes and couplers were soon developed too. In 1869 George Westinghouse invented an air brake that was vastly superior to the hand brake, but the railroads proved reluctant to adopt it. When Westinghouse tried to demonstrate the merits of his invention to "Commodore" Cornelius Vanderbilt of the New York Central, the latter snorted: "Do you pretend to tell me that you could stop trains with wind? I'll give you to understand, young man, that I am too busy to have any time taken up talking to a damn fool!" The air brake and the automatic coupler, developed in the 1870s, were not universally adopted until 1893, when they were made mandatory by federal law.

Certain train wrecks have a prominent place in the romantic tradition of the American railroads, chiefly because of the popular ballads that were sung about them. One of these occurred on the Toledo, Peoria and Western line near Chatsworth, Illinois, on August 10, 1887. That afternoon a crew had been burning weeds along the tracks at Piper City Culvert, a ravine spanned by a small wooden bridge about two and a half miles from Chatsworth. Prairie fires were a threat to trains during the summer months, and the railroad tried to protect its tracks by burning out vegetation around them. Foreman Timothy Coughlan told his track laborers to be sure the fires were completely stamped out before they left for the day. After their departure, the area around the culvert was deserted for hours. An excursion train to Niagara Falls, New York, was due to pass along the track later that night.

The Niagara Falls special, with fifteen cars drawn by two engines, left Peoria at 8:00 P.M. and picked up more passengers at stations on the way. In all, there were nearly a thou-

An artist who was dispatched to the scene of the "Angola Horror" created a visual image of the burning railroad car for the weekly newspaper. Publicity given to the terrible accident led to the standardization of railroad gauges in the United States.

sand people on the train. After passing through Chatsworth, the engineer in the first locomotive noticed a small fire burning ahead of him but thought it must have been someone burning leaves. He had almost reached the culvert before he saw that the bridge itself was on fire. It was too late to stop. His engine made it across, but the flaming bridge disintegrated under the second engine, which fell into the culvert along with six of the cars. Two other cars were derailed before they reached the bridge. The engineer who reached the other side went on to Piper City, where he reported the accident and returned with help three-quarters of an hour later.

Meanwhile, many of those who had not been hurt did their best to free the injured from the overturned passenger coaches. Some of the survivors were thankful; others were angry. Among the latter was E. N. Armstrong, the general superintendent of the railroad, whose private car was attached to the end of the train. When Tim Coughlan arrived on the scene, Armstrong furiously accused him of being responsible for what had happened. A subsequent inquiry did censure Coughlan but also criticized the company's practice of burning along the tracks. To commemorate this tragedy, an anonymous balladeer wrote a song called "The Chatsworth Wreck" in the lugubrious style of the period. It ended with the words; "The bridge was burned at Chatsworth, and a hundred lives were lost." The actual toll was eighty-two.

Equally famous was the wreck of Old 97, a Southern Railway mail train that ran between Washington, D.C., and Atlanta, Georgia, from 1902 to 1907. In that short time it became a great favorite with the people who lived along its route. What made the train immortal was an accident that occurred on the stretch between Monroe, Virginia, and Spencer, North Carolina, on Sept. 17, 1903. The hero of the episode was engineer Joseph A. (Steve) Broady, who took over the throttle when Old 97 stopped at Monroe. The run was an hour late, which was considered unacceptable for a mail train, and Broady was expected to try to make up the time on the way to Spencer. As a result, he was traveling much too fast when he reached the curve leading to the Stillhouse Trestle outside of Danville, Virginia. Broady ignored the sign directing him to reduce speed. His engine jumped the tracks going around the curve and landed in the mud a hundred feet from the trestle, with five cars strung out behind it. In a few moments, cinders from the locomotive's firebox set the mail cars ablaze. Broady and twelve others were killed.

A ballad called "The Wreck of Old 97" was popular among the mountain people of Virginia and North Carolina for many years. Three different men claimed to have written it, and later, when it was recorded and used in the motion picture *Scarface*, it became the subject of a legal battle that dragged on for more than a decade, reaching all the way to the Supreme Court in 1939. The Court refused to consider the

On August 10, 1887, the second locomotive on the Niagara Falls special fell into a ravine near Chatsworth, Illinois, dragging six cars behind it, derailing two more, and killing 82 persons. Unhurt passengers help their injured relatives and companions (above), and later the debris from the wreck is cleared away (below).

case, and the question of authorship was never settled.

It is a curious fact that American folklore seems to have a special fondness for engineers whose trains were destroyed because they were going too fast. Broady was one of these. But an even more familiar example is John Luther (Casey) Jones, the engineer of the Illinois Central fast mail train Number One, "The Cannonball," who died when he plowed into another train at Vaughan, Mississippi, on April 30, 1900. Because Jones was the only fatality in that crash, however, it cannot be considered a major disaster—except insofar as he himself was concerned.

The Tay Bridge Disaster

Great Britain, where railroads originated, also had its share of accidents in the early years. The most spectacular, like many of those in the United States, took place on a bridge.

The first bridge across the estuary of Scotland's Tay River was considered a marvel of modern engineering. Its designer and most persistent advocate was Thomas Bouch, who had built several bridges and viaducts in England before spanning the Tay. He came to Scotland in 1849 as the traffic manager for the Edinburgh and Northern Railway. In those days, travelers going from Edinburgh to Dundee had to cross the Forth Estuary by boat, transfer to a train, and then transfer back to a ferry to cross the Tay. Although the two cities were only forty-six miles apart, the journey took more than three hours. Bouch argued that bridges should be built over the Forth and the Tay so that the trip could be made quickly and comfortably by rail all the way. Although the idea was repeatedly rejected because of its expense, he continued to promote it for two decades.

In 1870 the North British Railway, successor of the Edinburgh and Northern, finally agreed to finance Bouch's project, even though there was still considerable opposition to the proposal among the public. The Tay Bridge was to be constructed first. The Tay Estuary at Dundee was more than a mile wide, and no bridge of that length had ever been built before. Many said it was impossible, especially since the mud and gravel that covered the bottom of the river offered a poor foundation. But after making some borings, Bouch claimed to have reached bedrock eighteen to twenty feet below the gravel. If the foundations were extended to the bedrock, he said, the bridge would stand firm. The citizens of Perth, farther up the Tay, feared that the bridge would make it impossible for seagoing vessels to ascend the river, thereby cutting off their trade. This objection was handled by agreeing to make the central part of the bridge high enough to allow shipping to pass under it.

Work on the structure began in 1871, but there were a good many delays before the bridge could be completed. The solid rock turned out to be much deeper in some places than Bouch had predicted, and artificial rock beds had to be constructed to support the piers. There were also a number of accidents in which a total of twenty workmen were killed. Nevertheless, little by little, the bridge was extended from the south shore of the estuary toward Dundee. The structure consisted of eighty-five separate spans, the highest of them nearly ninety feet above the surface of the water, each one supported by four iron piers or columns.

The bridge was finally completed in 1877. On September 26 of that year the first crossing was made by a trainload of dignitaries and their wives. Although it was a festive occasion, everyone was a little nervous. Halfway across there was a sudden jolt and the sound of splintering wood, and the ventilator housings were torn off the roof of the first carriage. The passengers leaped from their seats, and some of the women screamed. They were relieved to learn that the train had only run into some wooden staging the workmen had left on the track. The rest of the trip was made without incident.

Early in the following year, the bridge was inspected by Maj. Gen. Charles S. Hutchinson representing the Board of Trade, which was responsible for approving such facilities. Hutchinson went over every part of the structure before writing his report. He found no fault with the bridge but suggested that trains crossing it should observe a speed limit of twenty-five miles an hour. At the end of the report he added this note: "When again visiting the spot, I should wish, if possible, to have an opportunity of observing the effects of a high wind when a train of carriages is running over the bridge." Despite the frequency of gales in the Tay Estuary, this additional observation was unfortunately never made.

With the approval of the Board of Trade, regular passenger and freight service was inaugurated on June 1, 1878. The immediate result was a boost to the economy of the Dundee area and to the profits of the North British Railway Company. Later in the same month, Queen Victoria crossed the bridge on the way to Windsor Castle in England from her Scottish residence at Balmoral. Ships in the Tay fired salutes and bands played in her honor as the royal train passed through Dundee. The Queen was evidently impressed by what she saw because Thomas Bouch received a knighthood a few days later.

Before long, however, some people began to feel uneasy about the Tay Bridge and the way it was being used. Passengers noticed that the trains were frequently exceeding the speed limit of twenty-five miles an hour, and the bridge vibrated in an alarming manner in rough weather. Henry Noble, an ex-bricklayer employed by the railway company as an inspector for the bridge, found narrow cracks in the iron piers, some of them several feet in length. Noble reported the cracks to Bouch, who did not seem overly disturbed by the report but told Noble to have the faulty areas reinforced with iron bands. The repairs were carried out, and the bridge continued in use with no serious problems.

The month of December 1879 was remarkable for severe and stormy weather in the area, but during most of Sunday the twenty-eighth the skies were clear and the temperatures moderate. The people of Dundee enjoyed a relatively pleasant day for a change. Later in the afternoon, however, the barometric pressure fell rather suddenly, and around four o'clock it began to rain. By five o'clock a heavy gale was blowing, with winds of up to seventy-five miles an hour.

In deference to Scottish respect for the Sabbath, railway service was kept to a minimum on Sundays. A single train made the round trip from Dundee to Burntisland on the north shore of the Forth Estuary, leaving at 1:30 P.M. and starting back at 5:20. On this night the train reached St. Fort, the last station before the Tay Bridge, at about seven o'clock. The rain was coming down in torrents as the engine and five cars stopped at the platform to pick up people who were waiting to go to Dundee. A few minutes later the train passed the signal cabin at the south approach to the bridge. The signalmen watched it go by and saw its lights move across the bridge in the darkness. All at once there were several bright flashes, and the lights of the train disappeared. Alarmed, two signalmen ran onto the bridge to find out what had happened but were forced back by the howling gale. Then, as the two men ran back and forth along the shore peering out across the water, the moon broke through the clouds, revealing a terrible sight. The central portion of the bridge was gone.

Across the river in Dundee, stationmaster James Smith was puzzled when the 5:20 from Burntisland failed to arrive on time. He had received the signal indicating that it was on the bridge at 7:13. By 7:30 he was sure that something was wrong. James Roberts, a locomotive foreman, volunteered to go onto the bridge and investigate. Unable to stand up in the wind, he crawled out along the tracks on his hands and knees. After proceeding this way in the dark for a couple of hundred yards, he suddenly froze as he saw the rails ahead of him hanging down into the waters of the Tay. Beyond that was a thousand-yard gap, with only the stumps of twelve iron piers where the fallen section of the bridge had been. Roberts crawled back and reported to the stationmaster. There was

The Tay Bridge collapsed on the stormy evening of December 28, 1879, and all 75 persons aboard the 5:20 train from Burntisland to Dundee, Scotland, were lost in the icy waters of the estuary.

no longer any doubt about what had happened to the 5:20.

The next day, as thousands gathered on both shores to watch, local officials began searching the river for the bodies of the dead. With the primitive diving equipment then available, it was three days before they even found the wreckage of the train. Recovering the bodies took much longer. Seventy-five people had been on the train, and there were no survivors, but only forty-five of the bodies were ever found.

The news of the bridge's collapse galvanized Great Britain, and the Board of Trade appointed a court of inquiry to investigate the causes of the disaster. The facts that emerged from the inquiry were even more shocking. As travelers on the line had noticed, trains using the bridge had often exceeded the speed limit set by the board; in fact, they had been in the habit of racing boats across the Tay. The real surprise was the revelations about the construction and maintenance of the bridge. Workmen from the Wormit Foundry, where the iron for the structure had been cast, testified that faults in the iron columns destined for the bridge had frequently been filled with a substance called Beaumont Egg, which was made of "beeswax, fiddler's rosin, iron filings and lamp black." Sir Thomas Bouch and his associates had exercised little supervision over the work at the foundry; they had just assumed that the iron was of good quality. The court was also astonished to discover that Noble, the bridge's inspector, had no experience or qualifications for the job. Bouch himself, the last witness to testify, was forced to make the humiliating admission that he had neglected to allow for wind pressure when he designed the bridge. He died a few months later, a broken and discredited man.

The lessons learned from this fiasco were remembered in the construction of the second Tay Bridge, completed in 1887, and the Forth Bridge, which was opened in 1890. Both bridges are still in use today.

The Wartime Trains of Modane and Balvano

Although the improvement of safety standards in the twentieth century has helped to reduce the railroad accident rate, mishaps—sometimes very serious ones—have continued to occur. In terms of human lives, the worst train wreck on record was the crash of a World War I troop train at Modane, France, on December 12, 1917.

The train was greatly overloaded with more than 1,200 soldiers who were returning from the war front for Christmas leave. Before it got under way, the engineer objected to the unsafe overcrowding and refused to move the train. Only after he had been threatened by an army officer—first with a court-martial and then with execution for failure to carry out a wartime order—did the engineer begin the journey.

The engineer's premonition had been correct. Near the southeastern town of Modane the overweight train moved through the Mont Cenis Tunnel and down a steep grade. As it reached a sharp curve at the bottom of the grade, the train derailed; the cars fell onto one another in a deep gorge and burst into flames.

The French officially listed 543 persons as dead and 243 as injured. Other officials claimed, however, that nearly twice this number had died. (The engineer, who had tried to prevent the calamity, survived.) The accident occurred at a time when France's war morale was at a low ebb, and the full news of the tragedy was suppressed. Officials apparently felt that a disclosure of the details would be a reflection on the military. Only fifteen years later were the complete facts of the holiday accident made public.

Allied troops of World War II invaded Sicily in July 1943; by October they had won control of Italy as far north as Naples, and they spent the following winter trying to drive the Germans back toward Rome. In the area south of the war zone, civilian rail traffic came to a halt. All railroad equipment was seized by the Allied forces. People who had to travel got around by whatever means they could—legal or illegal. One of the most common ways was to steal a ride on one of the freight trains that went out from the cities to bring supplies in from the countryside. Railroad employees seldom hindered anyone from riding in empty boxcars.

There were forty-two such cars on Train 8017, which left Salerno for Potenza on the evening of March 2, 1944, as well as an engine, four coaches, and a caboose. A number of illegal passengers were forced off the train by MP's at one of the junctions outside Salerno, but many more piled on when it stopped at Eboli, Persano, and other towns along the way. Food was in short supply, and many of the hitchhikers were black-marketeers carrying cigarettes and chocolate purchased from British and American soldiers, which they planned to trade for meat, oil, eggs, wine, and other staples in the farm country around Potenza. With only one engine and so many unauthorized riders the overloaded train began to have difficulty making it up the steep grades when it got into the Appenine Mountains. To help out, a second locomotive was added at Romagnano.

Shortly after midnight 8017 reached the village of Balvano, when it had to stop and wait because another train was stalled on the single track ahead. The Balvano station is situated in an open area between two mountain tunnels, and during the wait, the last half of 8017 remained in the tunnel west of the station. The coal used to fire the two steam locomotives was the best that could be obtained under wartime conditions, but it was not very good, tending to give off an unusually large amount of carbon monoxide. There was no wind, and the tunnel was still full of smoke from the engines that had passed through.

It was nearly 1:00 A.M. before the track was cleared and the train moved slowly forward again. Between Balvano and the next station, Bella-Muro, there were two short tunnels, a viaduct, and a longer tunnel known as the Galleria delle Armi. It was on an upgrade and was nearly two miles in length. After the entire train had entered the tunnel the wheels of the two engines apparently began to lose traction. The train stopped, rolled back a few yards, and then stopped again, leaving half of the caboose outside the tunnel entrance. No one knows precisely the sequence of events, but within minutes the Galleria delle Armi was filled with smoke from the funnels of the engines, and most of the crew and passengers were asphyxiated by the poisonous carbon monoxide. The engineers were evidently among the first to die. Most of the passengers were asleep and just never woke up. Many of those who were awake were not aware of the danger and simply stayed where they were.

A brakeman in the caboose, curious as to the long delay, finally got out and walked into the dark tunnel. After finding dead bodies and realizing that the peculiar odor he smelled was gas, he dashed into the open air and across the viaduct. Sick and struggling to remain conscious, he inched along through the darkness, following the track back through the tunnel to the Balvano station where he blurted out the story of the disaster.

Police and rescue workers from Balvano, bringing with them another engine to pull the train out of the tunnel, and U.S. military personnel from Potenza, sixteen miles to the west, rushed to the scene. They were appalled by what they found. Car after car was filled with corpses; one had so many inside that the door would not slide open—it had to be broken off. Most of the dead, except for the traces of blood around their nostrils that indicated carbon monoxide poisoning, looked as though they were sleeping peacefully. In all, 521 persons were dead. The 193 of them who were unidentified were buried in three common graves near the Balvano station. At least six individuals are known to have survived, although there may have been more since most of the passengers would have been reluctant to admit that they had been on the train because of the penalties for violating regulations.

The story went almost unnoticed in the midst of the war news, but a U.S. military board of inquiry called it the most unusual catastrophe in the history of railroading since neither a derailment nor a collision had occured. Until 1959, when the use of steam locomotives was discontinued, special precautions were taken at the Galleria delle Armi to make certain that nothing of the sort happened again.

Commuter Collisions

One of the worst train wrecks of recent decades occured on the night of May 3, 1962, when a steam-driven freight train sideswiped a commuter train near Mikawashima Station, three miles north of the center of Tokyo. Several of the commuter cars were derailed, and as the dazed passengers were climbing out onto the tracks their train was hit by yet another, which was also carrying a full load of commuters. Many of those who had escaped from the derailed cars tried to get out of the way by jumping down a thirty-foot embankment alongside the tracks and were killed when carriages from the third train fell on them. Some of the bodies were found buried under five feet of earth.

The casualties among those inside the trains at the time of the second collision were aggravated by what was supposed to have been a safety measure. Following an accident some years before in which scores of people had been trapped inside a burning train, new doors designed to open automatically in case of emergency had been installed in all passenger cars. In the Mikawashima crash, many of the passengers were catapulted through the open doors to their deaths. Shoji Iwasaki, a young factory worker, described what had happened to him:

> When the first crash came, blue electric sparks filled the air, and then everything went dark. People stumbled about, wailing and screaming. I broke a window glass and jumped out and started to climb down the embankment. Then the other train came crashing into our wreckage. The leading car toppled down and pulled four others after it. . . . It was horrible.

In all, 163 persons were killed in the disaster, and more than 300 others were injured. Shinji Sogo, the president of Japan National Railways, was overcome with emotion when he made a public admission that the company had been at fault. The freight had run through a blocking signal before colliding with the first commuter train. Nine railwaymen were indicted for criminal negligence in connection with the crash.

Another commuter train collision occurred ten years later in Chicago. In the late 1960s the Illinois Central Gulf commuter railroad, which serves the Chicago metropolitan area, had not bought any new passenger cars for more than three decades. The cars it had in use, built in the mid-1920s, were for the most part still in good condition and were well maintained. But the company, which was being forced by rising costs to increase its fares, felt that it should make some effort

A rescue team searches for victims of a commuter railway collision in Tokyo, Japan, on May 4, 1962, the day after a fatal crash killed 163 persons.

to modernize. It contracted to purchase 130 double-deck commuter cars from General Steel Industries, Inc. The new cars were more elaborate than the old ones and were air conditioned, but they were lighter in weight and were generally less sturdy. The first cars were put in service in June 1971. About sixteen months later, on October 30, 1972, a new four-car double-deck commuter train was headed for the Randolph Street Station in Chicago's Loop during the morning rush hour. About three miles south of the Loop, the motorman overshot the platform at a station, stopped, and backed up to allow passengers to board. As he was doing so, the train was hit from the rear by a train of six of the older heavyweight cars. The lead car of the train coming from behind rammed through the last of the double-deckers, virtually demolishing it. The older car was relatively undamaged. The weight of the older train caused the newer, lighter cars to telescope into one another.

It was the passengers in the rear car of the newer train who received the full impact of the crash. Bodies were mangled in the wreckage; some were impaled on pieces of twisted steel. One passenger said, " . . . the other train was inside our car. When I looked down, the floor was gone. It was just twisted steel with arms and legs sticking out." Firemen were called to the scene, and they were joined by the staff members of a hospital located only a few blocks away. Assisted by the medical personnel, the firemen began the difficult task of freeing the injured and removing the dead, a process that took as long as five hours. Another passenger later said to reporters that "some of the passengers tried to dig out those trapped. It was terrible. Those that were pinned in just kept screaming."

The firemen did not know that the windows of the new cars could be opened by prying them from above. When they broke the windows in order to gain access to the cars, the flying glass caused additional injuries. Holes were cut in the two most heavily damaged cars; doctors and nurses entered with the firemen and gave emergency treatment to some of the injured. One doctor said that "human limbs were hanging out of windows. . . . About the only thing doctors and nurses could do at the scene was apply tourniquets and splints, and give sedatives." Forty-five persons were killed and about 350 were injured in the accident, the first involving any fatalities on the Illinois Central since 1926.

In many ways the Illinois Central accident was symptomatic of the problems faced by most American railroads in the 1970s. A declining volume of business coupled with rising costs frequently necessitated economies that posed new safety hazards and increased the risk of accidents. The subsequent report of the National Transportation Safety Board indicated that the newer Illinois Central cars were not, in fact, safe. Tests showed that posts at the end of the cars were not substantial enough to absorb the impact of a high-speed crash.

But the agency's final report also indicated that human error—specifically the failure to follow established safety regulations—had contributed to the Illinois Central crash. The second train had been traveling too fast, perhaps ten miles over the limit for the conditions. The inability of the engineer to see the train ahead of him was also a factor.

The first train, however, had violated an even more serious rule in backing up. Railroad signals show an approaching

On October 30, 1972, in Chicago, 45 passengers were killed and 350 were injured as an old-style lead car on the Illinois Central Gulf commuter line rammed into a new double-deck car on a commuter train that was backing into the station. Firemen (above) work to free survivors from the wreckage as policemen (below) administer first aid to the injured.

train whether the signal block or section of track ahead is occupied (red), has been cleared only recently by a train ahead (yellow), or is completely clear (green). If a train backs into a block that it has just left it is required to send a flagman to the rear to warn oncoming traffic—a safety rule that grew out of early rail accidents in similar circumstances.

When the first train backed up, reentering the block it had just left, it triggered a red signal at the entrance to that block. The second train, however, had already entered the block while a yellow signal showed it was unoccupied. In failing to dispatch a flagman to the rear, the backing train neglected the single action that might have prevented the crash.

Other Train Wrecks, 1959–78

1959

May 28

Western Java. A passenger train plunged into a ravine, killing 91 persons.

June 5

São Paulo, Brazil. The collision of two trains killed at least 60 persons and injured an estimated 200.

June 18

Rio de Janeiro, Brazil. A train collision killed 12 persons and injured at least 30 others.

July 6

Sivas, Turkey. A collision of two freight trains killed 10 persons.

Aug. 27

Near Banja Luka, Yugoslavia. A train plunged into a river, killing 14 passengers and injuring 42 others.

Dec. 17

Cañada de Gómez, Argentina. A bus-train collision killed 13 persons and injured 24.

Dec. 24

Near Freetown, Sierra Leone. A railway crash killed 13 persons.

1960

Jan. 5

Monza, Italy. A train derailment killed 15 persons.

Jan. 6

Opole, Poland. A train rammed a bus, killing 16 persons.

Feb. 1

Near Devon, South Africa. A freight train rammed a standing passenger train; there were 15 reported deaths.

Feb. 7

Sewell, Chile. A train jumped the rails on a steep incline, killing 25 persons.

March 1

Bakersfield, California. A passenger train collided with an oil tank truck, killing a reported 14 persons and injuring 55 others.

May 15

Leipzig, Germany. A collision of an express train with a local killed 59 persons.

Nov. 14

Near Steblova, Czechoslovakia. Two passenger trains traveling at high speed collided, killing 110 persons.

1961

Jan. 9

Near Barcelona, Spain. The head-on collision of an express and a freight train killed at least 25 persons and injured more than 50 others.

June 13

Esslingen, West Germany. Two local trains collided, killing at least 34 passengers.

June 18

Near Vitry-le-François, France. The Strasbourg–Paris express jumped the tracks and plunged down a 30-foot embankment; 24 persons were killed, and more than 100 were injured.

Aug. 27

Northwest Moravia, Czechoslovakia. A train crash killed 18 persons and injured 10 others.

Oct. 4

Hamburg, Germany. A suburban passenger train rammed into a halted train loaded with bridge-building material; 33 persons died, and 31 others were injured.

Oct. 20

Near Calcutta, India. A train derailment, about 135 miles west of the city, killed more than 50 passengers and injured 300 others.

Dec. 23

Catanzaro, Italy. The rear coach of a two-car interurban train broke loose on a bridge and fell 100 feet into the Fiumarella River gorge; 71 persons were killed, and 30 others were injured.

1962

Jan. 8

Woerden, The Netherlands. An express speeding through dense fog rammed into a commuter train; 91 persons died, and almost 200 others were injured.

Feb. 22

Near Cali, Colombia. The head-on collision of a freight and a passenger train killed 40 persons; 67 others were injured.

March 8

Castel Bolognese, Italy. A speeding express jumped the tracks; at least 12 persons were killed, and more than 100 were injured.

May 31

Voghera, Italy. The halted Milan–Genoa express was rammed by a speeding freight train; at least 63 persons were killed, and more than 20 others were injured.

July 21

Buxar, India. The Amritsar–Howrah fast mail train rammed into a standing freight, killing 69 persons.

July 22

Bucharest, Romania. A passenger train jumped the tracks in speeding around a curve; 32 persons were killed, and 54 others were injured.

July 23

Dijon, France. The Paris–Marseilles express, crowded with 900 vacationers, derailed on a viaduct; one coach plunged 160 feet into a deep ravine, killing 40 persons.

July 28

Steelton, Pennsylvania. Derailment of a baseball excursion train bound for Philadelphia caused three cars to plunge into the Susquehanna River; 20 persons died, and about 116 others were injured.

Sept. 18

Belo Horizonte, Brazil. One coach of a passenger train jumped the tracks, killing 13 persons and injuring 40 others.

Oct. 2

Kroonstad, South Africa. A passenger train jumped the tracks, killing 17 persons.

Oct. 2

Potchefstroom, South Africa. A passenger train collided

head-on with a freight; 12 persons were killed, and 12 others were injured.

Oct. 5

Moszczenica, Poland. A Balkan–Poland express train en route to Warsaw jumped the tracks, and as passengers detrained and swarmed over the adjoining tracks they were plowed into by the Chopin express headed for Vienna; 34 persons were killed, and 67 others were injured.

Nov. 5

Kabanovce, Yugoslavia. A Belgrade–Skoplje train jumped the tracks, killing 27 persons; 17 others were injured.

Nov. 12

Northern India. Passengers riding on the roof of an overcrowded train were swept off by a low girder of an overhead bridge; all 25 were killed.

Dec. 20

Buena Vista, Guatemala. A speeding freight rammed into a stationary passenger train, killing 20 persons and injuring 41 others.

Dec. 26

Minshull Vernon, England. The London-bound Scot express crashed into the rear of another passenger train standing at the station; 18 persons were killed, and at least 60 others were injured.

1963

Jan. 4

Katihar, India. A fast mail train crashed into a standing passenger train, causing an explosion and fire; 38 persons were killed, and 90 others were injured.

March 18

Rio de Janeiro, Brazil. A crowd protesting a delay in train service swarmed over the tracks and interfered with the operation of signals to stop an oncoming train, which plowed into the mob and killed 12 persons, injuring 5 others.

April 11

Jakarta, Indonesia. A derailment caused by faulty brakes plunged the engine and a coach of the Jakarta–Bandung express into a 200-foot ravine; 37 persons were killed, and 126 others were injured.

July 13

Surabaja, Indonesia. A passenger train coach was derailed by a faulty switch; 21 persons were killed, and 40 others were injured.

Aug. 2
Montevideo, Uruguay. A passenger train ran through an open switch and crashed into a string of freight cars on a siding; at least 30 persons were killed, and another 100 were injured.
Nov. 9
Yokohama, Japan. A passenger train en route to Tokyo crashed into a derailed freight, jumped the tracks, and rammed a moving commuter train; 162 persons were killed, and at least 70 others were injured.
Dec. 24
Szolnok, Hungary. A passenger train carrying holiday crowds rammed into a standing freight, unseen in a dense fog; 43 persons were killed, and at least 36 others were injured.

1964
Jan. 1
Cairo, Egypt. A suburban train crashed into the side of a bus at a crossing, killing 32 persons and injuring 22 others.
Jan. 4
Jajinci, Yugoslavia. A crowded commuter train bound for Belgrade rammed into a passenger train stalled on the tracks; 66 persons were killed, and at least 300 were injured.
Feb. 1
Altamirano, Argentina. The "Firefly Express," en route to Buenos Aires with more than 1,000 homeward-bound vacationers, piled head-on into a standing freight; both engines exploded, and two of the passenger coaches burned completely; an estimated 70 persons were killed, and 70 were hospitalized.
March 8
Bhadrakh, India. A two-train head-on collision at Baudpur station killed 22 persons and injured 30 others.
April 30
Western Java. A night train jumped the tracks and plowed into a ravine, killing 21 persons and injuring 108 others.
July 26
Oporto, Portugal. A train carrying weekend visitors from the seaside resort of Pòvoa de Varzim derailed, killing 94 persons; at least 78 others were injured.
July 29
Randfontein, South Africa. Derailment of a speeding passenger train brought death to 21 persons.
Nov. 1
Near Langhagen, East Germany. Overrunning a stop signal

at full throttle, a freight train crashed into the oncoming Berlin–Rostock express; at least 39 persons were killed, and more than 100 were injured.

Nov. 30

Saigon, South Vietnam. A locomotive idling with no one at the controls suddenly started up and crashed through the main station building and into a waiting crowd, killing at least 17 persons.

Dec. 20

Tacotalpa, Mexico. Surrounded by dense fog, a sleepy engineer rammed his freight train into a standing passenger train, killing 41 persons and injuring 75 others.

1965

Feb. 10

Saragossa, Spain. Three wooden coaches of the Madrid–Barcelona mail train were destroyed by fire; at least 30 persons died, and 33 others were injured.

Feb. 20

Skultorp, Sweden. A speeding express rammed into a halted train, killing 10 persons; 51 others were hospitalized.

Feb. 26

Near Port Sudan, Sudan. A passenger train collided with a freight; at least 15 persons were killed.

March 29

Nova Iguassu, Brazil. A commuter train smashed into a derailed freight, killing 21 persons and injuring 40 others.

April 5

Paraíba do Sul, Brazil. A head-on collision between a passenger train and a freight killed 40 persons.

April 11

Mage, Brazil. A speeding passenger train crashed into a bus, killing at least 20 persons.

June 16

Luzon, Philippines. A head-on collision of two trains killed 10 persons.

Aug. 28

Pont d'Héry, France. The Milan–Paris express rammed into the rear of the Lombardy express, halted in the station; 12 persons were killed, and 32 others were hospitalized.

Oct. 4

Durban, South Africa. Derailment of the last three coaches of a rush-hour commuter train killed at least 81 persons; another 130 were injured.

Dec. 8

Toungoo, Burma. The Rangoon–Mandalay night passenger-mail express rammed into a standing freight train, killing more than 80 persons and injuring 100 others.

Dec. 18

Villar de Los Alamos, Spain. A head-on collision between the Paris–Lisbon express and a local train killed 30 persons and injured 60 others.

Dec. 20

Algoeirão, Portugal. A Lisbon commuter train crashed into a freight; at least 22 persons died, and 12 others were seriously injured.

1966

Feb. 14

Near Rangoon, Burma. A speeding passenger train jumped the tracks and plunged into a deep ravine; at least 22 persons were killed.

Feb. 16

Northeastern India. Two time bombs exploded in the mail coach of the Assam express train in the Indian state of Nāgāland; 36 persons were killed, and 53 others were injured.

Feb. 16

Split, Yugoslavia. Brake failure caused a nineteen-car coal train to collide with a passenger train; at least 29 persons were killed, and 27 others were injured.

April 20

Lumding, India. An explosion blasted a passenger train stopping at the junction; at least 64 persons died, and 120 others were injured.

April 23

Diphu, India. The second passenger train explosion in Assam within three days killed 40 persons and injured 60 others.

May 26

Near Belgaum, India. An express train sped off the rails, killing 22 passengers and injuring 20 others.

May 31

Near Bucharest, Romania. A collision between the Bucharest–Galati express and a local train killed 38 persons and injured 65 others.

June 13

Bombay, India. Two suburban trains collided on the outskirts of the city; 65 persons were killed, and 200 others were injured.

Oct. 12

Hyderabad, India. A passenger train rammed into a freight train; 70 persons died, and another 65 were injured.

Oct. 21

Cosne-sur-Loire, France. The last car of the Montagis–Nevers local train jumped the tracks and toppled over; 10 persons were killed, and 15 others were injured.

Oct. 23

Lakhisarai, India. A nonstop express plowed into a group of passengers crossing the tracks to the station as they left a halted train; 35 persons died, and at least 12 others were injured.

Nov. 11

Siliguri, India. Derailment of a troop train killed 14 persons and injured 35 others.

Nov. 16

Nilópolis, Brazil. Two high-speed commuter trains crashed head-on when one engineer failed to heed a signal; 34 persons died, and at least 100 others were injured.

Dec. 17

Near Bombay, India. A passenger train jumped the tracks and toppled down a 20-foot embankment; 18 persons died, and 50 others were injured.

Dec. 18

Teruel, Spain. A two-car diesel train slammed into a freight obscured by fog; the burning wreckage claimed 28 lives.

Dec. 28

Everett, Massachusetts. A one-car train collided with an oil truck stalled on a crossing; 12 passengers died, and 18 others were injured.

1967

July 6

Langenweddingen, East Germany. A double-deck commuter train demolished a 4,000-gallon-capacity gasoline tanker truck as it pulled into an unguarded grade crossing; the ensuing explosion and fire killed 83 persons (including 44 children) and injured more than 50 others.

Aug. 10

Fyn Island, Denmark. A speeding passenger train slammed into the rear of another passenger train as it stood on an overpass; 14 persons were killed, and at least 45 others were injured.

Sept. 10

Ndola, Zambia. A freight train ran into the rear of a passenger-freight and killed at least 11 persons.

Sept. 28

Alipur Duar, India. A train derailment brought death to 14 persons and injury to 38 others.

Oct. 4

Fexhe-le-haut-Clocher, Belgium. A passenger train, slowly pulling away from the station, was struck from the rear by a second passenger train; the first train's engine was thrown onto adjacent tracks and into the path of the oncoming Brussels express, traveling at 75 mph; in the tangle of wrecked coaches at least 12 persons perished, and 75 others were injured.

Nov. 5

London, England. The Hastings–London electric express struck a broken rail and hurtled off the tracks at Hither Green in south London; 49 passengers were killed, and 78 were injured.

1968

Jan. 1

Northeastern Transvaal, South Africa. A two-train collision killed at least 13 persons; 25 others were injured.

Jan. 6

Hixon, England. A Manchester–London express traveling at 70 mph over a grade crossing struck a truck loaded with a 125-ton transformer; 13 train passengers were killed, and 50 others were injured.

Jan. 27

Fanfa, Brazil. A combined passenger-freight train and an all-freight crashed into one another at the station; at least 40 persons were killed, and 60 others were injured.

Feb. 16

New Delhi, India. The crack New Delhi–Calcutta express plowed into a group of pilgrims on the way to bathe in the sacred waters of the Ganges River; 16 persons were killed.

March 18

Hubli, India. A speeding express crashed into a standing passenger train and killed 52 persons.

Sept. 30

Corinth, Greece. A stationary passenger train was rammed by another crowded express; 10 persons died, and at least 100 others were injured.

Dec. 22

Near Budapest, Hungary. A head-on collision between a heavy freight and a fast passenger train caused death or injury to over 100 persons.

1969
Jan. 31

Ch'onan, South Korea. An engineer failed to see a red signal light obscured by blinding snow and rammed his Seoulbound express into the rear of another passenger train stopped on the tracks; at least 135 persons were killed, and 102 others were injured.

Feb. 4

Tamil Nadu State, India. As a train glided beneath the girders of a bridge, 28 persons died when they were swept off the roof upon which they were riding.

Feb. 7

Violet Town, Australia. A head-on collision of the Sydney–Melbourne passenger express and a freight train, both traveling at 60 mph, killed at least 10 persons and injured 85 others.

March 21

São Paulo, Brazil. A packed electric train halted by a power failure was plowed into by a locomotive coming to its aid when the power surged on suddenly; 30 to 40 persons were killed, and 300 were injured.

March 25

La Louvière, Belgium. Early morning mist caused two passenger trains to crash head on; 20 persons died, and 70 others were injured.

June 21

Near Benares, India. A ten-coach train jumped the tracks as it passed over a bridge across the Maghai River; 60 persons perished, and at least 150 others were injured.

June 22

Hanover-Linden, West Germany. A railroad car loaded with ammunition exploded as the train was stopped at the suburban station; at least 12 firemen and railroad workers were killed, 3 others were missing, and 10 were injured.

July 15

Near Cuttack, India. A train filled with pilgrims on their way to Puri for the "juggernaut" festival was halted by a passenger who pulled the emergency brake to get off where there was no stop; before the train could get under way it was rammed from the rear by a speeding freight; at least 81 persons were killed, and more than 150 others were injured.

1970

Feb. 1

General Pacheco Station, Argentina. A cross-country express traveling at 65 mph rammed into the rear of a commuter train stalled on the Bartolomé Mitre tracks 18 miles north of Buenos Aires; 141 persons died, and 179 others were injured.

Feb. 16

Kaduna, Nigeria. A train wreck south of the town claimed the lives of at least 80 persons; an additional 52 injured passengers were killed when a truck transporting them to a hospital crashed.

Aug. 9

Plencia, Spain. The head-on collision of two trains at the Plencia station killed 40 persons and injured 136 others.

Aug. 22

Tamouh, Egypt. An Aswan–Cairo express train overturned and killed 13 persons; 54 others were injured.

Oct. 31

Near Johannesburg, South Africa. A crammed passenger train ran into the rear of an equally crowded commuter train, killing 13 persons and injuring more than 100 others.

Dec. 27

Belo Horizonte, Brazil. Two passenger trains fell from the tracks and plunged into a ravine, killing 17 persons and injuring 25 others.

1971

Feb. 9

Aitrang, West Germany. The Trans-Europe Bavarian express jumped the tracks and killed 28 persons; 35 others were injured.

Feb. 14

Near Zenica, Yugoslavia. The engine of a local passenger train caught fire as the train was passing through the Vranduk tunnel; ensuing flames and gas fumes killed at least 34 persons and injured 113 others.

May 27

Near Wuppertal, West Germany. A two-coach train returning a senior class group from an outing was rammed head-on by a freight as it rounded a blind curve between Oberbarmen and Radevormwald; of the 46 persons killed, 41 were students.

June 10

Tonti, Illinois. An Amtrak southbound streamliner traveling

up to 95 mph tore up 1,200 feet of track as it derailed into a twisted mass of flame and metal; 11 persons were killed, and 164 others were injured.

July 6

Mograhat, India. A collision of two trains resulting from the theft of electrical wires from the interstation communications system brought death to at least 16 persons and injured 50 others.

July 21

Near Karlsruhe, West Germany. The Switzerland express with 300 to 400 passengers aboard derailed on a curve and killed at least 25 persons; about 100 others were injured.

Aug. 4

Belgrade, Yugoslavia. A six-car passenger train collided with a freight, possibly due to poor visibility after a heavy rainstorm, about 16 miles south of the city; at least 40 persons perished in the wreckage, and 100 others were injured.

Oct. 25

Near Tsu, Japan. Two electric-powered passenger trains collided in a single-track tunnel, killing at least 23 persons; 9 others were missing, and at least 214 received injuries.

1972

Jan. 16

Larissa, Greece. A head-on collision between an international express and a freight train killed 15 persons and injured at least 60 others.

March 31

Potgietersrus, South Africa. A nine-coach passenger train jumped the tracks as it passed over a small bridge; 38 persons died, and another 174 were injured.

June 4

Jessore, Bangladesh. A crowded passenger train running at full speed was misdirected as it entered the station and crunched into a stopped train, killing at least 76 persons; more than 500 others were injured.

June 16

Vierzy, France. A partial collapse of the Vierzy railway tunnel caused the derailment of a six-coach Paris–Laon train when it piled into the heaps of debris; about an hour later a Laon–Paris express entered the opposite end of the tunnel at 60 mph and smashed into the first jackknifed train; at least 107 persons were killed, and about 90 others were injured.

July 21

Lebrija, Spain. The fourteen-coach Madrid–Cádiz holiday express with 500 passengers collided head-on with a four-coach local that had apprently run a red signal light a few miles down the track; 76 of the 200 persons riding the local were killed, 103 others were injured.

Aug. 6

Liaquatpur, Pakistan. A passenger train bound for Karachi from Rawalpindi plowed into the rear of a freight train standing at the Liaquatpur station and killed 57 passengers; more than 100 others were injured.

Sept. 29

Malmesbury, South Africa. Seven coaches of the Cape Town–Bittefontein train jumped the tracks in rounding a curve and threw three cars and the locomotive over a steep embankment; 48 persons died, and more than 150 others were injured.

Oct. 5

Saltillo, Mexico. Speeding downhill, a 22-coach passenger train carrying pilgrims returning from a religious fiesta at the Shrine of St. Francis in Catorce swerved off the tracks, overturned, and caught fire; 208 persons perished in the wreckage, and almost 700 others were injured.

Oct. 30

Karl-Marx-Stadt, East Germany. Two East German passenger trains collided, killing 25 persons and injuring 70 others.

Oct. 31

Eskisehir, Turkey. A Konya–Istanbul passenger train sped head-on into a track-repair train and burst into flames, killing at least 30 persons; dozens of others were severely injured.

Dec. 10

Venchan, Bulgaria. A Sofia–Tolbukhin passenger train slammed into a stationary freight, killing 26 passengers.

1973

Feb. 1

Medjez-Sfa, Algeria. A train running down a slope 50 miles from the Tunisian border crashed and killed 35 persons; 30 others were injured.

Feb. 16

Megara, Greece. A passenger train jumped the tracks and overturned, killing at least 10 persons and injuring 17.

March 16

Las Villas Province, Cuba. Derailment of a Santiago de Cuba–Havana passenger train as it crossed a bridge near Santa Clara caused one car to fall into the river; 24 of the 400 passengers were killed, and 31 others were injured.

Dec. 19

Ealing, England. A crowded express commuter train returning to Oxford from London with Christmas shoppers left the tracks, plowed into an embankment, and overturned; 14 of the 600 aboard were killed, and 40 were injured.

1974

Jan. 7

Zeytinlik, Turkey. Two passenger trains collided at a station in southern Turkey, killing at least 25 persons and injuring some 50 others.

March 27

Near Lourenço Marques, Mozambique. A Mozambique freight train, loaded with petroleum products, collided with a Rhodesian passenger train about 31 miles north of the Mozambique capital; of the estimated 60 persons who died, most were burned to death in a raging fire; about 50 others were hospitalized in serious condition.

May 29

Rio de Janeiro, Brazil. Two suburban freight trains passing each other created a powerful slipstream that tore loose the grip of habitual free riders clinging to the sides of the cars; 16 persons were killed, and many others were injured.

June 17

Banha, Egypt. A crowded train bound for Alexandria collided with a truck at the Banha crossing, about 30 miles from Cairo; 18 persons died, and more than 98 others were injured.

Aug. 30

Zagreb, Yugoslavia. An eight-car passenger train derailed when the engineer, probably dozing with fatigue, failed to slow the train down as it swept into Zagreb station and hit a curve; 124 persons were reported killed, and about 100 others were injured.

Dec. 20

Near Bamako, Mali. A speeding passenger train jumped the tracks as it rounded a curve before entering Bamako station; 20 persons were killed, and 180 were injured.

1975

Jan. 18

Egypt. A train, so overcrowded that some passengers were

riding on the locomotive, derailed north of Cairo while traveling at great speed; 27 persons were killed, and more than 50 were injured.

Feb. 17
South Africa. An express train traveling from Cape Town to Johannesburg crashed into a freight train, killing 16 persons and injuring about 30 others.

Feb. 22
Near Tretten, Norway. Two twelve-car trains carrying mostly skiers to and from a winter resort crashed head-on when neither pulled onto a siding to let the other pass; 27 of the 800 passengers lost their lives.

Feb. 28
London, England. A six-car subway train roared into Moorgate station during the morning rush hour, plowed through a barrier of sand at full speed, then struck the dead-end wall of the tunnel with devastating impact; the disaster took 41 lives.

March 25
Argentina. A freight train heading for Paraná, 300 miles northeast of Buenos Aires, lost traction on a hill and rolled backward into a passenger train; 12 persons died, and 30 were injured.

March 31
Linköping, Sweden. An automobile was demolished at a railroad crossing by an oncoming express train, which derailed on impact; at least 14 persons were killed, and 39 were injured.

June 8
Near Munich, West Germany. Two passenger trains traveling in opposite directions on a one-track section of the Munich–Bad Toelz line crashed with such violence that several cars telescoped on impact; at least 25 persons died, and more than 50 were injured, some critically.

July 17
Near Rio de Janeiro, Brazil. A speeding commuter train carrying over 1,000 passengers left the track and hurtled into a suburban dance school; the death toll was estimated at 30 and the number of injured at more than 200.

July 19
Near Belgrade, Yugoslavia. A fast-moving express train crashed into the back of a passenger train standing motionless in a suburban station; 16 persons were killed, and 37 were injured.

Sept. 29

Near Río Lujan, Argentina. A collision involving two passenger trains about 35 miles from Buenos Aires killed some 30 persons and injured about 16 others.

Oct. 20

Mexico City, Mexico. A subway train carrying work-bound commuters into Mexico City smashed into another train that was standing motionless at a station stop; more than 20 persons died, and dozens were severely injured.

Dec. 14

Fornos de Algodres, Portugal. A Lisbon express heading for Paris, France, crashed headlong into a train carrying migrant workers home from France for the Christmas holidays; at least 16 persons were killed, and some 60 were injured.

1976

Feb. 17

Near Alexandria, Egypt. At least 11 persons died when a speeding train smashed into a train that was not in motion; about 50 other persons were seriously injured.

Late February

Near Caborca, Mexico. A collision between a train and a bus killed 30 persons and injured 50 others.

April 21

Near Ta-ch'eng, Taiwan. An express train that crashed into a bus in central Taiwan killed 40 persons.

April 27

Northeast Egypt. A collision between two trains about 90 miles from Cairo took the lives of 12 persons and injured more than 50 others.

May 4

Schiedam, The Netherlands. The ten-coach Rhine Express, on a run from the Hook of Holland to West Germany and Austria, crashed head-on into a slowly moving local train during the morning rush hour. All 23 fatalities, some of them children, were aboard the badly damaged Dutch train.

May 23

Near Seoul, Korea. A truck loaded with 200 drums of fuel oil exploded in flames after striking a commuter train; flaming oil was mainly responsible for killing 19 persons and injuring 95 others.

June 14

Jasen, Bulgaria. A passenger train collided with a freight train about 100 miles from Sofia, killing 10 persons and injuring 3.

June 27

On May 23 a truck carrying fuel oil exploded after colliding with a commuter train near Seoul, South Korea.

Neufvilles, Belgium. A crowded express train traveling from Amsterdam, The Netherlands, to Paris, France, jumped the tracks in southern Belgium; 11 persons were killed.
Sept. 6
Benoni, South Africa. A commuter train crashed into an express train that had halted for a red light at the Benoni station 16 miles from Johannesburg; most of the 31 fatalities and 70 injured were aboard the express train.
Sept. 9
Cameroon. Two passenger trains collided in southern Cameroon; though initial reports were sketchy, more than 100 persons were feared killed and about 300 injured.
Sept. 20
Near Ljubljana, Yugoslavia. An express train traveling to Trieste collided head-on with a local passenger train; at least 17 persons were killed and about 40 others were injured.
Oct. 10
Northwestern Mexico. A glass-domed passenger train traveling through scenic Sierra Madre Occidental slammed into a freight train after the engineer failed to heed a stop signal; the Red Cross reported 24 fatalities.
Nov. 3
Near Czestochowa, Poland. A passenger train, making a scheduled stop at the small town of Julianka, was struck by

an express train during a heavy fog; 25 persons were killed.

Nov. 10

Near Zagreb, Yugoslavia. An express train, speeding past a crossing that had not been closed off by the attendant, crashed into the back half of a bus, killing 10 passengers.

Nov. 29

Near Kathekani, Kenya. An express train traveling from Mombasa to Nairobi plunged into the Ngaineithia River when the weight of the train caused a bridge, already weakened by swirling floodwaters, to give way; of the nearly 650 persons aboard, 14 were killed, and about 200 were injured.

1977

Jan. 18

Near Sydney, New South Wales, Australia. A commuter train derailed and rammed into a steel bridge pier causing 500-ton concrete deck slabs from the overhead roading to collapse onto the third and fourth cars of the train, flattening them like matchboxes; 82 persons were killed.

Feb. 4

Chicago, Illinois. A Dan Ryan route elevated train, rounding a curve during the early-evening rush hour, smashed into a halted Ravenswood route train in Chicago's Loop; two cars

The Mombasa–Nairobi express derailed on November 29 and plunged into the floodwaters of the Ngaineithia River, Kenya.

Two crowded elevated train cars tumbled from the tracks during the evening rush hour on February 4 in Chicago.

of the Dan Ryan train crashed 30 feet onto the street below, and two others dangled precariously from the metal structure; 11 persons were killed and 189 were treated for injuries.

Feb. 28
Near Barcelona, Spain. Two suburban commuter trains filled to capacity crashed head-on near San Andrés de la Barca some 20 miles west of Barcelona, in a collision so intense that the engine and first passenger car of one train bounced atop the two cars of the other train; the casualty list included 2 engineers and 22 passengers killed and 85 commuters injured.

May 2
Belorussia, U.S.S.R. A collision involving two passenger trains at Krizhovka Junction, 400 miles southwest of Moscow, claimed the lives of 19 persons.

May 30
Assam State, India. An express train plunged into a flood-swollen river in northeastern India as a result of a rain-weakened rail line; there were 44 fatalities.

June 27
Near Lebus, East Germany. A passenger express train, traveling from Zittau in the southeast to Stralsund on the Baltic, burst into flames as it smashed into the rear of a freight train after inadvertently being switched from a main line onto a minor track; 29 persons were killed, and 7 were injured.

July 9
Near Wroclaw, Poland. A train traveling from Prague, Czechoslovakia, to Moscow, U.S.S.R., by way of Warsaw slammed into a diesel locomotive near the suburban station of Wroclaw Psie Poli; 11 persons were killed.

July 24
Pusan, South Korea. Two passenger trains crashed when an express train carrying vacationers from Seoul to Pusan rammed into the rear of another train standing at the station; 53 persons were injured, and at least 12 were killed.

Sept. 8
Near Assiut, Egypt. A passenger train carrying 700 persons and traveling at 80 mph derailed near Assiut, 220 miles south of Cairo, after the locomotive crew ignored the restricted speed zone; hundreds of passengers were trapped under overturned cars, 150 persons were injured, and 40 were killed.

Sept. 18
Tukh, Egypt. Two trains, so overloaded that passengers were clinging to the outsides, roared past each other in northern Egypt; 15 persons were crushed to death.

Oct. 10
Near Allahabad, India. A passenger express train traveling to Delhi rammed into the rear of a stationary freight train in northern India; more than 60 persons were killed.

Nov. 23
Near Rewari, India. The derailment of the locomotive and ten cars of a mail train 50 miles from its Delhi destination claimed the lives of more than 20 persons.

Dec. 3
Near Vereeniging, South Africa. Two locomotives, four passenger coaches, and two freight cars derailed when a freight train slammed into the rear of a standing passenger train at Kleigrond Station; at least 14 persons were killed.

1978
Feb. 24
Waverly, Tennessee. A derailed railroad car loaded with propane gas exploded while workers were preparing to transfer the gas to trucks; the blast leveled at least 14 buildings, destroyed two downtown blocks and killed 15 persons.

Feb. 25
Sa Pereyra, Argentina. A speeding express train carrying more than 2,000 passengers to Buenos Aires struck a heavy truck when the driver failed to respond to flashing signals at the crossing; all eleven cars of the train were derailed, resulting in more than 120 injuries and nearly 50 deaths.

March 22
Libiri, Zaire. A train crash in eastern Zaire killed 22 persons and injured many others.

April 16
Pueblo, Mexico. A passenger train crashed into a bus carrying 37 persons from the nearby town of Tlaxcala; 10 passengers on the bus were killed, and 16 others were injured.

April 17
Near Bologna, Italy. A southbound Venice–Rome luxury express train collided head-on with a northbound Lecce–Milan local train during a blinding rainstorm that triggered a mudslide across the tracks and steered the local into the path of the express; 43 persons were killed.

Early May
Vasai, India. The Ahmedabad Express train slammed into a stationary suburban train; more than 100 persons were injured, and 31 persons were killed, most of whom were women.

Dec. 13

Firemen carry the body of one of the victims of a train crash near Bologna, Italy, after a mudslide slid across the tracks during torrential rains on April 17.

Near Mexico City, Mexico. A passenger train rammed a bus loaded with pilgrims on their way to a religious observance; at least 20 persons died, and dozens of others were injured.

Dec. 21

Near Muñoz, Spain. A train locomotive slammed into a school bus carrying more than 90 children to a Christmas party, splitting the vehicle in two; 28 children and one adult were killed, and another 63 children were seriously injured.

6
Motor Vehicle Accidents

In its first half century the mass-produced automobile has changed the world, its economy, its politics, and its ways of life, as well as its ways of death. The impact of the motor vehicle on life and death, although evident everywhere, is most conspicuous in the United States, where man's infatuation with the automobile was the world's first and where it remains its most extravagant. For every three Americans—including infants, the aged, and the incarcerated—there are two motor vehicles.

In the United States motor vehicles are the number five killer—behind heart disease, cancer, stroke, and pneumonia. Cars, buses, trucks, and other vehicles killed Americans at the rate of 21.3 per 100,000 in 1976, triple the mortality of the next most dangerous kind of accident—falls—and at a higher rate than diabetes, arteriosclerosis, and cirrhosis of the liver. Motor vehicles killed more people than suicide and homicide together—which some investigators believe are the categories under which traffic deaths should be recorded.

United States losses in the Vietnamese war, from the first casualty to the pullout in 1973, included about 46,600 killed in battle. In the same period, more Americans were killed in auto accidents—653,000—than were killed in battle in all American wars from the Revolution to Vietnam. In 1973, the final year of the Vietnam war, the death toll on U.S. highways was more than 54,000. That was several thousand more than all the Americans killed in action in Vietnam from beginning to end.

Such statistics, however, represent the enormous number of cars and drivers in the United States rather than the quality of highway safety itself. In effect, they represent the number of cars and drivers per unit of population, and not accidents per thousand cars or automobile deaths per unit of population. Austria and Japan, for example, lead the world in number of accidents per 1,000 cars—followed by Belgium, West Germany, and Great Britain. Australia, Canada, and France have the highest traffic death rate per 100,000 population—followed by Austria, Belgium, and West Germany.

Passenger Cars and Buses

Accidents involving passenger cars—usually designed to car-

Ten motorists lost their lives in 1971 when 200 cars and trucks collided in a patch of fog on a busy highway near Thelwall, England (above). The death toll rose during 1973 in weather-related accidents on superhighways; during a blinding snowstorm 12 persons were killed in a fiery pileup in Ontario (below), a chain-reaction crash in the midst of dense fog and smoke claimed the lives of 9 people on the New Jersey Turnpike (right).

ry from two to five or six persons—do not often claim more than a handful of lives at one time. For that reason, they rarely attract much public attention except in the location of the crash and the homes of the victims. Noteworthy exceptions occur when a great many cars are involved, or when vehicles are grossly overcrowded.

England's superhighway M-6 runs northward from Birmingham to Lancaster. Outside the village of Thelwall, in the Cheshire Plain near Liverpool, the highway crosses a network of canals. On September 13, 1971, patches of fog shrouded segments of highways in the region. A single collision on a murky stretch of the heavily traveled M-6 quickly grew into a tangle of vehicles of every description, and before it stopped the mass pileup involved two hundred cars and trucks and left ten motorists dead, with sixty-one others taken to hospitals.

A similar accident in a similar situation in 1973, when sixty-five vehicles collided amid fog and dense smoke on the New Jersey Turnpike, claimed nine lives and forty injuries. Also in 1973, on Ontario highway 400, thirty-two cars came together in a flaming wreck that resulted in the death of twelve persons.

Overcrowding has led to even higher death tolls in one- and two-car accidents. Eleven of twelve passengers in a single car died near Whitesburg, Kentucky, on July 31, 1954, when the car in which they were riding ran into a cliff and caught fire. In Mexico on March 24, 1967, seventeen members of one family were in a car that tumbled into the Gulf of Mexico near Tecolutla; fourteen were killed. On June 21, 1971, seventeen persons bound for an Egyptian festival were crammed into a taxi that left the road and plunged into a lake outside Cairo. Only one person escaped drowning.

Onyang, South Korea. Flaming wreckage is perhaps the most gruesome—and one of the most common—settings for traffic fatalities. A bus loaded with seventy-six boys was on the way home from a midweek school excursion near Onyang, South Korea, on October 14, 1970. Momentarily distracted while negotiating a blind curve on the road, the driver failed to notice a train approaching an unguarded railroad crossing.

The locomotive struck the bus broadside, and shoved it a hundred yards along the tracks before the train was able to come to a halt. As the bus careened along the tracks and ties

A bus transporting 76 schoolboys was struck by a locomotive at an unguarded crossing near Onyang, South Korea, on October 14, 1970, and all of the 24 survivors were injured.

its fuel tank ruptured, and sparks from the screeching steel instantly turned the bus into an inferno. The driver and fifty-two of his young passengers perished. Although twenty-four of the boys managed to escape death, all of the survivors were injured, many suffering severe burns.

Asbestos, Quebec. An especially poignant bus tragedy claimed the lives of most of the handicapped residents of the Canadian mining town of Asbestos, Quebec, in the summer of 1978. It was nearly midnight of Friday, August 4, and the members of the Society of the Sick and Handicapped of Asbestos, Ltd., were on their way home from a theater outing to Eastman, Quebec.

Not far from Eastman on the sixty-mile trip home, their twenty-year-old bus was traveling down a steep hill on a road that turned sharply along the shore of small, spring-fed Lac d'Argent. Suddenly the bus's brakes failed, and the vehicle began gathering speed. The driver realized that he would be unable to negotiate the sharp turn at the bottom, and, picking his course by headlight in the night, he steered across a local road, dodging an enormous tree on one side and a utility pole

Divers search in the early morning mist (left) for a bus that plunged into the icy waters of Lac d'Argent on August 4, 1978, near Eastman, Quebec. After searching for hours the mud-coated bus (above) was located and hauled out; 37 of the 41 victims, most of them severely handicapped, were found trapped in the bus (below).

on the other, and headed across fifty feet of sandy beach, which he hoped would slow him down enough so the bus would come to rest in shallow water.

The momentum of the careening course down the long hill, however, carried the bus into deeper water, where it finally slowed and floated to a stop 260 feet from shore. The screams of the passengers roused summer residents in their cottages along the shore. Alain Pouliot, the twenty-four-year-old director of the society, was one of only two swimmers among the forty-eight persons on the bus. He managed to open a door and get into the water, and he struck out for a moored sailboat that he could make out in the dark about 200 feet from shore, thinking that he could get it back to the bus for service as a rescue vessel.

Meanwhile, the awakened residents were running to the scene, including two young men who jumped into a pair of dinghies and rowed as fast as they could toward the floating bus, which was sinking lower in the water. Pouliot was unable to free the sailboat from its mooring. The screaming continued as the bus settled further.

Most of the occupants were handicapped mentally, and some physically as well; four were in wheel chairs and many were on crutches. Lucie Pouliot, the wife of the director, got out of the bus. A young parish priest from Asbestos, Rev. Raymond Cloutier, got into the water too and found himself grasping Lucie Pouliot for support.

"He said to me, 'I don't want to die; save me,'" she recalled. "I told him, 'I want to live, too, but I can't swim.' Later Father Raymond let go of me," she said. He drowned trying to get to shore. Lucie Pouliot and the bus driver and three elderly passengers, two women and a man, who managed to get out of the bus, were able to stay afloat dog paddling and floating on their backs, until the two boys in the dinghies reached the scene, hauled them in, and took them ashore.

The bus continued to sink, and the screaming stopped. Before the dinghies could return, the bus had disappeared. Alain Pouliot and the only other swimmer, Rev. Gaston St. Jean, of St. Isaac's Catholic Church in Asbestos, reached shore safely.

The next day, after fourteen hours of searching, divers found the bus balanced on an underwater ledge, forty feet down, settled in silt up to its gas tank. By Sunday morning the bus had been pulled ashore, and when police opened the door, thirty-seven bodies were jammed together in the front.

Searching continued elsewhere in the lake, and by late Sunday the remaining four bodies were found—Father Cloutier and three others who had managed to escape the bus but could not stay afloat.

No one knew how long the bus remained afloat after it had slid to a stop in the lake. To those in the water it seemed a long time, perhaps fifteen minutes. Watchers on shore put the time at three or four minutes. But it was time enough to turn a merry outing into a tragedy. The mayor of Asbestos, a physician who had treated most of the passengers, declared Sunday a day of mourning, and the town scheduled a two-day wake for the victims.

"We were trying to get them out into the world," reflected one of the sponsors of the society. "The world belonged to them too."

Trucks

Trucks are often used instead of buses to carry passengers, and the results are sometimes catastrophic. India's state of Maharashtra stretches eastward from Bombay and the Arabian Sea. In its rural reaches about forty miles east of Poona in May 1975, more than eighty wedding guests were riding on a truck en route to the ceremony. The driver either did not see or misjudged the speed of an approaching train, which smashed into the truck, leaving a toll of sixty-six dead and eighteen injured.

In the spring of 1962 a truck loaded with farm workers and farm supplies was negotiating a mountain road near Trikkala in central Greece. It missed a turn, bouncing down the mountainside and finally plunging 1,500 feet into a mountain ravine. Thirteen passengers who were lucky enough to be thrown off suffered only injuries. Thirteen others died at various stages of the descent, which took more than ten seconds (long enough for a television commercial to sell a product, long enough for a so-so high school sprinter to run a hundred yards, or long enough for an airliner to fly a mile and a half).

Less spectacular truck plunges have wrought even more havoc. Turkish laborers aboard a truck in 1965 were thrown about when the truck slid over a cliff; thirty-one were killed and fifteen injured. On the day after Christmas in 1947 a truck carrying skiers in the Italian Alps went off a mountain road, killing twenty-one and injuring twenty-nine. In Mexico in 1952 a truck loaded with Holy Week pilgrims shot off the road and into a ravine, resulting in at least forty deaths.

Explosive Cargoes

Dangerous cargoes constitute grave potential danger for other vehicles, pedestrians, and nearby property. In developed countries, and increasingly in others, government regulations sharply restrict the kinds of explosives or other dangerous materials that may be carried by motor vehicles. Often these regulations are revised on the heels of a particularly serious accident.

Chicago, Illinois. A tank truck loaded with between 7,000 and 8,000 gallons of gasoline was proceeding carefully northward on South State Street in Chicago, Illinois, during the evening rush hour on May 25, 1950. A southbound streetcar approached, loaded with homebound passengers.

A flooded underpass in the area had necessitated rerouting the streetcar, and an open switch ahead would direct it into a left turn, squarely in the path of the oncoming tanker. A transit company flagman, Charles G. Kleim, waved a frantic warning to the motorman, who either ignored or did not see the urgent signals. The truck driver did not notice that the switch was set to project the loaded streetcar into his path. Just as the truck drew opposite the switch, the streetcar swung into its left turn, going, so the flagman estimated, at about thirty miles an hour.

Peter Simadis, the owner of a tavern in the block, heard a loud crash and looked out of his window to see a wall of flame rolling up the street. Within seconds, thousands of gallons of gasoline coursed and blazed in the street, pouring onto and under the streetcar and producing an inferno. Windows in nearby stores began to melt, and buildings caught fire.

The doors of the streetcar were jammed shut and passengers struggled vainly to get out the windows. A Baptist minister who had been getting gasoline for his car at the corner filling station ran as close to the scene as the searing heat would permit.

"One woman got her head out but couldn't get her body through the opening," he recounted. "She raised her clenched fists over her head and just shuddered, and then slumped to the floor. I saw people with their hair on fire. It was miserable."

Parked automobiles and eight buildings on the block burned out of control. Bricks and concrete in the street cracked and buckled. One passenger who survived was Edward White, Jr. "The whole car was in flames," he said. "I kicked the glass out of the back door and jumped out. The flames were right behind me." Another survivor, Ora Mae Bryant, said, "We couldn't get the door open, Finally someone broke a window and we crawled out."

Those who could reach a broken window jumped from the blazing streetcar, their clothing in flames and their faces and bodies bleeding from the broken glass. At last the back door was forced open, and more badly burned passengers escaped. Thirty were injured.

It was too late for thirty-four, including the motorman and the truck driver, who died in the flaming wreckage. Firemen sprayed water on the car for an hour before it cooled off enough to enter. The bodies were charred, most of them beyond recognition. Firemen placed the incinerated remains on the sidewalk until they could be removed to the county

During rush hour in Chicago on May 25, 1950, a streetcar burst into flames following a disastrous collision with a tank truck loaded with gasoline. Rescue workers removed bodies of victims from the charred remains of the streetcar to the sidewalk.

morgue for identification, a morbid ritual rendered more difficult because wallets and identification papers had been destroyed by the flames.

Tortosa, Spain. In the summer of 1978 the most volatile liquefied gas permitted to be transported in pressurized tank trucks over Spanish highways was an industrial product called propylene. The substance is used in the manufacture of plastics. At midday on Tuesday, July 11, a 38-ton tank truck with a full load of liquefied propylene was en route to a refinery complex at Puerto Llano.

The weather was beautiful as the tanker breezed along the Castellón-Tarragona highway under the hot early afternoon sun. A few yards of white sand separated the highway from the blue Mediterranean. On the other side of the road a huge campsite was placid with siesta, bikini-clad sunbathers stretched drowsing on their towels and air mattresses.

Suddenly, something went wrong. The tank truck, cruising at about forty miles per hour, went out of control. It overturned, smashed through a thin cement wall separating the road from the campsite, and exploded in a ball of fire. The blast dug a sixty-foot crater some fifteen feet deep and sent rivers of flaming liquid gas in every direction into the campsite. The heat and the concussion of the blast set off a chain reaction of smaller explosions of campers' tanks of cooking gas.

The force of the initial explosion was so great that it destroyed a discotheque across the highway from the camp. The body of a four-year-old girl was found in the ruined building. Other vacationers were blown into the sea or onto the beach where they were buried by sand. Some were blown to pieces.

Of eight hundred campers, more than a hundred were killed immediately, and at least fifty were burned so critically that death was assured. Hundreds more were injured. Some were still missing days after the catastrophe, despite the efforts of divers, who did recover a number of bodies from the sea.

Hurriedly assembled rescue crews evacuated the injured—many of them beyond hope—in military helicopters, ambulances, buses, and private cars. The injuries of some survivors were so serious that doctors would not let them be moved. Those who could be moved were rushed by air to burn centers in France, Belgium, and West Germany.

Twelve nearby summer homes were destroyed and some of their occupants killed and maimed in the explosions and fires.

Approximately one hundred cars and trailers were destroyed. Tents were left flattened, sundered, charred, and shredded.

The truck driver was completely incinerated. Enough remained of his watch to read the time at which it had stopped: 2:36 P.M. In the cemetery at nearby Tortosa, the bodies of the victims, some of whom had succumbed after being broiled alive, many of whom were literally carbonized, were laid out in open coffins along paths shaded by pines from the hot Mediterranean sun. Embalmers worked over them in the open air as the stench of burned flesh pervaded the area.

Even before the survivors finished packing to leave the ruined campsite, and before the embalmers finished their work, relatives of the dead and missing began arriving to trace—or try to trace—their kin through rings, watches, and other personal effects. Camp records were often inadequate, and many bodies were unrecognizable.

The day after the explosion the province of Tarragona banned all trucks carrying dangerous cargoes from its public roads. A police officer summarized the event with a simple sentence: "It resembles Hell, or what we think Hell is like."

Tepeji del Rio, Mexico. Widespread and increasing shipment of liquefied gases for industrial uses and domestic heating raises the specter of repetitions of the Spanish holocaust. Indeed, as if to emphasize that grim prospect, chance dictated a repetition on the other side of the world within a week, albeit on a slightly smaller scale.

Early on Sunday, July 16, 1978—only 102 hours after the Spanish catastrophe—a tractor-trailer with twenty-two tons of liquid butane gas was headed for Mexico City from a state refinery at Tula. At Tepeji del Rio the pressurized tanker turned south onto highway 57. Even at a little after 2 A.M. traffic was heavy on the rain-swept highway, the major artery to the capital from San Luis Potosí and Queretaro.

Outside Tepeji, only about forty-five miles from Mexico City, tragedy occurred. Police speculated that it may have been a blowout, or possibly simply a skid on the wet road. The truck began to zigzag, struck a highway rampart, overturned, and exploded. In the hills to the west, villagers at Jilotepec de Abasolo awakened and ran screaming into the streets as flames lit the black sky, shooting up 100 to 150 feet in the air from the blazing truck ten miles away.

A bus speeding along behind the tanker plowed into its flaming wreckage, followed by two more buses, two other trucks, and a passenger car. Liquid butane spewing from the

In the summer of 1978 a truck carrying propylene gas exploded into a campsite near Tortosa, Spain, setting off a chain reaction of smaller explosions and devastating the seaside vacation area (above and below). Open coffins containing the bodies of victims, many burned beyond recognition, were laid out in rows along shaded paths (opposite page) of the local cemetery.

tanker vaporized and burned, engulfing the mass collision in flames. Four more buses crashed into the fringes of the growing conflagration. Within minutes of the explosion eighty-five persons died in the vehicles closest to the tank truck.

There were 123 passengers on the first three buses that hit the fiery wreck. Most of them were among the eighty-five people killed in the first minutes. The lucky ones escaped by leaping out of the bus windows, their clothing afire. One of them, who had been sleeping, awakened to watch the driver of his own bus perish. "I opened my eyes when the bus was fifty feet from the burning tank truck," Sergio Olmeda Uribe said. "Then there was an explosion. The bus driver became a human torch. He died at the wheel without even being able to take his hands off it. I was breathing fire and I barely managed to get out through one of the windows. All my clothes were on fire."

"There were five explosions in all," recalled Aurelio Montes Acevedo, a passenger on one of the other buses. "When we got on the bus I noticed a young woman carrying two small children in her arms. After the explosion I saw the same woman with a baby in one arm and a burning baby in the other. I never saw them again."

By sunrise, fire fighters from three nearby villages, after battling the flames for three hours, finally brought them under control. After five more hours—at around 10 A.M.—the burned-out wreckage, although still too hot to touch, had nevertheless been dragged off the asphalt so that the highway could be opened again. The blackened shells of burned-out vehicles lined the median strip among the charred stubs of what had been shade trees. On either side of the road for half a mile, woodlands and cornfields had been burned to the ground, and debris littered the charcoal earth everywhere. The death toll stood near 100, and 150 injured survivors lay in three Mexico City hospitals.

A witness invoked the same sinister image employed by the policeman who summed up the Spanish inferno: "I saw passengers turned into torches. It was like the damned coming out of Hell."

Cali, Colombia. When a major motor vehicle explosion occurs in the very heart of a city, massive economic change can augment the toll in human lives and the damage to the vehicles involved. Just after midnight on August 7, 1956, seven trucks of a military convoy loaded with ammunition, high explosives, and gasoline blew up in the center of downtown

On July 16, 1978, seven buses, two trucks, and a car plowed
into the flaming wreckage of a gasoline tractor-trailer
(above) in a mass collision on a highway in Mexico. Most of
the nearly 100 victims were passengers in the first three
buses that rammed the burning truck (below).

Cali, Colombia, a city of nearly 89,000 about 185 miles south-west of Bogotá, the country's capital. Cali's railway terminal, where the vehicles had been parked, was completely leveled, and eight city blocks surrounding the blast were almost total-ly razed. Nearby, a military police headquarters and an army barracks were destroyed, killing at least five hundred persons.

Rubble from the exploding trucks rained down on streets and buildings. Automobiles were buried beneath the falling debris. Window panes within a three-mile radius of the blast were blown out by its tremendous force. The large, heavy doors of St. Peter's Cathedral, thirteen blocks from the explo-sion, were torn from their hinges. A huge cloud of dust hov-ered over the smoldering ruins, the center of which was an enormous crater where the blast had occurred.

Rescuers later dug through the destruction, which included hotels, cafés, and the local American offices of Abbott Laboratories, the Ford Motor Company, and General Mo-tors. Overall, the final casualty count stood at approximately 1,200 persons dead and several thousand injured. Damage was estimated in the tens of millions of dollars.

City officials examine the ruins in the downtown area of Cali, Colombia, the day after a military convoy exploded in the center of the city, killing at least 500 persons.

In his message of condolence, Colombian President Gustavo Rojas Pinilla said that the catastrophe was "the gravest the country has suffered." He called the explosion of the vehicles the work of anti-government conspirators, vowed not to rest until "the material and intellectual culprits are severely and justly punished," and declared an official three-day period of mourning.

Bystanders

Vehicular catastrophes have brought injury or death to many innocent spectators and pedestrians in the age of the automobile. Few have been as macabre as the event of December 6, 1965, that befell the village of Soutouboua in central Togo, the small republic on Africa's Gulf of Guinea.

It was a day of festivities; hundreds of merrymakers danced in the streets. Then two trucks, both out of control, came speeding into the village and plowed into the crowd. The trucks mowed down nearly 250 persons, killing 125 or more and injuring at least another hundred.

Le Mans, France. The world's most celebrated sports car race, the Le Mans Grand Prix, became the site of racing's worst catastrophe and bloodiest carnage on June 11, 1955. A two-car collision sent flaming automobile parts hurtling over a retaining wall into a crowd of spectators, killing eighty-three and injuring at least a hundred others. The accident occurred as more than 250,000 racing fans watched three cars speeding abreast down the half-mile straightaway at approximately 160 mph. Suddenly there was a collision between a British Austin-Healy, driven by Lance Macklin, and a French Mercedes-Benz, driven by Pierre Levegh.

Split seconds before the accident, Mike Hawthorne in a Jaguar somewhat in front of Macklin and Levegh had swerved abruptly to the right, apparently responding to a signal for a pit stop. Macklin veered his Austin-Healy to the left, to go around Hawthorne's car. The oncoming Levegh, racing at full speed, smashed into Macklin. Macklin's car went out of control, brushing against the pit wall, breaking up, and flinging auto parts into the crowd with explosive force. The car then caromed off the pit wall and headed across the track at a right angle. The Austin-Healy was engulfed in flame, but Macklin managed to escape.

Levegh's Mercedes-Benz plowed into the retaining wall, disintegrating into metal fragments that flew like shrapnel into the crowds, killing and maiming. Some sections of the car, including the hood and chassis, soared into the air, slicing through the screaming spectators like giant cleavers. Two children were decapitated, as was Levegh, whose body was burned beyond recognition.

The dead and injured were carried away two to the stretcher. Last rites were administered to the dying by a priest who wandered among the dazed, bloody victims. Farm trucks were commissioned to assist ambulances in bringing the injured to nearby hospitals. French Minister of Public Health Bernard Lafay left Paris after receiving the news of the disaster to take charge of the hospital and first aid facilities. It took workers more than two hours to remove the dead.

American racing driver John Fitch, Levegh's teammate, along with other drivers including British ace Stirling Moss, urged officials to stop the race. "I'm sure it would have been stopped if such a tragedy occurred at Indianapolis," said

At the Le Mans Grand Prix on June 11, 1955, at least 100 spectators were injured and 83 were killed as flaming fragments from a sports car collision were sent hurtling over the retaining wall.

Fitch. The entire Mercedes-Benz team withdrew from the competition in mourning for Levegh.

Officials declined to cancel the race, however, and pleaded with spectators to donate blood for transfusions to the injured. The following afternoon the twenty-four-hour Le Mans race was won by British driver Mike Hawthorne in the Jaguar that had begun the chain of fatal events.

Asse, Belgium. Few accidents involving pedestrians have been as ironic as one that struck down a group of Belgian schoolboys in the spring of 1966. At Asse, northwest of Brussels, a class of twenty boys, accompanied by their teacher, was walking to a special lesson. A truck running out of control smashed into the group, killing eleven students and injuring the teacher and four more boys.

The subject of the class was highway safety. And the special lesson was to have been a drill in crossing streets safely.

Other Motor Vehicle Accidents, 1959–78

1959
Jan. 5

United States. Press associations reported 377 persons killed in traffic accidents over the four-day New Year's holiday.

March 3

Near Cortazar, Mexico. A bus crashed into a truck, killing 28 persons.

April 5

West Pakistan. A bus plunged down a ravine, killing 20 persons and seriously injuring 11 others.

April 26

Ootacamund, India. A bus overturned; 18 persons were killed.

May 10

Mexico City, Mexico. A train and crowded bus collided, killing 16 persons and injuring 29.

June 1

United States. A total of 310 persons were killed as the result of traffic accidents over the Memorial Day weekend.

June 1

Santiago, Chile. An express train crashed into a bus, killing 11 persons and injuring 39.

June 2

Schuylkill Haven, Pennsylvania. A gas truck crashed and exploded; 11 people died.

June 8

Phoenix, Arizona. A bus smashed into a tree, killing 16 persons and injuring 32.

June 21

Lauffen, West Germany. A train-bus collision killed 43 persons.

July 1

Salar del Carmen, Chile. A truck overturned, killing 12 persons.

July 2

Central Taiwan. A truck crashed through a wooden bridge, killing 18 persons and injuring 23.

July 6

United States. Traffic accidents resulted in the death of 276 persons during the Independence Day weekend.

Aug. 17

Columbia, Missouri. A two-car collision killed 10 persons.

Aug. 26

Dahanu, India. A bus plunged into a rain-swollen irrigation canal; 30 persons drowned.

Sept. 7

United States. Traffic deaths on U.S. highways for the three-day Labor Day weekend totaled 438 persons.

Oct. 2

Warsaw, Poland. A truck and train collision killed 23 persons.

Oct. 4

Near Svatyn Martin, Czechoslovakia. A train hit a bus at a crossing, killing 15 persons.

Oct. 5

Salvador, Brazil. Two buses collided head-on; 16 persons died.

Oct. 8

New Brunswick, New Jersey. An empty truck rammed into a bus, causing the gas tank in the rear of the bus to explode; 12 persons were killed, and 10 others were injured.

Oct. 29

Buenos Aires, Argentina. A train-bus collision killed 11 persons and injured 40.

Nov. 8

Near Guadalajara, Mexico. A bus-truck collision killed 23 persons.

Nov. 13

Jalisco State, Mexico. A bus crashed into a station wagon and fell into a river, drowning at least 23 persons.

Nov. 21

Mombasa, Kenya. A truck carrying children collided with a truck loaded with stone, killing 13 persons and injuring 21.

Dec. 10

Cuernavaca, Mexico. A bus overturned and caught fire; 20 persons died.

Dec. 22

Casablanca, Morocco. A bus carrying tribesmen to see U.S. President Dwight D. Eisenhower collided with a truck, killing 15 persons.

Dec. 31

Pucallpa, Peru. A bus plunged over a cliff; 22 persons died.

1960

Jan. 9

Near La Paz, Bolivia. A truck plunged over a mountain road; 37 persons died.

Jan. 11

Near Reynosa, Mexico. A bus went over a cliff, killing 29 persons.

Jan. 30

Sativa Norte, Colombia. A bus overturned, killing a reported 42 persons.

Feb. 15

Diamantina, Brazil. When the truck in which they were riding plunged into a chasm, 20 workmen perished.

March 4

Chunkok, Korea. A bus plunged off a 100-foot cliff; 20 persons died.

March 4

Torreon, Mexico. A bus smashed into a gasoline tank which had fallen from a truck; 8 children and 2 adults burned to death.

April 1

Beirut, Lebanon. A bus overturned, killing 22 teenage students.

April 10

La Paz, Bolivia. A truck bringing Indians for Palm Sunday services slid off a mountain road into a ditch, killing 37 persons.

April 18

Bombay State, India. A bus smashed into a tree, killing 23 persons.

May 28
Rawalpindi, Pakistan. A bus swerved off the road into a canal;
22 of 34 persons aboard were drowned.

June 1
United States. A total of 367 persons were killed as the result
of traffic accidents over the Memorial Day weekend.

June 23
Sabre, Transvaal, South Africa. A truck overturned, killing 18
persons.

July 4
United States. Traffic accidents resulted in the death of 442
persons during the Independence Day weekend.

July 19
Near Taxila, Pakistan. An army truck fell into a flooded
stream, killing 22 soldiers.

July 28
Near Huancayo, Peru. A bus plunged off a mountain road
into a gorge, killing 29 high school students.

July 30
Trabzon, Turkey. A truck plunged off a mountain road; 33 of
its 65 occupants died.

Aug. 2
Vienna, Austria. A two-streetcar collision killed 18 persons.

Aug. 4
Macaé, Brazil. A bus fell off a bridge into a river, killing 15
persons.

Aug. 24
São José do Rio Prêto, Brazil. A bus plunged into the Turvo
River, killing 60 persons.

Sept. 5
United States. Traffic deaths on U.S. highways for the Labor
Day weekend totaled 415 persons.

Oct. 17
Near Mancha Grande, Ecuador. A bus went over an embankment into a deep gully; 35 persons were killed, and 22 others
were injured.

Nov. 29
Near Lamont, Alberta, Canada. A freight train struck a
school bus, killing 17 high school students and injuring 24
others.

Dec. 11
Near Buenos Aires, Argentina. During the running of the
Argentine Grand Prix auto race, a series of accidents resulted
in the death of 17 persons.

The wreckage of a school bus is strewn across the railroad tracks after a freight train smashed into the bus near Lamont, Alberta, on November 29.

1961

Feb. 8

Bilbeis, Egypt. A bus careened from a highway into a canal, killing 21 of the 43 passengers.

May 22

Seville, Spain. A bus plunged into a 60-foot ravine and caught fire; 21 persons were killed, and 46 others were injured.

July 9

Chiayi, Taiwan. An express train crashed into a bus at a crossing, killing 48 persons and injuring 28 others.

Aug. 2

Herziswil, Switzerland. A bus loaded with U.S. tourists collided with a truck and plunged into Lake Lucerne; 16 of the 22 persons aboard drowned.

Sept. 10

Monza, Italy. A Ferrari racing car, hit from behind by another racer in the Grand Prix of Italy, spun through the track barrier; the driver, Count Wolfgang von Trips, and 14 spectators were killed, and at least 25 others were injured.

Sept. 26

Istanbul, Turkey. A truck loaded with workmen slid over a

cliff; 31 persons were killed, and 15 others were injured.
Oct. 22
Prijepolje, Yugoslavia. A Titograd–Belgrade bus ran off the
road and fell 300 feet into a canyon; 39 of the 52 passengers
were killed.
Dec. 14
Near Evans, Colorado. A passenger train struck a school bus
on a grade crossing; 20 children were killed, and 13 others
were injured.

1962
March 3
Latakia, Syria. A car collided with a gasoline truck; 31 persons
attempting to collect the spilled gas were killed when the
truck exploded, 39 others were injured.
March 7
Mexico City, Mexico. A loaded bus, out of control, hit a
station wagon; 30 persons were killed, and 28 others were
injured.
April 8
Tel Aviv, Israel. An express train crashed into a truck; 11
persons were killed, and 6 others were injured.
May 31
Bombay, India. An overloaded bus careened into the Mahor
River 40 feet below; 69 persons were killed, and 18 others
were injured.
June 11
Buenos Aires, Argentina. A commuter train hurtled into a
crowded school bus at a fog-covered crossing; 33 persons
aboard the bus (mostly children) were killed, and 83 others
were injured.
June 11
Jaipur, India. A bus collided with a passenger train, killing 25
persons and injuring 23 others.
July 8
Pigg Peak, Swaziland. A truck carrying a group of Africans
to a religious meeting overturned; 21 persons were killed, and
10 others were injured.
July 9
Garmsar, Iran. The collision of a crowded bus and a freight
train killed 49 persons and injured 29 others.
Aug. 27
Faiyum, Egypt. A tractor-drawn trailer loaded with farm
workers snapped its coupling and rolled into a canal; 27 per-

sons (mostly children) drowned, and 23 others jumped to safety.

Oct. 14

Cuenca, Ecuador. A bus hit a rock jutting from the side of the road and burst into flames; 36 passengers died, and 8 were severely burned.

Oct. 18

Near Bristol, England. A multiple crash involving four vehicles on the fog-covered Gloucester–Bristol highway brought death to 11 persons; 5 others were injured.

Dec. 14

João Pinheiro, Brazil. A washed-out highway bridge collapsed, plunging a busload of Brazilians into the raging Prata River; at least 38 persons were killed.

Dec. 21

Lima, Peru. An Ayacucho–Huancayo bus went off the road, killing 29 persons; one seriously injured child survived.

1963

Jan. 8

Near Recife, Brazil. A truck and a train collided; 16 religious pilgrims died.

Feb. 6

Near Belo Horizonte, Brazil. A bus traveling between Belo Horizonte and Varginha went off the road into a ravine; of the 35 passengers at least 28 were killed.

Feb. 7

Auckland, New Zealand. A bus returning a group of Maori to their homes, after welcoming ceremonies for visiting Queen Elizabeth II, plunged down a 130-foot embankment; 15 persons were killed, and 21 others were injured.

Feb. 17

Lagos, Nigeria. A "mammy wagon" (passenger truck) hurtled into the Majidun River, killing at least 30 persons.

Feb. 26

Abidjan, Ivory Coast. A bus and a truck collided on a bridge across the Nzi River about 150 miles north of the city; the bus fell into the river, killing 18 persons.

Feb. 28

Tecununmán, Guatemala. An overcrowded bus traveling at high speed turned over and burned; 64 persons (including 16 children) perished.

March 14

Near São Paulo, Brazil. Two trucks collided on a bridge

and fell into the river below; at least 30 road workers were killed, and another 39 were injured.

April 7

Near Nairobi, Kenya. A loaded bus swerved off a bridge and plunged into the Tiva River; at least 58 persons died, and 14 others were injured.

May 18

Pahokee, Florida. A bus loaded with migrant farm workers ran off the road into a 25-foot-deep canal; 27 persons drowned.

June 10

Near Escalante, Utah. An open-bed truck loaded with Boy Scouts on their way to the Hole-in-the-Rock campsite overturned and plunged down a steep embankment; 12 in the party (5 adults and 7 scouts) were killed, and 35 others were injured.

June 29

Near Yarumal, Colombia. A bus careened off the road and over a 300-foot cliff; 40 persons were killed, and 30 others were injured.

July 31

Near Toledo, Ohio. A station wagon belonging to migrant farm workers ran head-on into a tractor-trailer, killing 10 persons (8 were children).

Aug. 5

Near Istanbul, Turkey. A gasoline truck exploded upon colliding with a bus on the Istanbul–Ankara highway; 21 persons were killed, and another 17 were injured.

Aug. 19

Near Santiago, Chile. Mechanical failure caused a bus to careen off the road into the Cachapoal River; 23 persons were killed, and 15 others were injured.

Sept. 17

Chualar, California. A work bus crossing in front of an oncoming freight train was hit broadside; 30 Mexican farm workers were killed, and 33 others were injured.

Sept. 17

Recife, Brazil. A speeding truck loaded with farm workers smashed into a roadside embankment; 15 persons were killed, and another 16 were injured.

Sept. 20

Viña del Mar, Chile. Brake failure resulted in a bus accident that killed 14 persons and injured 12 others.

Nov. 3

Bronx, New York. An automobile carrying a family group crashed through the barrier of a dead-end street and plunged into the Harlem River; 11 of the 12 persons drowned.

Dec. 3

São Roque, Brazil. A truck loaded with Roman Catholic pilgrims en route to a church festival overturned, killing 20 passengers; 25 others were injured.

Dec. 5

Angola. A truck transporting native workers plunged off a bridge and into the Cutato River on the border between the Bie and Huambo districts; 52 men were killed.

Dec. 8

Yilmaz, Turkey. A train and small bus collided at a grade crossing; 17 persons died.

Dec. 24

Near Calca, Peru. A bus plunged off a mountain road, killing 15 passengers.

1964

Jan. 29

Timgad, Algeria. Floodwaters inundated a bus attempting to cross a river ford and swept away 28 of the 31 passengers.

Feb. 14

Resende, Brazil. A bus careened off the road into a river, carrying 36 persons to their deaths.

Feb. 18

Kuahab District, West Pakistan. A passenger truck loaded with children skidded into the Jhelum River; 26 persons drowned.

March 13

Near Narino, Colombia. A school bus loaded with pupils bound for Narino flew off the road, over a precipice, and into the Guaitará River; about 30 children died.

April 6

Near Sebinkarahisar, Turkey. A Siran–Ankara bus plunged into the Aucura River, killing all 35 persons aboard.

June 14

Rize, Turkey. A truck filled with children tumbled off a mountain pass into a flooded river; 23 children drowned, and 13 others were injured.

July 11

Bergerac, France. A group of spectators watching the Tour

de France bicycle race were rammed by a speeding gasoline truck which swerved out of control and plunged over a bridge railing, taking about 30 persons with it into the canal below; 10 persons were killed, and 20 others were injured.

July 27

Vittel, France. A bus transporting a group of folk dancers from an art festival fell off a bridge onto the railroad tracks below; all 19 occupants were killed.

Aug. 16

Bourg St. Maurice, France. A bus filled with children returning to a summer camp, after attending a mountain festival, was forced off the road by an oncoming vehicle and plunged 200 feet down the mountainside; 17 persons were killed, and 30 others were injured.

Aug. 19

Near Cuernavaca, Mexico. A truck went over a mountain embankment, killing 14 persons.

Aug. 30

Zempala, Mexico. A bus loaded with pilgrims, homeward bound from a religious festival, went out of control on a hill as the brakes failed; 20 persons were killed, and 56 were injured.

Aug. 31

Near Belo Horizonte, Brazil. A bus crash killed 11 persons.

Sept. 20

Near Pasto, Colombia. A bus sped over the edge of a cliff and fell 500 feet, killing 25 persons.

Nov. 9

Van, Turkey. A truck carrying a group of farm people sped off a mountain road into a deep ravine; 25 persons died.

Dec. 20

Near Vidago, Portugal. A bus-truck collision killed 15 persons.

1965

Jan. 3

Southern Peru. A Huancayo–Ayacucho bus ran off a mountain road and tumbled down a 300-foot ravine into the Mantaro River; 28 persons were killed.

Jan. 10

Dolores Hidalgo, Mexico. A chartered bus, taking soccer players and their families to a game, developed engine trouble and plunged into a 450-foot ravine, killing 19 passengers and injuring 22 others.

Jan. 31

Malang, Indonesia. A bus ran off the highway and sank in a river; 36 persons perished.

Feb. 3

Zacatecas, Mexico. A bus, veering off the highway, fell over a 300-foot cliff, killing 25 persons and injuring 40 others.

Feb. 10

Ayyat, Egypt. A truck missed a fog-obscured turn in the road and plunged into a canal; 36 of the 66 workers riding in the vehicle were killed.

Feb. 13

Near Guadalajara, Mexico. A bus wreck on the winding road between Cocula and Tecolotlán caused 19 deaths; 38 other persons were injured.

Feb. 18

Naples, Italy. A bus crowded with commuters sped off the Naples–Pompeii highway and fell into a ravine, killing 16 passengers and injuring 29 others.

Feb. 28

Semdinli, Turkey. A bus plunged into a deep crevasse, killing 15 persons and injuring 11 others.

March 12

Near Brasilia, Brazil. A bus overturned on the Brasilia–Belem highway and slid into a river, killing 12 persons.

April 15

Near American Falls, Idaho. A head-on collision of two cars speeding on a narrow stretch of road killed 10 persons.

May 5

Abshaway Al Malak, Egypt. A trailer loaded with farm workers overturned, fell into a canal, and drowned 19 persons.

May 9

Ixtapan de la Sal, Mexico. A passenger bus plunged off the road into the jagged 450-foot Calderon ravine, killing at least 30 of the 40 persons aboard.

June 29

Near Chinchallote, Honduras. A bus loaded with members of a Costa Rican children's ballet, en route for a performance in Tegucigalpa, crashed on the Pan American Highway and killed 35 persons, most of them children.

July 1

Seville, Spain. A Seville–Granada bus was struck by a train at a grade crossing; 12 persons were killed.

July 31

Near Lima, Peru. An overloaded bus plunged over a cliff; 27

persons were killed, and 29 others were injured.

Aug. 11

Hendek, Turkey. An Istanbul–Ankara bus crashed into a tank truck; 23 persons were killed by acid spraying from the truck, and 17 others were injured.

Aug. 17

Tbika, Kenya. A collision of two buses killed 23 persons (including 10 children) and injured 29 others.

Aug. 27

Vinton, Louisiana. A truck loaded with heavy timber slammed head-on into a Greyhound Scenicruiser; 11 persons were killed, and 28 others were injured.

Aug. 30

Seoul, South Korea. A bus went over a cliff, killing 15 persons and injuring 12 others.

Sept. 2

Adana, Turkey. A bus was struck by a freight train at a crossing; 17 persons in the bus were killed, and 25 others were injured.

Sept. 2

Near Jammu, Kashmir. A bus plunged over the edge of a mountain road, killing 27 persons.

Sept. 6

Teloloapan, Mexico. Fire consumed a bus after it careened off the road and over an embankment; 30 persons died.

Sept. 8

Cairo, Egypt. A bus and a truck collided near the outskirts of the city, killing 16 persons.

Sept. 11

T'ai-nan, Taiwan. An excursion bus fell off a highway bridge, killing 15 persons; 13 others were injured.

Sept. 21

Havana, Cuba. A collision between a motorized railway car and a bus killed 14 persons.

Nov. 1

Cairo, Egypt. A trolley bus crammed with students and shoppers swung out of control, dived over a 20-foot embankment, and sank into the Nile River; 72 persons (most of them high school students) drowned.

Nov. 2

Near Mexico City, Mexico. A passenger train en route to Veracruz crashed into a bus at a grade crossing; 29 persons died, and 13 others were injured.

Dec. 8

Koru, Kenya. A bus plunged into a dry river bed, killing 29 persons; 36 others were injured.

Dec. 23

Near Middleburg, South Africa. A truck loaded with young farm workers went out of control on a mountain road, crashed, and killed 37 youths.

Dec. 23

Medford, Oregon. An interstate bus carrying Christmas travelers skidded on a patch of ice and overturned; 13 persons were killed, and 26 others were injured.

1966

Jan. 6

Surigao del Sur Province, Philippines. A passenger bus sped off a mountain road and into a 100-foot ravine, killing 35 persons.

Jan. 11

Near Buenos Aires, Argentina. A train struck a bus and pushed it across a bridge, killing 11 pedestrians on the bridge.

Jan. 23

Tochutla, Mexico. A laborers' bus plunged off the road and landed in a deep ravine; 20 child farm workers died, and 18 others were injured.

Feb. 1

Near Miami, Florida. The collision of a train with a bus carrying Puerto Rican farm workers killed 18 of the workers and injured 14 others.

March 7

Calginia, South Africa. A bus taking workers to a road construction site left the road and fell into a ditch, killing 23 men.

March 26

Sokoto, Nigeria. A truck carrying a group of riders toppled off a bridge and killed 37 persons; 9 others were injured.

June 17

Moscow, U.S.S.R. A bus accident killed 64 persons; the driver, who survived, was given a jail sentence for his "lack of discipline."

June 27

Shahrud, Iran. A bus sped off the road and crashed into a deep gorge, killing 42 passengers; another 20 were injured.

June 27

Near Agra, India. A bus fire killed 40 persons and injured 30.

July 1
Ozark, Alabama. A converted school bus, used to transport migratory farm workers, blew a tire and careened down an embankment; 12 persons were killed, and 12 others were injured.

July 25
Niederbrechen, Germany. A tour bus, taking a group of Belgian children home from a vacation, ripped through the guardrail of an autobahn overpass and landed upside down on the road below; 28 children and 5 adults were killed, and, of the 10 survivors, 6 were severely injured.

Aug. 17
Narayanpur, India. A skidding bus slipped into a canal; 29 persons died.

Aug. 28
Near Istanbul, Turkey. A collision between a train and a bus killed 25 persons; another 23 were injured.

Sept. 18
Near Bucaramanga, Colombia. A bus left the road and plunged into a ravine, killing at least 20 persons and injuring 15 others.

Oct. 7
Dorion, Quebec, Canada. A freight train struck a chartered school bus carrying students to a dance; 19 teenagers were killed, and 21 others were injured.

Nov. 19
Ngomweni, South Africa. An overloaded bus shot off the road, down an embankment, and into the flooded Jmhloti River; more than 40 persons were killed, and another 31 were injured.

Dec. 11
Qum, Iran. Two highway buses collided on the Tehran–Isfahan road, killing 25 persons and injuring 41 others.

Dec. 15
Near the Syrian border. An Iraqi Air Force plane crashed into the Baghdad–Damascus bus as it traveled across the desert; the plane's pilot and 26 bus passengers were killed.

Dec. 19
Near Belo Horizonte, Brazil. A bus-truck collision killed 11 persons and injured 18 others.

Dec. 29
Near Celaya, Mexico. Two buses collided, killing 24 persons and injuring 48 others.

1967

Jan. 6

Manila, Philippines. A convoy of 57 buses loaded with Roman Catholic pilgrims met with tragedy when the ninth bus in line went out of control, rammed the bus ahead, and both careened into a deep gorge; 83 persons died, and at least 60 others were injured.

Jan. 23

Rosario, Argentina. A school bus hit a train, killing 16 of the children and injuring 15 others.

March 24

San Antonio, Texas. A car-station wagon collision killed 10 of 15 members of two families.

March 28

Dacca, East Pakistan. A bus, swerving to avoid a car, skidded off the road and caught fire; 16 persons burned to death.

March 28

Saint-Denis, Réunion. A bus loaded with many children went out of control and slid into a river; 24 passengers were killed, and 32 were injured.

April 30

Kiev, U.S.S.R. A bus fell off a bridge into a river, killing 27 persons and injuring 5 others.

May 8

Teloloapan, Mexico. A bus plunged over a cliff and killed 15 of the 41 passengers aboard.

May 31

Stuttgart, West Germany. A car, speeding on the rain-slick Stuttgart–Munich autobahn, cut in front of a chartered bus carrying elderly British tourists, forcing the driver to brake and skid off the road; 12 passengers were killed, and 31 were injured.

July 6

Near Nakhon Ratchasima, Thailand. An express train smashed into a bus, killing at least 43 of the bus passengers and injuring scores more.

July 13

Genoa, Italy. A collision of two autos and an Italian Army truck on the Riviera road knocked the truck over a cliff and into the sea; 13 soldiers died, and 12 other soldiers and auto passengers were injured.

Aug. 2

Near Nagpur, India. The flooding Wainganga River covered

the road and concealed a low place into which a truck was driven; all 20 persons aboard drowned.

Aug. 26

Lima, Peru. A truck careened down a mountainside, killing 35 persons; 28 others were injured.

Sept. 13

Near Belo Horizonte, Brazil. A bus dropped 300 feet from a viaduct and killed 12 persons; 7 others were injured.

Oct. 13

Near Izmir, Turkey. An intercity bus plunged off the road into a ravine; 25 persons died, and 18 were injured.

Oct. 16

Near Kimchon, South Korea. A sightseeing bus shot off the road and fell 60 feet down a mountainside; 42 elderly tourists were killed, and 10 others were injured.

Nov. 12

Mae Sariang District, Thailand. A lumber truck loaded with festival-goers plunged into a ravine, killing 25 riders.

Dec. 15

Near Jhelum, Pakistan. The head-on collision of two buses caused the death of 42 persons.

Dec. 22

Near Manila, Philippines. An out-of-control bus spun over a cliff and into a 30-foot ravine, killing 47 passengers, mostly students homeward-bound for Christmas.

Dec. 25

Near Tafidel Valle, Argentina. Some 16 persons drowned when their bus sank in the Tala River.

1968

Jan. 21

Cuernavaca, Mexico. Brake failure caused an overloaded bus to ram into a wall, killing 18 persons and injuring 45 others.

Jan. 26

Near Conquista, Brazil. En route from Ihéus to São Paulo, a bus skidded off the highway and into a lake; 13 passengers drowned.

Feb. 22

Bogotá, Colombia. A bus carrying more than 80 persons went out of control on a steep incline and crashed into a house; 11 persons were killed, and 32 others were injured.

March 7

Near Baker, California. A Las Vegas, Nevada-bound Greyhound bus collided with an automobile, overturned on the rain-slick highway, and burst into flames; 19 bus passengers and the driver of the car were killed.

March 16

North of Lagos, Nigeria. A collision between a bus and an oil truck killed 19 persons; 12 others were injured.

March 17

West of Istanbul. Two passenger buses collided on the Istanbul–Edirne highway, killing 35 persons and injuring 45 others.

March 17

Near Lagos, Nigeria. A bus-truck collision killed 19 persons.

March 18

Near Rampur, India. A bus ran off the road and slid into the Jhelum River, drowning 27 persons.

April 30

Benares, India. Transporting a wedding party of about 50 persons, a truck hit a tree and careened into a ravine; 19 persons died, and at least 25 others were injured.

May 4

Northern Colombia. A Pamplona–Cucuta bus skidded over a 1,200-foot cliff, killing more than 20 persons.

May 17

Bercha, India. Passing over a grade crossing, a heavily loaded bus was struck by an express train; 27 bus passengers were killed, and 38 others were injured.

May 18

Near Manipur, India. Plunging into a ravine, a bus overturned, killing 10 persons and injuring 33.

June 13

Near Kisumu, Kenya. A bus crash killed 38 persons.

June 21

Colombia-Venezuela border. A bus transporting 60 schoolgirls plunged over a precipice, reportedly killing between 20 and 25 of the girls.

Aug. 14

Near Lima, Peru. A bus ran off a mountain road, killing 12 persons.

Aug. 18

Gifu, Japan. Earth loosened by the torrential rains of Typhoon Polly slid down over the highway and swept two sightseeing buses into the churning Hida River; at least 102 women and children perished in the muddy waters.

Sept. 21

Turkey. A bus accident on a mountain road killed 14 persons.

Oct. 3

Near Pracmuap Khiri Khan, Thailand. A truck crashed over a riverbank and into the water; 11 persons were killed, and many others were missing.

Oct. 14

Northern Kashmir. Plunging off the road, a bus fell 1,000 feet into a ravine, killing 21 persons and injuring 20 others.

Nov. 11

Accra, Ghana. A bus-tank truck collision killed 22 persons, most of them children.

Dec. 6

Near La Paz, Bolivia. Three trucks were swept away by a swollen river; 50 persons drowned.

1969

Jan. 1

Ismailia, Egypt. A Cairo–Suez passenger bus collided with a truck, killing 14 riders and injuring 35 others.

Jan. 7

Cairo, Egypt. A bus, swerving to miss an oncoming car, smashed through a fence and plunged into the Nile River; 15 passengers perished, and 20 others were missing.

Jan. 10

Seoul, South Korea. A crowded bus collided with a train at a grade crossing; 18 persons died, and 70 were injured.

Jan. 15

Tuzla, Turkey. A Zonguldak–Istanbul bus toppled off a bridge into the ravine below, killing 22 riders; 14 others were injured.

Feb. 5

Near Casablanca, Morocco. The collision of a truck and a bus, traveling between Safi and Marrakech, killed 17 persons and injured 17 others.

March 2

Covington, Georgia. A drag-racing car pushing 180 mph spun off the track, hurtled into a group of spectators, and killed at least 11 of them; as many as 50 others were injured.

March 17

Fresno, Colombia. A bus accident accounted for 30 deaths; 19 persons were injured.

May 19

Northern Turkey. A passenger bus ran off the highway into a stream, killing 18 persons.

May 27

Northern Philippines. A speeding bus overtook a jeep carrying about 30 persons, piled into it, and killed 10 riders; another 15 were injured.

June 4

Corum, Turkey. A loaded truck plowed into a group of pedestrians, killing 13 and injuring 6 others.

June 21

Central Syria. A truck transporting 35 girls to the harvest fields overturned; 25 of the girls were killed.

July 15

Dinant, Belgium. Dutch vacationers were dumped into the Meuse River when their tour bus left the road because of faulty brakes; 21 passengers died, and 4 others survived.

August 5

Himalaya Mountains, India. A bus went down a canyon, killing 27 pilgrims.

Sept. 8

Ankara, Turkey. An Artvin–Samsun bus, pullling onto the shoulder to make way for a passing truck, fell into a 600-foot ravine; 13 occupants of the bus died, and 50 others were seriously injured.

Sept. 22

Swalior-Bhopal, India. A bus plunged into the Parbali River; 33 passengers died.

Oct. 2

Casma Province, Peru. An intercity bus collided with a heavily loaded truck and burst into flames; 21 passengers perished, and 25 others were severely burned.

Oct. 4

Toumba, Mexico. A trolley car sliced through a bus and killed 15 of the bus riders; 2 others were injured.

Oct. 5

Near Madurai, India. A mountain-road collision between a bus and a jeep propelled the bus down the mountainside and killed 26 persons; 40 others were injured.

Oct. 5

Vranje, Yugoslavia. A bus careened off the road and overturned, killing at least 10 riders.

Nov. 1

South of Cairo, Egypt. A skidding bus landed in an irrigation ditch, killing 18 of the 40 passengers.

Dec. 8

Northern Dahomey. A truck carrying 140 refugees from Ghana overturned, killing 15 persons and injuring 73 others.

Dec. 12

Bulawayo, Rhodesia. A bus flipped off a bridge and fell 100 feet into the 20-foot-deep Gwaai River; 21 persons perished, and many others were missing and presumed dead.

Dec. 17

Guatemala City, Guatemala. A bus collided with an auto, and both vehicles were thrown into a 1,200-foot ravine; 26 persons died, and 25 others were injured.

Dec. 23

Erivan, Armenia, U.S.S.R. A bus crash reportedly killed as many as 100 persons.

Dec. 29

Southwestern Colombia. A bus veered off the mountain road between Popayán and Pasto, killing 10 persons; 29 others were injured.

1970

Jan. 8

Near Montes Calaros, Brazil. A bus-truck collision killed 23 persons.

Feb. 21

Kafanchan, Nigeria. While being taken to a hospital, after having been injured in a railroad accident, 52 persons were killed in a bus crash.

March 6

Katmandu, Nepal. Swerving to avoid hitting a small girl, a speeding truck overturned and killed 14 persons riding on top of its load of cement; 14 other riders were hurt.

March 14

Pachuca, Mexico. Two buses collided, then were smashed into and set afire by a truck loaded with industrial alcohol; 27 persons perished, and 32 others were injured.

March 20

Ambato, Ecuador. An overloaded bus plunged through the guardrail of a bridge and into the Ambato River, killing 56 of the passengers; 61 others were injured.

May 3

Near Managua, Nicaragua. A truck and bus collision caused 13 deaths.

Aug. 21

South Korea. A Seoul–Pusan bus plunged over a 130-foot cliff, killed 25 persons, and injured 22 others.

Sept. 18

Ceara State, Brazil. Loaded with pilgrims returning from a religious festival, a truck lost its brakes, and veered off a hilly curve and into a lake, killing 19 pilgrims and injuring 33.

Oct. 9

Chamba, India. A bus went into a mountain ravine, killing 45 passengers.

Oct. 24

Near Bangkok, Thailand. About 70 miles southeast of the city, a truck smashed into a bus carrying Buddhist pilgrims; 27 persons were killed.

Nov. 3

Takane, Japan. A construction minibus ran off the road and plunged into a reservoir, killing all 10 passengers.

Dec. 18

Rawalpindi, India. A bus ran into a canal; 27 persons drowned.

1971

Jan. 3

Benue Plateau, Nigeria. A truck smashed into a bridge; 26 passengers were killed, and 34 others were injured.

Feb. 5

Near Ibjar, Iran. A bus careened into a deep gorge, killing 30 persons.

March 25

Near Davao, Philippines. A bus plunged into a river; 12 persons were killed, and 38 others were injured.

May 10

Near Chongpyong, South Korea. Trapped in a bus that settled into a reservoir after falling off the roadway, 77 persons drowned; 14 others survived.

May 11

Lashkargah, Afghanistan. Careless driving put a bus into an irrigation ditch and killed 21 persons; 6 others were injured.

May 24

Panama Canal. A bus smashed through the guardrail of a bridge, killing 38 passengers.

June 20

Near Afyion, Turkey. A collision between a truck and a bus resulted in 33 deaths; 24 persons were injured.

June 27

Cairo, Egypt. Swerving to avoid another vehicle, a truck veered into a canal, killing 15 persons and injuring 17 others.

July 11

Nainital Hill district, India. A bus fell into a lake; 21 persons were drowned.

July 12
Roi-Et Province, Thailand. A bus ran head-on into a truck and killed 12 persons.

July 26
Simla, India. Dropping into a 100-foot gorge, a bus caused the deaths of 14 persons and injured 45 others.

Aug. 7
Central Ghana. A truck slammed head-on into a bus on the Accra–Cape Coast road; 16 persons were killed, and 18 others were injured.

Aug. 18
Near Casablanca, Morocco. Plunging into a deep gorge, a rural bus brought death to 45 persons and injured 30 others.

Sept. 11
Bronkhorstspruit, South Africa. A collision between a truck and a school bus killed 19 children.

Sept. 17
Near Valdepeñas, Spain. A tourist bus traveling the main road to Andalusia collided with a brick-loaded truck, killing the truck driver and 17 Canadian women tourists.

Oct. 24
Walla Walla, Washington. A two-car collision caused 11 deaths; one other person was seriously injured.

Dec. 19
Aswan, Egypt. An accident caused an overturned trailer to land in an irrigation ditch, drowning 50 laborers.

1972
Jan. 21
Bogotá, Colombia. A collision between a bus and a tanker truck 45 miles east of the city killed 20 of the 37 passengers aboard the bus.

Feb. 5
Mahasu, India. A bus lurched off the road and into a Himalayan mountain gorge, killing 19 persons.

Feb. 18
Kafr Saad, Egypt. A Port Said–Cairo bus blew a front tire, careened into a rock wall, then plunged into the Tefiki irrigation canal; most of the 77 persons who died were students.

March 4
Minab, Iran. In attempting to ford the Kae River a bus was swept away by the strong current; 32 persons drowned, and 37 others were rescued.

March 19

The mangled wreckage of a double-decker bus clutters the highway in Bean Station, Tennessee, after the bus collided with a tractor-trailer on May 13; both drivers and 12 others were killed.

Carsamba, Turkey. A passenger bus collided head-on with a minibus and killed 17 persons; 15 others were injured.

May 13

Taipei, Taiwan. Transporting a group of schoolgirls, a bus veered off the roadway into a ravine and killed 14 persons.

May 13

Bean Station, Tennessee. A double-decker Knoxville–New York Greyhound bus, behind schedule and speeding along in the early dawn on a wet U.S. 11W, a winding two-lanc highway, whipped into a tractor-trailer outfit and was split in half; 14 persons were killed (including the drivers of both vehicles), and 15 others were injured.

May 15

Minia, Egypt. On its way to a monastery with a group of Christian pilgrims, a bus skidded from the road and fell into the Nile River; more than 50 persons drowned.

June 11

Shady Nook, Louisiana. A wheat-laden semitrailer truck ripped into the rear of a pickup truck as the small vehicle turned off the highway on its way to a swimming hole with a load of children; the young woman driver and 11 of the 13 children were killed.

June 25
Cáceres, Spain. A bus plunged down a mountainside, killing 22 passengers.

July 3
Amritsar, India. A bus-truck collision killed 27 persons.

July 10
Ayacucho, Peru. A passenger-filled truck toppled into a ravine, taking the lives of 15 persons.

July 19
São Domingos, Brazil. A bus fell from a ferry ramp into the Capim River; 30 persons were killed.

July 28
Burgas, Bulgaria. A bus plunged into a river, killing 40 persons and injuring 9.

Aug. 4
South Iran. A bus-truck collision reportedly killed 18 persons and injured 23 others.

Aug. 8
Zarand, Iran. Two buses crashed head-on, killing 39 persons and injuring 40 others.

Aug. 27
Northern Ecuador. A crowded bus went over an embankment and into a 150-foot ravine, killing 19 persons; 5 others were seriously injured.

Sept. 8
Crete, Greece. En route to a religious ceremony, a passenger bus left the road and dropped over a 150-foot cliff in southeastern Crete; 21 pilgrims died, and 28 others were injured.

Sept. 21
Pernik, Bulgaria. A transport bus carrying a team of Czechoslovak parachutists to the Warsaw Pact parachute jumping championship was hit by a train at a grade crossing; 11 team members were killed.

Sept. 30
Saraburi Province, Thailand. Failing in an attempt to pass another vehicle, a truck rammed head-on into a bus, killing 20 passengers; 15 others were hospitalized.

Oct. 6
Kericho, Kenya. A crowded bus racing through the night careened off the road and into a flooded ditch, taking the lives of at least 25 persons; 63 others were hurt.

Oct. 11

Medenine, Tunisia. An army truck collided with another vehicle, killing 20 persons.

Oct. 23

Belo Horizonte, Brazil. A collision between a coal truck and a bus killed 12 persons and injured at least 25 others.

Nov. 4

Greytown, South Africa. An open truck filled with riders veered off the road and rolled down a slope, killing 18 of the occupants; 4 others were seriously injured.

Dec. 26

Near Glorieta, New Mexico. A bus transporting a Baptist Church youth group from Austin, Texas, to the Vadito ski resort in New Mexico collided with a cattle trailer when the two vehicles attempted to squeeze past one another on an extremely narrow bridge; 19 passengers were killed.

1973

Jan. 14

Zonguldak, Turkey. Blinded by heavy snow, the driver of a bus steered over a cliff; 16 occupants of the bus died, and 25 others were injured.

Jan. 21

Suva, Fiji. A bus carrying a group of wedding guests collided with another bus, killing 15 guests, mostly women and children; another 48 guests were injured.

Jan. 29

Near Cordoba, Argentina. A bus fell into a 90-foot ravine and killed 11 persons; 25 others were injured.

Jan. 30

Kecskemet, Hungary. Traveling over a crossing, a bus was rammed by a passenger train; 24 persons died, and 20 more were severely hurt.

Feb. 15

Uvita, Colombia. A bus burst into flames as it fell to the bottom of a ravine, killing 20 persons and injuring 6 others.

March 12

Baquedano, Chile. A head-on crash of two buses accounted for the death of 45 persons, with another possible 50 hurt.

May 2

Near Salvador, Brazil. Out of control on a rural road after hitting a donkey, an overloaded bus crashed head-on into a truck; 39 persons, 13 of whom were children, were killed.

May 3

Dacca, Bangladesh. A bus waiting for a ferry to take it across the Bansi River rolled off the dock and into the river, drowning at least 52 persons; 8 others scrambled out of the bus before it went under.

May 16

Kyongju, South Korea. An overloaded bus attempting to cross some railroad tracks was struck by a train and hurled into a stream; 23 persons, mostly high school students, were killed, and more than 60 others were hurt.

June 10

Near Buenos Aires, Argentina. Caught on the train tracks, a standing bus was rammed by a train and dragged 100 feet; 13 persons died, and 30 others were injured.

June 21

Pindamonhangaba, Brazil. A multiple crash involving four buses, five trucks, three trailers, and six cars occurred in a thick fog on Brazil's busiest highway; a group of pilgrims on their way to a holy shrine on Corpus Christi Day were among the 14 fatalities resulting from the pileup.

July 2

Alwar, India. A bus attempting to ford a swollen stream stalled in the swirling waters; two differing high-caste groups of passengers refused to share the single rescue rope brought out from shore and stayed on the bus as it was swept downstream; 78 lives were lost, and 8 persons survived.

July 9

Bogor, Indonesia. Colliding with another bus, a crowded bus veered off the road and into a river, killing 18 persons and injuring 33 others.

July 15

Japalpur, India. Crashing through a collapsing bridge, a bus fell into the Kopra River, killing 31 of 40 passengers.

July 22

Iran. A bus speeding around a curve in northeast Iran hit a pedestrian, crashed through a bridge guardrail, and plunged into a river; 48 persons died, 22 of whom were children.

Aug. 17

Monterrey, Mexico. A highway bus collided with a car and trailer truck on the Monterrey–Monclova highway, sending 18 persons to a fiery death and seriously injuring 40 others.

Sept. 21

Isparata, Turkey. An open truck careened off a highway and overturned; 23 farmers, who were on their way to market, were killed, and 4 others were seriously injured.

Sept. 26

New South Wales, Australia. Brake failure caused a tourist bus to roll backward and down a mountainside in the Australian Alps before plunging into a hydroelectric dam; 18 elderly persons from Adelaide were killed, and 21 others were injured.

Sept. 29

Guadalajara, Mexico. A bus traveling from Tepic to Mexico City collided with a truck near Guadalajara; 22 persons were killed, and 16 were injured.

Oct. 29

Nagpur, India. A bus traveling in the Chanda district of central India plunged into a rain-swollen river, drowning 30 persons.

Nov. 3

Sacramento, California. A Greyhound bus carrying 43 passengers to Reno, Nevada, gambling casinos was totally demolished when it crashed head-on into a highway abutment near Sacramento; 13 persons were killed, and 31 were injured.

Nov. 20

San Nicolás Coatepec, Mexico. A drunken driver lost control of a bus overloaded with religious pilgrims, as it moved along a twisting mountain road about 70 miles southwest of Mexico City, and sent it plunging into a ravine 150 feet below; 15 persons died, most of them children, and 43 others were injured.

1974

Jan. 19

Karachi, Pakistan. When a gasoline tanker truck collided with a bus, leaking fuel set fire to nearby buildings; at least 24 persons were killed, and 40 others were injured.

Jan. 28

Peru. A bus that plunged into a river in the Andes was swirled 400 yards downstream; at least 35 persons died.

Jan. 29

Colombia. A bus toppled over a precipice and into the Ovejas River, killing 17 persons and badly injuring 10 others.

Feb. 11

Banphot Phisai, Thailand. Two buses collided about 165 miles north of Bangkok; 25 persons were reported killed and 50 injured.

March 14

Nigeria. A truck, moving along the road between Kontagora and Zura, went off the road and plunged into a river; 23 persons were killed, and 14 were injured.

April 12

Near Acapulco, Mexico. A double-level truck, swerving to avoid a horse, went off the road and into a 21-foot gully; 14 passengers, returning home from Good Friday services, lost their lives, and more than 100 others suffered injuries.

May 20

Eastern Tabasco State, Mexico. A bus filled with vacationers crashed into the Carizales River, killing 36 persons.

May 21

Ganges River, India. A crowded bus, being driven onto a tug that served as a river ferry, slid off the boat and into the Ganges; at least 50 persons were believed drowned.

June 29

San Mateo Atenco, Mexico. A bus slammed into a bridge, killing 29 persons.

July 25

Near Mexico City. Two bus crashes, both near Mexico City, took the lives of 24 persons and injured 71.

July 28

Near Belém, Brazil. A bus collided with a truck, killing 69 persons and injuring 10.

Aug. 11

Near Bolu, Turkey. A collision between two buses traveling along the Ankara–Istanbul highway took the lives of 21 persons and injured 41.

Sept. 9

Lusaka, Zambia. A bus accident caused the death of 26 persons.

Dec. 20

Sterkstroom, South Africa. A truck overturned near Sterkstroom, killing 33 African railway workers and injuring 26 seriously.

Dec. 27

Nova Iguaçu, Brazil. An interurban train passing a suburban railroad crossing north of Rio de Janeiro crashed into a bus; 18 persons died, and 18 others were injured.

1975

Jan. 1

Japan. A bus slid off an icy road into a lake, killing 23 vacationers on their way to a ski resort.

Jan. 30

Near Quito, Ecuador. A bus ran over a steep embankment; 30 persons were killed.

Feb. 8

Tultepec, Mexico. A passenger bus, carrying more than twice its approved capacity, was struck by a train when the driver tried to speed over a crossing; 29 persons died, and 28 others were injured.

Feb. 24

Medellin, Colombia. A bus, plunging down a mountainside, killed 20 persons.

March 7

Munich, West Germany. A seven-car electric commuter train traveling 75 mph hit a public bus when it went past a protective gate that opened prematurely; of the 12 persons who died, 6 were young students.

March 10

Near Manila, Philippines. An express train smashed into a passenger bus, killing 10 persons and injuring 28.

March 14

Near Buenos Aires, Argentina. A truck and bus collided in bad weather, killing at least 11 persons and seriously injuring 5 others.

March 25

Near Rio de Janeiro, Brazil. A suburban bus plunged into a muddy river and sank, killing 26 of the 32 persons aboard.

March 27

Bahía Blanca, Argentina. During a heavy rain, a bus was hit broadside by a freight train at an unguarded crossing; 12 persons died, and 22 were injured.

April 2

Vizille, France. A crowded bus with faulty brakes missed a sharp turn, smashed through a stone barrier, then plunged off a bridge onto a river embankment about 100 feet below; 27 persons returning from a religious pilgrimage died, and 16 were injured.

April 25

Near Plovdiv, Bulgaria. A collision at an unguarded railroad crossing caused a freight car to derail, then strike a bus carrying workers to a mountain resort; 11 persons were killed, and 16 were seriously injured.

May 20

Roseau, Dominican Republic. A truck fell 500 feet into a ravine, killing 28 persons.

May 27

North Yorkshire, England. A chartered bus smashed through the stone siding of a bridge and dropped upside down onto a field 25 feet below; 31 of the 45 women passengers, and the driver, were killed.

June 15

Villach, Austria. Brake failure caused a tour bus to plunge off a steep mountain road and hurtle 120 feet into a rocky ravine; 21 retirees were killed, and 23 others were injured.

July 5

Near Bandar-Abbas, Iran. A head-on collision between a truck and a bus killed 21 persons.

July 21

Near Culiacán, Mexico. A bus burst into flames after colliding with a car near the capital of Sinaloa State in western Mexico; 30 persons trapped inside the burning bus died.

Aug. 20

Near Mexico City, Mexico. In a head-on collision between two buses, 15 persons were killed and 78 others injured.

Sept. 20

Near Ciudad Obregón, Mexico. A crowded bus plunged into a canal and submerged; at least 18 persons lost their lives, 7 of whom were children.

Oct. 14

Eastern Hungary. A crowded bus crashed into a train at an unmanned crossing, killing 12 persons.

Oct. 30

Zitacuaro, Mexico. A truck that moved into the lane of oncoming traffic smashed into a school bus; 15 students and the bus driver were killed.

1976

Jan. 4

Natal State, South Africa. A bus plunged into the Umtawalumi River, killing 19 persons and injuring 38 others.

Jan. 26

Near Nongoma, South Africa. A bus crash in a remote area of eastern South Africa killed 19 persons and injured 76 others.

Feb. 7

Beckemeyer, Illinois. A camper truck that was crossing an unguarded railroad track at night was hit by a fast-moving Baltimore & Ohio 67-car freight train; a grandfather and 11 young children, on their way to a skating rink, were killed.

Feb. 7

Konya Province, Turkey. A driver lost control of his bus on an icy road in central Turkey, killing 10 persons and injuring another 8.

Feb. 10

Near Kinshasa, Zaire. A truck transporting workmen to their jobs crashed when the driver lost control of the vehicle; 23 persons were killed, and dozens were injured.

March 5

Shivalli, India. A bus, jam-packed with guests traveling to a wedding reception, went off the road, overturned, and plunged into a deep irrigation canal when the driver swerved to avoid a bullock cart; 79 persons were killed.

March 29

Near Hoshiarpur, India. A reported 20 persons were killed and 40 injured when a bus crashed into a tree in northwestern India.

Late March

Near Poona, India. A tractor-drawn wagon transporting wedding guests between villages fell into a canal; 45 bodies were recovered.

April 29

Luzon Province, Philippines. A bus heading for the resort city of Baguio in northern Luzon crashed into a tree and burned; 22 persons were killed, and 7 others were injured.

April 30

Near Baguio, Philippines. A bus carrying trade school employees and their families to Baguio slipped over the edge of a 250-foot cliff that bounds the zigzag MacArthur Highway; casualties included 29 persons dead and 27 seriously injured.

May 21

Near Martinez, California. A bus carrying members of a Yuba City high school choir smashed through a guardrail and landed upside down 30 feet below a bridge ramp that was part of a freeway exit; 28 students and one adult were killed, and many teenagers were seriously injured.

May 28

Near Rishikesh, India. A bus skidded and plunged into the Ganges River; 40 persons were killed.

Aug. 25

Northeastern Iran. A passenger bus and a tank truck crashed into each other some 50 miles from Shahrud in northeastern Iran; the accident claimed 21 lives.

September

Near Trinidad, Cuba. A bus exploded in flames after colliding with a truck near Trinidad; 27 persons were reported killed.

Sept. 2

Near Mexico City, Mexico. A passenger bus went over a 150-foot embankment about 25 miles west of the nation's capital; at least 15 persons died in the mishap, and some 30 others were injured.

Sept. 19

Santiago, Chile. A runaway truck crashed into a crowd of people celebrating Chile's independence day; 23 persons died, and 62 were injured.

Oct. 15

Eastern Cuba. Two freight cars that broke away from an ore train at the Nicaro nickel mines smashed into a crowded bus at a lower level crossing; 54 persons were reported killed.

Nov. 14

Near Manaus, Brazil. A bus loaded with voters failed to stop at an Urubu River ferry crossing and was swept downstream after plunging into the water; 38 persons were killed in the mishap.

Nov. 29

Near Van, Turkey. A bus and taxi fell over a precipice and into Lake Van after colliding on a road; 25 persons were killed, and 15 others were injured.

Dec. 12

Near São Paulo, Brazil. A bus traveling between São Paulo and Igautu plunged into the Pardo River when the driver swerved to avoid hitting a group of pedestrians; 20 persons were killed, and 16 were injured.

Dec. 21

Lyon, France. A school bus transporting handicapped children went off the road in heavy fog as the driver attempted to make a sharp turn; 17 persons died in the waters of the Rhône River, and 2 others were reported missing.

1977

Jan. 23

Near Kumanovo, Yugoslavia. A bus traveling from Turkey to Yugoslavia crashed through an overpass guard barrier as it was overtaking a truck; 24 passengers were killed and 19 injured, some critically.

March 31

Dera Ghazi Khan, Pakistan. A bus carrying 30 persons plummeted into the Indus River in Punjab Province, when a drawbridge collapsed; 22 persons died, 4 were rescued, and 4 others were missing.

April 3

Cairo, Egypt. A bus carrying some 100 persons plunged into an irrigation canal after swerving to avoid hitting a child; 19 persons died and 15 were injured in the mishap.

June 28

Near São Paulo, Brazil. Two trucks crashing into one another on the fog-shrouded highway that links São Paulo to the coastal city of Santos created a chain reaction of collisions involving 46 buses, 12 trucks, and 74 automobiles; at least 15 persons were killed and 229 were injured.

Aug. 21

Near Hermosillo, Mexico. A bus traveling on a highway between Hermosillo and Nogales toppled into a water-filled ditch after rain washed out the roadway; 20 persons were killed, and 27 were injured.

Sept. 24

Near Dera Ismail Khan, Pakistan. A bus veered off a road while making a sharp turn and plunged into a ravine; 14 persons were killed in the crash.

Oct. 2

Near Tampa, Florida. A St. Petersburg-bound Amtrak passenger train collided with a pickup truck about 15 miles west of Tampa; all 10 persons riding in the truck were killed.

Nov. 9

Near Pietermaritzburg, South Africa. A tractor-trailer traveling along the highway to Pietermaritzburg killed 11 persons in a crowd that had gathered where an accident had occurred moments earlier.

Dec. 25

Azuay Province, Ecuador. A bus traveling on a mountain road in the southern province of Azuay plunged over the side of the road; 26 persons were killed, and 30 others were injured.

1978

Jan. 3

Sariaya, Philippines. A bus traveling to Manila smashed into a parked truck about 50 miles east of the capital; 21 passengers were killed, and 38 others were injured.

Feb. 5

Aguas Buenos, Puerto Rico. A school bus transporting students in rural areas to public schools toppled off a narrow road into a 500-foot ravine about 13 miles south of San Juan; of the estimated 60 children aboard the bus, 11 were killed, and 30 others were injured.

Feb. 16
Tarma Province, Peru. A bus plunged over a precipice; 40 persons were killed, and 25 others were injured.

March 22
Near Birjand, Iran. A collision between a bus and a road tanker in eastern Iran claimed the lives of 28 persons and injured 26 others.

March 27
Near San Luis, Mexico. A head-on collision between two buses, about 40 miles south of the border town of San Luis, killed at least 30 of the 81 passengers; many of the victims burned to death in a fire that broke out following the crash.

March 30
Near Tehran, Iran. In Iran's second major traffic accident in nine days, an oil truck, a bus, and a car collided west of Tehran on the Karaj–Qazvin road; 26 persons were killed, and 18 others were injured.

May 4
Southern Colombia. A tourist bus carrying university students on an excursion to Pasto, a city near the Ecuador border, went over a precipice; 11 students died, and 18 others were injured.

May 8
Near Gwalior, India. A bus transporting members of two wedding parties skidded off a bridge in central India and plunged into a river; 31 persons, including the 2 grooms and 9 children, were killed, and 35 others were injured.

June 10
Near Chechaouene, Morocco. A bus plunged into a 500-foot ravine about 30 miles east of this Rif Mountains resort in northern Morocco; at least 23 persons died, and 22 others were injured.

July 16
Near Mexico City, Mexico. A truck carrying propane gas flipped over, exploded, and spewed fiery gas onto a four-lane highway; two trucks, two buses, and a car crashed into the wreckage; at least 11 persons died, and nearly 200 others were severely burned.

July 17
Near Cairo, Egypt. An overcrowded bus plunged into the Nile River after colliding with a truck; 11 passengers and the

After a deadly plunge into the Han River near the center of Seoul, Korea, on July 23, a bus is hauled to the surface by rescue workers.

driver escaped injury, but 56 others, many of them soldiers, drowned.

July 23

Near Mungling, Nepal. A bus carrying 38 passengers tumbled into the swollen Trusuli River; 25 persons were killed.

July 23

Seoul, South Korea. A swerving bus hurtled through a bridge guardrail and plunged 60 feet into the Han River; 36 persons were killed, and 7 others were rescued with serious injuries.

Aug. 12

Northern Uganda. A bus traveling between Arua and Moyo plunged into a river, killing at least 40 persons; many of the victims were children returning from school to their villages on holiday.

Mid-September

Maputo, Mozambique. A truck transporting dozens of farm workers to the town of Xai Xai in Gaza province overturned and plunged into an irrigation canal; 65 workers were killed, and 11 others were injured.

Oct. 1

Basirhat, West Bengal, India. A bus traveling down one of India's muddy, flood-ravaged roads overturned and landed in a flooded ditch; 88 persons were killed, and 20 were injured.

7.
Miscellaneous Mishaps

Human failure, either in planning or in execution, underlies most of the so-called man-made disasters. In the majority of them technology or machinery has failed because of inadequate design, maintenance, or operation. Some man-made disasters, however, fall in other realms. They flow from human failures in the very areas that have been exalted variously as pinnacles of human understanding and experience: science, engineering, sports, politics, and religion. These "other" catastrophes include poisonings, building collapses, and stampedes.

Poisonings

Atlanta, Georgia, 1951. The manufacture and sale of bootleg liquor—or moonshine—continued to be a flourishing enterprise, particularly in the southern United States, long after Prohibition ended. Because such unlawful liquor was tax-free, and therefore inexpensive, it remained popular even though its danger was commonly known. Unscrupulous moonshiners sometimes created an absolutely lethal product.

In October 1951 a bootlegger named Jack Howell added a barrel of methyl alcohol to about 300 bottles of whiskey. The bottles of poisonous drink were sold in a black neighborhood. On the following day, October 23, 1951, more than four hundred blacks who had drunk Howell's moonshine went to a hospital in Atlanta with complaints of stomach cramps, respiratory difficulties, and loss of vision. The hospital was overwhelmed with the influx of the critically ill persons and had to use medical students to help treat them. Within a week thirty-nine persons died from the poisoning, and seven were permanently blinded. Howell was caught and eventually was sentenced to life imprisonment.

Al Basrah, Iraq, 1971. In September 1971 a huge shipment of American barley and Mexican wheat arrived at the port of Al Basrah. The grain had been treated with a mercury solution in order to prevent spoilage during shipment and storage. Although high levels of mercury are poisonous, the grain was intended for use only as seed. To indicate the presence of mercury the grain had been sprayed with a bright pink dye, and warnings had been attached in both English and Spanish. No warnings in Arabic, however, were given.

The grain was stolen from the loading docks and was repackaged and sold as food. Mass poisoning occurred throughout the country. Hundreds of persons died, and many thousands were crippled and blinded and suffered deafness and brain damage. The Iraqi government, however, did not make public any news about the poisonings. Two years after they occurred, U.S. newsman Ed Hughes discovered what had happened. His discoveries forced the Iraqi government to admit that hospitals had treated more than 6,500 cases of mercury poisoning. Government officials stated that 459 of those treated had died. Not satisfied with the government's figures, Hughes continued his investigation and concluded that as many as 6,000 persons may have perished and that 100,000 others may have been injured.

New Delhi, India, 1972. A gruesome instance of mass poisoning occurred in India on January 23, 1972. A bootlegger from one of the city's slums sold liquor containing wood alcohol and varnish for a wedding party in another slum.

Several hundred persons, including the bootlegger and his mother and brother, attended the party. At least a hundred persons died from drinking the poisoned liquor. Police traced it to the bootlegger, only to find him and his family dead in their house from poisoning.

Central Michigan, 1970s. It first appeared in 1973. By early the following year Michigan farmers were beginning to wonder if it was a mysterious epidemic. On many—but not all—farms, livestock began exhibiting peculiar behavior. Cows were producing less milk and soon began giving birth to dead calves. Occasional adult cattle began to die for no apparent reason. Chicken farmers found their flocks developing a kind of paralysis; the hens would flutter, fall over, and die. Pigs and sheep were also affected.

Farmers, apprehensively watching their animals die from an invisible cause, suspected their feed, but the suppliers scoffed at the suggestion that their products were contaminated. The plague swept on and soon human farm families began to report symptoms of fatigue, painful joints, headaches, sleeplessness, and dizziness. "I'm hungry all the time," one farmer said, "but when I eat I get cramps and dizzy."

The mystery was removed later in 1974, but the problem seemed almost impossible to eliminate; it seemed self-perpetuating. The symptoms reported by the farmers coincided exactly with those of poisoning by polybrominated biphenyl

(PBB), an industrial chemical. A belatedly urgent investigation did the necessary detective work. It had been contaminated feed after all.

In 1973 the Michigan Chemical Corporation had accidentally shipped a fire retardant containing PBB to a Michigan farm supply firm, Farm Bureau Services, Inc. Worse, the lethal fire retardant was included in a shipment of a livestock feed supplement widely used to enhance the nutritional value of natural feeds. Worse still, the two chemicals, one poison and the other highly nutritive, were in look-alike sacks.

At least 500 and perhaps as much as 1,000 pounds of the fire retardant was involved in the mixup. Along with the bona fide feed supplement, the poison was mixed with cattle, hog, and chicken feeds and sold to farmers all over Michigan.

By the time the nature and the scope of the problem were realized, livestock were dying on a large scale, hosts of farm families displayed symptoms of PBB poisoning, and tests were turning up traces of the chemical in mothers' milk. The Michigan legislature set strict standards on maximum permissible PBB presence in livestock. The state then set in motion a massive program of destroying and burying animals, especially cattle, that had been contaminated above the permissible level, and a two-year wave of slaughter saw 35,000 contaminated dairy and beef cattle and at least a million pigs, sheep, and chickens bulldozed into mass burial sites in a wooded northern county of lower Michigan.

When the slaughter ended in 1976 the topic dropped out of the news for a time, but all the contamination publicity led to flagging confidence in the purity of Michigan meat and dairy products in other states and Canada. The legislature set a new state PBB standard of only twenty parts per billion—far more stringent than the maximums allowed by any other state of the United States. New tests made necessary by the new standards found many animals with more PBB than the new limits and brought on new waves of slaughter and burial in 1978.

Meanwhile, bitter farmers, many suffering symptoms of PBB poisoning themselves, were finding that new animals bought to replace their slain and buried herds and flocks were becoming contaminated even though the tainted feed had not been used for years. It developed that a farm, once it was heavily contaminated, could be cleared of damaging residual levels of PBB only by the most herculean measures. Manure from poisoned animals if spread on fields as fertilizers—a

*Livestock contaminated with PBB, victims of human error,
are slaughtered and buried in mass burial plots in Oscoda
County, Michigan, in 1978.*

usual farm practice—would contaminate the fields it fertil-
ized, and this poison could only be purged by scraping off and
removing all soil to the depth that the field had been tilled.
Grazing animals could pick up PBB from plants, and chickens pecking and scratching in barnyards could be ingesting it.

The accidental confusion of a half-ton or less of PBB-laden

fire retardant with a nutritional feed supplement—each product by itself one of the miracles of modern science—had turned into a catastrophe that may have claimed more than two million animal lives, brought disease to as many as nine million humans who innocently ate poisoned meat or produce, and carried an economic price tag as high as $75 million.

Building Collapses

Boston, Massachusetts, 1919. The Paris Peace Conference was about to open, and Russia was torn by revolutionary strife, but what happened in Boston on January 19, 1919, took over newspaper headlines, at least temporarily. At the time Boston was a center for trade in molasses, used primarily in making rum. Ships carrying molasses regularly docked in the Boston harbor, and companies dealing in molasses had large storage tanks in the waterfront area. One such tank, owned by the Purity Distilling Co. and made of cast iron, was fifty feet high and ninety feet wide and held more than 2 million gallons of molasses. On a warm January afternoon, as Bostonians went about their work and shopping in the busy downtown area, there was a sudden rumbling followed by the sharp cracking sounds of bursting rivets on the Purity tank. Tons of molasses began to pour out.

A "tidal wave" of molasses, two stories high, swept through the North End of Boston and out to sea at a speed of thirty-five miles an hour. Office buildings, stores, warehouses, factories, and houses were crushed by the tons of liquid. People raced away from the surging wave, some on foot, and others in horse-drawn or motor vehicles. Many escaped the area, but others did not and were engulfed by the mass of molasses. Dozens of persons were killed, and about 150 were injured in what was one of the most bizarre catastrophes of history.

Diamond Harbor, India, 1946. In January 1946 multitudes of pious Hindus were heading for sacred Sagar Island in the mouth of the Hooghly River, an arm of the mighty Ganges. Sagar Island is where the sacred river itself once met the Bay of Bengal, and it is a major Hindu pilgrimage center and the site of an important three-day bathing festival.

The route to the island was by road some thirty-five miles south from Calcutta to Diamond Harbor, then forty or fifty miles by boat down the Hooghly, which at that point was from two to three miles wide. Temporary jetties had been constructed at Diamond Harbor to accommodate the crowds of pilgrims embarking for Sagar Island and the ceremonial bathing, which was to start on Monday, January 14. On the morning of Saturday the twelfth, while a crowd stood on the smaller jetty waiting to board a boat, the structure gave way and crashed into the river, carrying ten of the faithful to their deaths.

That afternoon the larger jetty was packed with pilgrims ready to embark when an ominous cracking sound came from beneath the center section. Suddenly the central supports gave way, and the temporary wharf collapsed in the middle, funneling hundreds of pilgrims into the current. The afternoon collapse killed about 150 persons, many of them crushed by planks as the structure tore apart or struck in the water by falling lumber. More than 200 of the survivors were injured.

Saint Marys, West Virginia, 1978. Collapse of a different kind of temporary structure killed fifty-one workmen in 1978 in a construction accident at Saint Marys, West Virginia. A power plant was being built on Willow Island in the Ohio River at Saint Marys, and a 428-foot-high cooling tower was about half completed. A twin tower had been finished earlier without event. The towers were 360 feet in diameter at the base, designed to resemble an inverted funnel with a large spout flaring slightly outward. They were fashioned of concrete that was poured one ring-shaped layer at a time. To each finished layer were bolted the forms into which the next-higher layer would be poured. To each layer was also bolted the circular wood and steel scaffolding inside the tower, on which construction crews worked to handle the pouring of concrete out of "baskets" suspended from cranes. A safety net inside the scaffolding protected workers from falling off.

The twenty-eighth layer of concrete had been poured on Wednesday, April 26. The forms and scaffolding had been raised and secured for the next layer, and the twenty-ninth was being poured on Thursday when suddenly the scaffolding began peeling away from the inside of the tower.

"The first thing I heard was concrete falling," said John Peppler, a laborer who had just sent a basketful of concrete up from the center of the tower. "I looked over my left shoulder and I could see it falling. I could see people falling through the air and everything falling." He and others on the ground in the center of the tower were uninjured.

Another witness inside the tower said the victims "just fell

On April 27, 1978, a group of workers plunged to their deaths as scaffolding collapsed on a partially constructed cooling tower for a power plant at Saint Marys, West Virginia.

like dominoes. I looked up and men were screaming and hollering." A co-worker said, "They knew what was happening, but there wasn't anything they could do about it."

The Monongahela Power Company, for which the plant

was being constructed, said "As the twenty-ninth [layer] was being poured today, the twenty-eighth disintegrated and the bolts that were holding the scaffolding pulled loose away from it."

The fifty-one dead were buried beneath a tangled circular heap of steel, boards, netting, and wet cement, which had followed them in their 168-foot fall as the circular scaffold—nearly 1,000 feet in circumference—peeled loose and spiraled to the ground.

Near the covered bodies of some of the victims, workmen clear debris from the construction site where a layer of concrete disintegrated, causing 51 workers to fall 168 feet.

"There was so much stuff there on the ground that you couldn't see the bodies," said Robert Hess, another survivor. "There wasn't a sound coming from it." When the bodies were recovered, Hess said, "they were torn up so bad I couldn't tell looking at them whether any of my friends had been killed. There will be no open caskets."

On the ground, there were no injured. On the scaffold, there were no survivors.

Stampedes

Indianapolis, Indiana, 1869. At the 1869 Indiana State Fair, one of the exhibits that attracted much attention was a portable sawmill operated by steam power. On October 1, 1869, while the fair was in progress, the steam boiler exploded, hurling pieces of metal so far that some landed outside the fairgrounds.

The explosion, however, was less destructive than the fright it created among the more than 15,000 persons attending the fair. Many of the fairgoers panicked and stampeded off the grounds. In all, twenty-seven persons were killed, and fifty-six were injured. Most of the killed and injured were women and children trampled by the fleeing crowd.

Sunderland, England, 1883. On June 16, 1883, about 1,500 children were attending a puppet show in Victoria Hall; nearly all of the city's children were present. About 1,200 children were seated in the gallery, chaperoned by only a few parents, mostly mothers. At the end of the performance, the children were invited to come to the stage to receive prizes. The children in the gallery, excited by the toys that awaited them on the stage, began to run down a staircase that led to the lower level. The staircase itself was narrow; furthermore, the doorway at the bottom had been purposely narrowed to less than two feet in order to insure that each child who passed through could be checked for a ticket. This measure, taken to control the movement of the children, became a death trap. The first children down the stairs became jammed in the doorway, and those behind continued to push forward, piling up on one another until the bodies were several feet deep.

A caretaker of the theater tried unsuccessfully to untangle the mass of children. He then ran up another stairway and led many of them to safety through another exit. About two hundred children at the bottom of the staircase, however, were crushed to death by the weight of others. Mass funerals for the victims were held in Sunderland the following day.

Caracas, Venezuela, 1952. A particularly gruesome human stampede occurred in a church in Caracas on April 9, 1952. A large crowd of parishioners had come to the church for prayers at the beginning of Holy Week. As they knelt, crowded together, a pickpocket attempted to work his way among them; but the thief apparently found his trade difficult in the quiet, closely packed throng.

In order to create confusion, a pickpocket's delight, the thief shouted "Fire, fire!" The crowd of worshippers rushed toward exits at the rear of the church. Many people fell and were trampled by their fellow parishioners who were rushing to escape the imagined fire. In all, fifty-three persons were killed, nearly half of whom were small children and infants.

Niigata, Japan, 1955. Shinto is the indigenous religion of Japan, which preserves and reflects Japanese culture and tradition, and many Japanese mark the coming of the new year at a Shinto shrine. Yashiko Shrine is situated at Niigata, Japan's major port on the Sea of Japan. There, in the last moments of 1955, 30,000 Japanese were crowded to pray and celebrate and see the new year in. Worshippers took turns in approaching the altar, where they knelt to pray, about a hundred at a time, heads bowed and hands clasped behind them. Behind them hundreds more waited their turns on a

In Niigata, Japan, a pine box coffin is carried into the Yashiko Shrine as the task of removing bodies begins. The New Year's celebration at the Shinto shrine had become a nightmare when the crowd stampeded shortly before midnight.

platform before the altar. Flowing down the steps behind those, and packing the temple compound all the way back to the gate, pressed the other thousands.

At five minutes before midnight, many children and some adults at the altar had finished their prayers and turned to melt back into the crowd, just as two priests mounted towers outside the altar. The priests began tossing traditional New Year's mochi, or rice balls, into the crowd, taking care to throw some back toward the gate, to the rear of the huge crowd.

The children leaving the altar scrambled down into the crowd after the mochi; so did the hundreds on the platform, surging into the thousands on the steps and the tens of thousands beyond them. People fell, then others. "Some stumbled off the stairs or were crushed under the oncoming human wave," said Tsuneo Togawa, a reporter for the newspaper *Asahi*.

Panic swept the temple compound. The men and women and children who had not fallen, struggling to keep their feet, stampeded, but there was no room to stampede, no place to go. The surging crowd broke through a six-foot wall, which collapsed.

When the panic subsided, shrine spokesman Hyoshio Takahachi said, "There was a pile of dead and injured at the bottom of the stairs. Some tumbled down, and some were trampled." The dead celebrants there, at the wall, and elsewhere in the compound numbered 124, many of them children, and 75 more were injured in what became the worst tragedy of any Japanese New Year on record.

Lima, Peru, 1964. What started as a soccer match ended in a murderous shambles when Argentina met Peru at Lima on May 24, 1964, to decide which team would compete in the coming Olympic Games. A tense and nationalistic crowd of an estimated 45,000 Peruvians watched as the match went against them. The score was 1–0 in favor of Argentina, and Peru was trying desperately to catch up. With two minutes to play, Peru kicked a goal—which the referee nullified, charging rough play by Peru.

Booing erupted from the crowd at once, and two spectators leaped the fence in front of the stands and dashed onto the field to attack the referee, R. Angel Pazos. A police detail of forty men charged onto the field and arrested the assailants. At this the crowd let out a roar of anger, and the air vibrated with tension. Surrounded by the enraged and now

Policemen fire tear gas into an angry crowd (above) in an attempt to disperse a riot that erupted during a championship soccer match in Lima between Argentina and Peru. Spectators were trampled (right) as the crowd tried to flee the stadium from the gas and smoke.

rabidly partisan Peruvians, with inadequate police protection, referee Pazos suspended the game.

Again the crowd thundered its anger, and a swelling tide of spectators began leaping the fence and pouring threateningly onto the field. A squad of police rushed the referee and both teams to a locker room deep within the stadium and slammed its steel door. Police then furtively hurried them out an exit to the street and into buses that took them to a distant part of the city.

Meanwhile in the stadium mounted police tried to herd the crowd toward the exits. Some charged their horses into groups of rioters. Others fired their guns into the air and lobbed tear gas grenades into the mob. These tactics only enraged the crowd further and fed a growing panic in the stadium. Rioters set fires in the stands, overturned benches, and hurled bottles and other missiles at the police.

Many exits from the stadium were locked, and bystanders

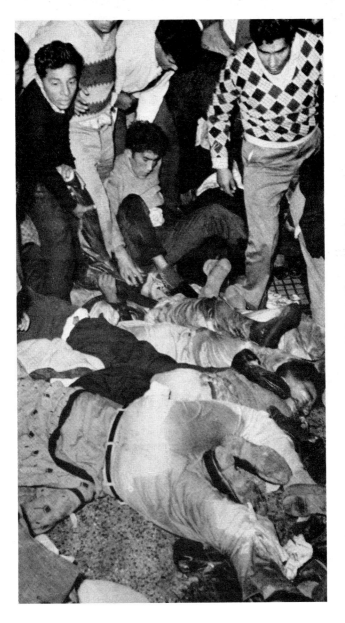

were trampled as crowds fleeing the tear gas and smoke from the fires bore down on them. The massed weight of the crowd thronging the locked doors burst them open. Already, dead bodies littered the field and the stands, and youthful bands of hoodlums swarmed over the dead, rifling their pockets and stealing anything of value.

The rampaging crowd spilled out of the stadium, putting vehicles and buildings to the torch, although firemen were able to put the fires out behind the mob as it moved along. Finally, the rioters began to break up, one band marching on the national palace to denounce the police brutality and urge Peruvian President Fernando Belaúnde Terry to have the soccer match declared a tie. Other segments of the disintegrating mob took up watches at hospitals and makeshift morgues, chanting "Revenge!" and "Down with the police!"

When the outpouring of rage subsided at last, the toll of the trampled, asphyxiated, and otherwise slain stood at 318 dead —four of them shot by police. It was impossible to count the wounded precisely, but the figure stood near 500. To restore order the government of Peru declared a state of emergency and suspended constitutional guarantees for thirty days.

Chandka Forest, India, 1972. Stampeding animals can also kill humans. During several hot, dry months of 1972, village farmers in the vicinity of Chandka Forest were afraid to work on their open farmland because, as they observed, elephants in the region had become crazed by the heat and drought.

On July 10 a herd of apparently mad elephants stampeded. It tore through five villages in the area, destroyed crops and huts, and killed twenty-four persons.

Cairo, Egypt, 1974. Mass stampedes of people have frequently occurred at sporting events, when emotions run so high that the slightest action or the prospect of being denied admission can set off a raging crowd. A soccer match had been scheduled for February 17, 1974, at the 100,000-seat Cairo Stadium, and the event was sold out. The promoters of the match, however, later switched the event to smaller Zamalek Stadium, which could seat fewer than half of the ticket purchasers.

When the gates were opened on the day of the match, the throng of ticket holders, in an attempt to insure that they would occupy the seats they had paid for, stampeded into Zamalek Stadium. Dozens were injured, and forty-nine persons were killed in the crush.

Other Mishaps, 1959–78

1959
Jan. 24
Kucuk Yali, Turkey. A motion-picture theater collapsed, killing 35 persons.
July 18
Pusan, South Korea. In a stampede set off by a sudden storm, 68 persons were trampled to death.
Aug. 19
Kandy, Ceylon. An elephant ran amok at a religious festival, killing 14 persons and injuring many others.
Sept. 16
Barletta, Italy. An apartment house collapsed, killing 59 of the occupants.
Sept. 20
Near Bombay, India. A crush created at the scene of a religious "miracle" killed a reported 75 persons.
Dec. 2
Fréjus, France. A break in the Malpasset Dam caused a flood which killed 421 persons.
Dec. 9
Recife, Brazil. A power line fell beside worshipers attending mass on a hillside; 10 persons were killed in the ensuing panic.

1960
Jan. 26
Seoul, South Korea. As crowds rushed to board a train, 32 persons were trampled to death.
March 2
Yokohama, Japan. A rush for theater seats led to 12 persons being crushed to death.
April 1
State of Pernambuco, Brazil. A dam on the Paraibo River burst; 15 persons in a canoe drowned.
June 12
Lahore, Pakistan. A bride and groom, along with 28 other persons, were killed when a house collapsed.
Aug. 17
Reocin, Spain. A dam burst at a zinc mining site, killing 23 persons.

1961
Feb. 3

Fléron, Belgium. A crumbling, rain-weakened rock pile buried about 15 houses and a passing bus; 21 persons reportedly were killed.

June 1

Clamart, France. About fifty homes, apartment buildings, and a factory collapsed after an earth cave-in; 20 persons were killed, and 37 others were injured.

Sept. 4

North Sikkim, India. A bridge under construction collapsed, killing 62 persons.

1962

Jan. 27

Volta Redonda, Brazil. A tipped-over crucible poured 70 tons of molten steel on a group of workmen; 17 died, and 33 others were severely burned.

March 1

Assuit, Egypt. A three-story hotel collapsed because of a weakened foundation; 29 persons were killed.

March 7

Idlib, Syria. Carbon dioxide seeping into a motion-picture theater brought death by suffocation to 14 children.

May 26

Montenegro, Yugoslavia. Construction scaffolding of a bridge collapsed into a river; at least 22 persons were killed, and 16 others were injured.

Sept. 3

Cairo, Egypt. A five-story housing unit collapsed during construction; about 60 workers were killed.

Sept. 17

Brussels, Belgium. A government office building collapsed and slid into an adjoining excavation; at least 17 persons were killed, and 20 others were injured.

Nov. 27

São Paulo, Brazil. Gale winds snapped a high-tension wire which fell into a crowd; 10 persons were electrocuted.

1963

Jan. 15

Naraj, India. A pneumatic pier-sinker burst, killing 47 workmen; 62 others were injured.

Jan. 29

Tripoli, Lebanon. A condemned five-story apartment house

collapsed and killed 20 persons; 7 others were injured.

Feb. 1

Biblian, Ecuador. During religious services, the rain-weakened walls of a Roman Catholic school collapsed, allowing the roof to fall in upon an estimated 450 children and nuns; 116 children and 4 nuns were killed, and 63 other pupils were injured.

Feb. 3

Granadilla, Canary Islands. An old house used as offices for issuing identity cards creaked as though threatening collapse; in the ensuing panic, 27 persons were killed and more than 100 others were injured.

Feb. 27

Rio de Janeiro, Brazil. The boisterous 1963 Carnival accounted for 50 deaths; 2,000 persons were injured.

May 16

Macao. Two ancient two-story buildings collapsed into rubble; at least 170 persons were buried under the debris.

May 28

Lisbon, Portugal. The roof of the Casi de Sodre railway station collapsed during the evening rush hour; 48 persons died, and 36 others were injured.

Aug. 20

Yeotmal, India. A mosque collapsed and tons of debris fell in upon a gathering of worshipers; 128 persons died, and more than 100 others were injured.

1964

Jan. 15

Rangoon, Burma. A harvest festival celebration brought death to about 30 persons who drowned while participating in bathing rites.

Jan. 15

Paris, France. The completed framework of eleven floors of a twelve-story apartment building under construction collapsed and buried more than 40 workmen beneath 100,000 tons of twisted steel and concrete; 23 of the men died, and 11 others were hospitalized.

April 4

Madurai, India. A two-story mud-brick school tumbled down upon 400 girls and teachers; 38 of the students and 2 adults were killed, and at least 137 others were injured.

May 2

Seoul, South Korea. A four-story slum building collapsed, killing 14 persons; 20 others were injured.

Aug. 23

Puerto Ordaz, Venezuela. A footbridge over a Caroni River gorge collapsed, dumping a group of sightseers into the rapids below; all 29 persons were presumed dead.

Nov. 6

Piracicaba, Brazil. The collapse of a building in the process of construction brought death to at least 41 persons.

Nov. 29

Jalapa, Mexico. A political rally erupted into a stampede when a speaker invited the crowd of 3,000 to the governor's residence; 24 persons were killed, and 33 others were seriously injured.

1965

Jan. 3

Rijo, Mexico. The roof of a newly built church collapsed during a dedication mass, killing 55 persons and injuring 63 others.

Jan. 31

Guadalajara, Mexico. A crowd of 7,000 persons leaving a music festival collided with incoming spectators for the next performance; in the ensuing crush, 20 persons were trampled to death.

April 10

Uttar Pradesh, India. The railings of a pontoon bridge over the Gogra River gave way during Hindu bathing rites; at least 70 pilgrims drowned.

Oct. 5

Seoul, South Korea. An overflow crowd, trying to see the opening ceremonies at a new stadium, forced the main gate and caused a stampede; 16 persons were killed, and scores were injured.

Dec. 18

Havana, Cuba. The old, residential Hotel Luz collapsed in the night, burying most of the 93 occupants; 28 persons were believed dead, and 50 others were injured.

Dec. 27

Off the Yorkshire coast, England. A British oil-drilling rig, the "Sea Gem," collapsed and sank 40 miles offshore, apparently when part of the ten-legged anchoring support buckled; of the 32 crewmen aboard, 13 were lost and presumed drowned.

1966

Jan. 19

Guaratinga, Brazil. Weakened by prolonged torrential rains, the municipal market collapsed upon hundreds of shoppers, killing at least 36 persons.

Jan. 22

Fresnillo, Mexico. Carbon-monoxide fumes from a gasoline-operated generator in a ranch house filled a closed room and killed 15 sleeping wedding guests.

Feb. 5

Tinsukia, India. Throngs of listeners stampeded to get closer to hear a speech by Prime Minister Indira Gandhi; 12 persons were crushed to death, and 23 others were injured.

Feb. 6

Johannesburg, South Africa. Panicked by the appearance of police with a dog, 200 persons attempted to flee a building by a narrow staircase; 10 persons died in the ensuing stampede.

March 27

North Sea. Winds of 100 mph buffeted the oil rig "Constellation" as it was being towed to an anchorage off Lowestoft, England, and made it impossible to rescue the 29 crewmen aboard before the rig sank; all were presumed dead.

April 24

Kabul, Afghanistan. The collapse of a two-story home killed 13 members of one family.

May 1

Near Karbala, Syria. The front ranks of a religious procession of 100,000 Shi'ite Muslims stopped suddenly when a woman darted across the road ahead of the line of march; in the resulting pileup 25 persons suffocated to death, and 49 others were injured.

July 18

Hardwar, India. Religious bathing rites in the Ganges River were interrupted by a sudden rainstorm; as the pilgrims stampeded for shelter, 17 persons were trampled to death.

Aug. 6

Southern Iran. A 30-man camel caravan, crossing the desert outbound from Shahabad, ran out of water; 16 members died of thirst.

Aug. 10

Near San Cristóbal, Venezuela. The collapse of a rain-weakened bridge plunged a bus into the river below, killing at least 30 persons.

Aug. 15
New Delhi, India. A 200-year-old building collapsed into a crowded alley; 14 of the 60 occupants were killed.

Oct. 27
Managua, Nicaragua. Following the opening game of the baseball season, spectators stampeded in the scramble to leave the stadium; 12 persons died, mostly of suffocation, and more than 100 others were injured.

Nov. 10
Cam Ranh Bay, South Vietnam. An old steel and concrete pier gave way as workers stood waiting for a ferry; at least 20 persons were killed, and about 59 others were injured.

1967
Feb. 8
Rio de Janeiro, Brazil. The four-day pre-Lenten Carnival occasioned various accidents that killed 93 persons.

April 23
Near Katmandu, Nepal. A 100-year-old rope bridge, strained by heavy pedestrian traffic, gave way and dropped at least 100 persons (mostly women and children) into the Sun Kosi River, where they drowned.

April 25
Erandio, Spain. The roof of an appliance factory collapsed, crushing the workers beneath its weight; 16 persons were dead or missing, and 30 others were injured.

Aug. 9
Madras, India. The drinking of varnish as a substitute for liquor, during three days of festival and parties in the prohibitionist state of Madras, accounted for at least 96 deaths; almost 140 other persons were hospitalized.

Aug. 27
Huron, Ohio. Sky divers, leaping through an overcast from an off-course B-25, hit Lake Erie instead of their scheduled drop target at Ortners Field, Birmingham, Ohio; 16 divers died, 2 survivors were fished from the lake, and 2 other divers hit the target on the second dropping run.

Sept. 27
Tijuana, Mexico. The mass poisoning of hundreds of persons was traced to accidental use of the lethal pesticide parathion in the mixing of bread; 17 deaths (mostly children) were reported, and more than 300 persons received treatment.

Nov. 25
Chiquinquirá, Colombia. The mass poisoning of food, also

caused by flour contaminated with parathion insecticide, resulted in the death of 80 persons.

Dec. 15

Kanauga, Ohio–Point Pleasant, West Virginia. Silver Bridge, spanning the Ohio River, collapsed during the evening rush-hour traffic and dumped at least 75 cars and trucks into the water below; the known dead numbered 38, with at least 25 other persons missing.

1968

Jan. 4

Guadalajara, Mexico. A continuing round of New Year's celebrations resulted in the deaths of 22 persons, mostly from drinking industrial alcohol.

Feb. 28

Rio de Janeiro, Brazil. The four-day pre-Lenten Carnival brought death to 89 persons.

June 24

Buenos Aires, Argentina. During a stampede of 90,000 spectators, fighting to get out of El Estadio Monumental following a soccer game, at least 70 persons were trampled to death; 67 others were hospitalized.

Aug. 1

Sutur Khana, India. Food eaten during a Muslim religious festival poisoned and killed at least 46 of the festival participants.

1969

Jan. 1

Indore, India. Rioting between Hindu and Muslim religious groups brought death to 12 persons.

March 12

Singida, Tanzania. Consumption of tainted meat caused 11 persons to die of poisoning.

June 15

San Rafael, Spain. An opening day celebration by 500 patrons of a new restaurant turned to horror as a second-story floor began to sag, the walls quickly crumbled and brought down the roof, crushing at least 57 persons; 140 were injured.

Nov. 26

Osaka, Japan. An air pipe broke loose from a caisson at a construction project 64 feet beneath the Shirinashi River; 11 workers drowned.

Nov. 29

Guadalajara, Mexico. The roof of the church of San Luis Gonzago collapsed upon 200 worshipers, killing at least 19 persons.

Dec. 25

Bukavu, Congo. The expected arrival of President Joseph D. Mobutu triggered a stampede among a crowd waiting outside the football stadium; 27 persons were killed, and more than 107 others were injured.

1970

Feb. 13

Kumaon Hills, India. A man-eating tiger, roaming a hilly area 50 miles northeast of New Delhi, was reported to have killed 48 persons.

June 21

Rio de Janeiro, Brazil. Celebration of Brazil's 4–1 victory over Italy in the World Cup soccer final game brought death to at least 44 persons and sent 1,800 others into hospitals; more than 10 deaths, and numerous injuries, were reported elsewhere in Brazil.

Aug. 2

Baltimore, Maryland. State health authorities reported that an outbreak of salmonella food poisoning at a city nursing home caused the deaths of 12 elderly patients; 60 others who were stricken recovered.

Oct. 15

Melbourne, Victoria, Australia. Construction on the new West Gate Bridge was disrupted when a span of the structure collapsed and plunged 150 feet into the Yarra River below; 34 workmen were killed, and at least 18 others were injured.

1971

Jan. 2

Glasgow, Scotland. The end of a closely contested soccer game brought the fans hurtling out of their seats and through a steel crowd barrier; in the ensuing pileup, 66 persons were trampled or crushed to death, and at least another 100 persons were injured.

May 15

Sallen, France. The floorboards of a rented hall gave way at the close of a wedding reception, plunging the guests into a well beneath the floor; 13 persons perished.

Nov. 10

Koblenz, West Germany. The collapse of a bridge under

construction across the Rhine River killed 10 workmen; 12 men were missing, and 10 others were injured.

Nov. 11

Kawasaki, Japan. A geological experiment to determine how heavy rainfall could trigger a landslide ended in the unexpected crumbling of a nearby cliff; 15 persons died in the mud and dirt slide, and 8 others were injured.

1972

Sept. 16

Naga City, Philippines. An 18-foot-wide wooden bridge gave way beneath the weight of hundreds of pilgrims observing a religious festival; 72 persons, mostly women and children, died as they plunged into the rocks and water below.

Nov. 21

Trujillo, Peru. Cakes made from cake flour containing a strong insecticide first killed 5 children in a family; more cake served later to mourners of the earlier victims caused another 6 persons to die for a final toll of 11 family members.

Dec. 20

Rio de Janeiro, Brazil. About 2,500 square yards of concrete roof collapsed upon the heads of shoppers and workers in the newly opened Ideal Supermarket; at least 16 persons died.

1973

Feb. 23

Andhra Pradesh State, India. Poisoning from drinking liquor sold in a store at Suryapet accounted for the deaths of at least 60 persons; more than 500 others became ill.

March 2

Baileys Crossroads, Virginia. The collapse of a partly constructed 24-story condominium building killed 14 workmen and injured 34 others.

Aug. 20

Sudan. A wild elephant, attacking a Sudanese village near the Zaire border, killed 11 persons, injured 3 others, and destroyed 10 homes.

Oct. 18

Ipoh, Malaysia. A gigantic piece of limestone, loosened by heavy rains and nearby blasting, went hurtling down a hillside and into a cluster of squatters' shacks; 40 or 50 persons were killed outright or buried alive.

Late November

Mozambique. A large quantity of methyl alcohol was washed

ashore in drums and mistakenly drunk as whiskey; 58 deaths were confirmed, but hundreds were believed to have succumbed.

1974
May 26
Central Kuwait. Three floors of an office building suddenly collapsed during construction; 14 workers were reportedly killed despite frantic efforts to rescue those trapped alive beneath the wreckage.
Dec. 5
Tehran, Iran. The concrete-slab roof above the main lobby of the newly enlarged airport terminal at Tehran collapsed after a heavy snowfall; 17 deaths were confirmed.

1975
March 9
Seoul, South Korea. A cement embankment supporting two buildings collapsed on several dormitories that housed young women employees of a nearby wig factory; 17 persons were killed, and 12 others were injured.

1976
January.
Jamaica. A shipment of imported flour contaminated by the insecticide parathion was blamed for the death of 17 persons.
March 9
Cavalese, Italy. A cable car, carrying vacationing skiers back to their lodgings at the end of the day, swung precariously when a cable loosened and then plunged 200 feet to the frozen ground; most of the 42 persons who died were from West Germany.
April 16
Gulf of Mexico. A survival capsule, launched from a storm-battered oil drilling rig that sank off the Texas coast, landed upside down in heavy seas; 13 workers, trapped inside the capsule, died.
June 5
Snake River Valley, Idaho. The 307-foot-high Teton Dam, criticized as potentially dangerous even before its construction began, collapsed as its reservoir was being filled for the first time; the vast quantity of water that roared into the upper Snake River Valley killed 14 persons and made some 30,000 others homeless.

Early July

Madras, India. Bootleg liquor containing methyl alcohol and other toxic ingredients killed 84 persons and hospitalized about 100 others.

Sept. 13

Karachi, Pakistan. A one-year-old, six-story residential building collapsed because of inadequate foundations; of the 140 persons who were killed, 6 belonged to the family of the man who owned the building.

1977

Aug. 17

Pushkino, U.S.S.R. A crowded footbridge over a main rail line collapsed under the weight of more than 100 persons who had arrived at Pushkino station about 20 miles northeast of Moscow; dozens were injured, and at least 10 persons were crushed to death by the wreckage of the bridge and by other victims who fell some 30 feet to the tracks.

Sept. 7

Near Jaipur, India. The roof of a village classroom collapsed under the weight of a troop of baboons; 15 schoolgirls were killed instantly.

1978

Jan. 19

Central India. A section of a bridge under construction collapsed; at least 70 workers died.

April 28

Beirut, Lebanon. A four-story building housing refugees from Israel's invasion of southern Lebanon collapsed, injuring at least 40 persons, many seriously; at least 13 persons were known dead, and many others were missing.

May 5

Jessore, Bangladesh. A banyan tree, uprooted during a storm, crashed into a marketplace; 30 persons were killed, and 100 others were injured.

Mid-May

Nicaragua. Lethal insecticides, sprayed during the cotton season, poisoned about 800 persons and killed at least 25 others who failed to take needed precautions while using the spray.

July 30

Tehran, Iran. The roof and second story of a 60-year-old hospital, in need of repair, collapsed and buried 28 patients on the first floor; 11 of these were killed, and 17 were injured.

Afterword:
Diminishing Death

Individual, small-scale accidents happen every day and kill more human beings than do wars—but they seldom attract notice beyond the bereaved families. The one positive thing that can be said for accidents on a catastrophic scale is that they attract substantial public notice. They force themselves on the attention of persons and agencies that can do something to minimize the likelihood that a particular kind of accident will recur.

The concept of casualty insurance to provide for payment of loss and damages in accidents grew out of marine insurance, which existed in some form in very ancient times. Not only did seafaring people of antiquity consider the economic perils of shipwreck but they also began to develop what amounted to national and international law regulating how ships might be built and used so as to afford maximum safety to freight, passengers, and crew.

Younger forms of transport have extended and developed further the kinds of protection initiated for marine transport, in terms of insurance and government regulation, including international regulation by treaty. Because of stringent regulations, accidents to passengers in air, rail, and sea transportation now constitute only a small fraction of total accidents in any country. In mass transportation, however, buses have continued to be more vulnerable to accidents than aircraft, trains, and ships because they face the same risks of the road as do the private automobile and the truck.

How much do accidents cost? One could add up the casualties in just the disasters recounted in these pages and come to more than 170,000 human beings—all with lives, families, friendships, and responsibilities. Then of course there is the inevitable "estimate" in cases of epic disaster, in which many bodies are dismembered, burned beyond recognition, or simply never found: the total may go as high as 200,000 or more. It would be infinitely more difficult, if not impossible, to calculate the cost in economic terms, even of the few dozen epic disasters. An accident to a single airplane has cost British insurers more than $40 million. Indeed, the potential loss on a single jumbo jet aircraft can be estimated to exceed $100 million. The world's private insurance market is put at more than $250 billion annually, and a large proportion of that market is concerned with insurance against the kinds of perils considered here.

Catastrophes change public attitudes, and public attitudes in time come to dominate and overrule even the arrogance of a tycoon or a dictator. Every landmark mishap has had its effect in law and treaty, whether on a global scale, as when the *Titanic* disaster led to twenty-four-hour radio watches on all the world's ships, or on so local a scale as the decision to ban the transportation of liquefied propylene from the highways of Tarragona Province in northeastern Spain. Commodore Cornelius Vanderbilt snorted at George Westinghouse's air brake—but a generation before Vanderbilt's rail empire was swallowed up by corporate and government conglomerates that would have stricken the old tycoon with horror, the air brake was universal on the world's trains, including those of the New York Central.

Catastrophes, indeed, communicate. They communicate the urgent need to take new steps in safety to keep pace with new steps in technology that continuously breed new dangerous cargoes or new perils for travelers. They communicate also a sense of immediacy and personal involvement perhaps best put by the English priest and poet John Donne—whose effigy, curiously enough, is said to be the only monument in St. Paul's Cathedral to have survived the Great Fire of London:

> *...Any man's death diminishes me, because I am involved in Mankinde; And therefore never send to know for whom the bell tolls; it tolls for thee.*

BIBLIOGRAPHY

The New Encyclopaedia Britannica (15th Edition)

Propaedia: This one-volume Outline of Knowledge is organized as a ten-part Circle of Learning, enabling the reader to carry out an orderly plan of study in any field. Its Table of Contents—consisting of 10 parts, 42 divisions, and 189 sections—is an easy topical guide to the *Macropaedia*.

Micropaedia: If interested in a particular subject, the reader can locate it in this ten-volume, alphabetically arranged Ready Reference of brief entries and Index to the *Macropaedia*, where subjects are treated at greater length or in broader contexts.

Macropaedia: These nineteen volumes of Knowledge in Depth contain extended treatments of all the fields of human learning. For information on *Catastrophe! When Man Loses Control*, for example, consult: Aerospace Industry; Aerospace Medicine; Aircraft; Air Law; Automobile; Bicycle; Bone Diseases and Injuries; Bridges, Construction and History of; Building Construction; Burns; Coal Mining; Compression and Decompression Injuries; Elevator; Explosives; Flight, History of; Health and Safety Laws; Icebergs and Pack Ice; Industrial Medicine; Instrumentation; Insurance; Life-Support Systems; Maritime Law; Mercury Products and Production; Motor Sports; Nuclear Reactor; Physiographic Effects of Man; Poisons and Poisoning; Price Systems; Radiation, Biological Effects of; Radioactivity; Roads and Highways; Safety Engineering; Security and Protection Systems; Ship; Ship Design and Construction; Steam Power; Torts, Law of; Traffic Control; Transportation, Air; Transportation, History of; Transportation, Water; Trucks and Buses; Wound.

Other Publications:

Accident Facts. Annual. Chicago, Ill.: National Safety Council.

Berman, Bruce D. *Encyclopedia of American Shipwrecks.* Boston, Mass.: Mariners Press, 1972.

Butler, Hal. *Inferno! Fourteen Fiery Tragedies of Our Time.* Chicago, Ill.: H. Regnery Co., 1975.

Eddy, Paul; Potter, Elaine; and Page, Bruce. *Destination Disaster: From the Tri-Motor to the DC-10.* New York: Quadrangle/ New York Times Book Co., 1976.

Hudson, Kenneth, and Nichols, Ann. *The Book of Shipwrecks.* New York: A & W Publishers, 1979.

Marx, Robert F. *Shipwrecks of the Western Hemisphere, 1492–1825.* New York: David McKay Co., 1975.

Shaw, Robert B. *History of Railroad Accidents, Safety Precautions and Operating Practices.* Potsdam, N.Y.: Northern Press, 1978.

Toland, John. *The Great Dirigibles, Their Triumphs and Disasters.* Original title: *Ships in the Sky: The Story of the Great Dirigibles.* New York: Dover Publications, 1972.

Picture Credits

Index

Facts at Your Fingertips!

- ☐ 11451   MOVIES ON TV (1978-79 Revised Ed.) $2.95
- ☐ 12419   THE BANTAM BOOK OF CORRECT LETTER WRITING $2.25
- ☐ 12850   THE COMMON SENSE BOOK OF KITTEN AND CAT CARE $2.25
- ☐ 12368   AMY VANDERBILT'S EVERYDAY ETIQUETTE $2.50
- ☐ 12993   SOULE'S DICTIONARY OF ENGLISH SYNONYMS $2.50
- ☐ 12713   DICTIONARY OF CLASSICAL MYTHOLOGY $2.25
- ☐ 12181   THE BETTER HOMES AND GARDENS HANDYMAN BOOK $2.25
- ☐ 12011   THE BANTAM NEW COLLEGE SPANISH & ENGLISH DICTIONARY $1.95
- ☐ 12370   THE GUINNESS BOOK OF WORLD RECORDS 17th Ed. $2.50
- ☐ 8481   MOTHER EARTH'S HASSLE-FREE INDOOR PLANT BOOK $1.75
- ☐ 12843   IT PAYS TO INCREASE YOUR WORD POWER $1.95
- ☐ 12427   THE MOTHER EARTH NEWS ALMANAC $2.50
- ☐ 11692   THE BANTAM COLLEGE FRENCH & ENGLISH DICTIONARY $1.95
- ☐ 12850   THE COMMON SENSE BOOK OF PUPPY AND DOG CARE $2.25
- ☐ 7890   SEARCHING FOR YOUR ANCESTORS $1.95
- ☐ 11529   WRITING AND RESEARCHING TERM PAPERS $1.95
- ☐ 02810   HOW TO PICK UP GIRLS $2.25

Ask for them at your local bookseller or use this handy coupon:

Bantam Books, Inc., Dept. RB, 414 East Golf Road, Des Plaines, Ill. 60016

Please send me the books I have checked above. I am enclosing $_____
(please add 75¢ to cover postage and handling). Send check or money order
—no cash or C.O.D.'s please.

Mr/Mrs/Miss_____

Address_____

City_____State/Zip_____

RB—6/79

Please allow four weeks for delivery. This offer expires 12/79.

The Inquisitive Mind

Bantam/Britannica Books were created for those with a desire to learn. Compacted from the vast Britannica files, each book gives an indepth treatment of a particular facet of science, world events, or politics. These accessible, introductory volumes are ideal for the student and for the intellectually curious who want to know more about the world around them.

☐	12486	**THE ARABS: People and Power**	$2.50
☐	12487	**DISASTER: When Nature Strikes Back**	$2.50
☐	12488	**THE OCEAN: Mankind's Last Frontier**	$2.50
☐	12485	**THE U.S. GOVERNMENT: How and Why It Works**	$2.50
☐	13106	**CATASTROPHE: When Man Loses Control**	$2.50
☐	23105	**ENERGY: The Fuel of Life**	$2.50
☐	13107	**HOW THINGS WORK: Aerosols to Zippers**	$2.50
☐	13108	**LAW IN AMERICA: How and Why It Works**	$2.50

Buy them at your local bookstore or use this handy coupon for ordering:

Bring out the books that bring in the issues.

☐	2677	GUILTY, GUILTY, GUILTY G. B. Trudeau	$1.25
☐	8151	WHO RUNS CONGRESS? Mark J. Green, James M. Fallows and David R. Zwick	$2.25
☐	02674	INSIDE THE COMPANY: CIA DIARY Philip Agee	$2.50
☐	10198	WHY NOT THE BEST? Jimmy Carter	$1.95
☐	12040	MY SOUL IS RESTED Howell Raines	$2.95
☐	11438	A HISTORY OF WOMEN IN AMERICA Carol Hymowitz & Michaele Weissman	$2.95
☐	10181	THE ECO-SPASM REPORT Alvin Toffler	$1.75
☐	11979	BURY MY HEART AT WOUNDED KNEE Dee Brown	$2.75
☐	10907	SOCIALISM Michael Harrington	$2.95
☐	12191	THE HOLOCAUST YEARS: Society on Trial Roselle Chartock & Jack Spencer	$1.95

Buy them at your local bookstore or use this handy coupon for ordering:

Bantam Books, Inc., Dept. EDM, 414 East Golf Road, Des Plaines, Ill. 60016

Please send me the books I have checked above. I am enclosing $_____ (please add 75¢ to cover postage and handling). Send check or money order —no cash or C.O.D.'s please.

Mr/Mrs/Miss_____

Address_____

City_____State/Zip_____

EDM—5/79

Please allow four weeks for delivery. This offer expires 11/79.

THE NAMES THAT SPELL GREAT LITERATURE

Choose from today's most renowned world authors—every one an important addition to your personal library.

Hermann Hesse

☐ 11916	MAGISTER LUDI	$2.25
☐ 12024	DEMIAN	$1.95
☐ 10060	GERTRUDE	$1.95
☐ 11978	THE JOURNEY TO THE EAST	$1.95
☐ 12529	SIDDHARTHA	$2.25
☐ 12758	BENEATH THE WHEEL	$2.25
☐ 12509	NARCISSUS AND GOLDMUND	$2.50
☐ 13174	STEPPENWOLF	$2.25
☐ 11510	ROSSHALDE	$1.95

Alexander Solzhenitsyn

☐ 10111	THE FIRST CIRCLE	$2.50
☐ 12677	ONE DAY IN THE LIFE OF IVAN DENISOVICH	$2.25
☐ 2997	AUGUST 1914	$2.50
☐ 11300	CANCER WARD	$2.50
☐ 12079	LENIN IN ZURICH	$2.95

Jerzy Kosinski

☐ 12465	STEPS	$2.25
☐ 12460	THE PAINTED BIRD	$2.25
☐ 2613	COCKPIT	$2.25
☐ 11899	BLIND DATE	$2.50

Doris Lessing

☐ 11870	THE SUMMER BEFORE THE DARK	$2.25
☐ 12759	THE GOLDEN NOTEBOOK	$2.95
☐ 12461	THE FOUR-GATED CITY	$2.95
☐ 11717	BRIEFING FOR A DESCENT INTO HELL	$2.25

André Schwarz-Bart

☐ 12510	THE LAST OF THE JUST	$2.95

Buy them at your local bookstore or use this handy coupon for ordering:

Bantam Book Catalog

Here's your up-to-the-minute listing of over 1,400 titles by your favorite authors.

This illustrated, large format catalog gives a description of each title. For your convenience, it is divided into categories in fiction and non-fiction—gothics, science fiction, westerns, mysteries, cookbooks, mysticism and occult, biographies, history, family living, health, psychology, art.

So don't delay—take advantage of this special opportunity to increase your reading pleasure.

Just send us your name and address and 50¢ (to help defray postage and handling costs).